Empowering the Poor

Why Justice Requires School Choice

David B. Van Heemst

ScarecrowEducation
Lanham, Maryland • Toronto • Oxford
2004

Published in the United States of America
by ScarecrowEducation
An imprint of The Rowman & Littlefield Publishing Group, Inc.
4501 Forbes Boulevard, Suite 200, Lanham, Maryland 20706
www.scicroweducation.com

PO Box 317
Oxford
OX2 9RU, UK

British Library Cataloguing in Publication Information Available

Library of Congress Cataloging-in-Publication Data

Van Heemst, David, 1966–
    Empowering the poor : why justice requires school choice / David Van
Heemst.
        p. cm.
    Includes bibliographical references and index.
    ISBN 1-57886-119-5 (pbk. : alk. paper)
    1. School choice–United States. 2. Poor–Education–United States.
I. Title.
LB1027.9 .V38 2004
371.1'11–dc22   2003027359

To April,
my bride,
your love flows
from the most
precious place in the universe,
from inside.

Contents

Acknowledgments   vii

Introduction   ix

1 How Are the Poor Doing in Our Current U.S. System?   1

2 Justice: A Philosophy of Empowering All Parents   29

3 The Supreme Court Aids the Poor   67

4 Elements of a Good School-Choice Plan   101

5 What Is Happening in the United States with School Choice?   137

6 The Poor Benefit from School Choice   165

Conclusion   195

Select Bibliography   199

Index   213

About the Author   219

Acknowledgments

I would not have been able to write this book without the assistance and guidance of many friends. Gary Streit, my academic dean, provided funding for the research. Jen Hatton and Jen Opperman surpassed all my expectations as research assistants. Tom Koerner, Amos Guinan, and Sally Craley from ScarecrowEducation provided encouragement and insight. I owe a large debt to my teachers, Roger Veenstra, John Vander Stelt, and Jim Skillen, who mentored me into a vision of justice for the "least of these." Most of all, my wife, April, and my twin daughters, Maggie and Ellie, have given me the greatest gift of all—a home filled with love and joy. To all I say, "Thank you."

Introduction

It's been two decades since the landmark report *A Nation at Risk* (1983) launched a nationwide effort to reform America's educational system. It's been a decade since a much-heralded Carnegie Foundation for the Advancement of Teaching Report (1992) declared, "The decade-long struggle to reform American education seems suddenly to hang on a single word: choice."[1] Now is the time to transform the United States' public educational system into a system of choice—one that will empower the poor, one that will offer them justice.

Many teachers, parents, administrators, and even students urge school choice because they are concluding that the old vision of America's public schools is obsolete. The old approach held that educational uniformity spearheaded by a common curriculum and teaching strategy could best meet the needs of every student. The new approach recognizes students' different learning styles, and would restructure America's educational system by creating a variety of schools to meet particular needs. Minnesota accounting teacher Kim Borwege says, "I've sat and dreamed of what the ideal school could be. I see so many students falling through the cracks. I get the feeling there are students who could be more successful with another approach."[2]

Only a few decades ago, parents from around the world dreamed of sending their children to schools in the United States. Recently, however, with school violence and drug sales increasing while graduation rates and SAT scores fall, this dream has faded.[3] Increasing numbers of parents and children perceive an educational crisis. The American educational system needs fixing.

Admittedly, some school problems find their origins in society. Crime, drugs, teenage pregnancy, unemployment, racism, poverty, and myriad other social ills enter the schools, creating seemingly insoluble problems. Yet trying to improve education by ending all social ills would be an exercise in futility. A more fruitful and concrete endeavor would be to restructure the American educational system. The present system is monopolistic and bureaucratic; it does not help children escape the cycle of poverty.

Because of the monopoly of public schools, family control over their children's education is compromised; parents who choose private or parochial schools are penalized by paying twice for their children's education; and public schools have little incentive to improve, given a lack of competition. Administrative red tape stifles teacher and student innovation. Finally, the doors to the better schools are closed to poor children, simply because their parents lack sufficient income.

School choice is not a panacea for America's educational crisis, but schools would improve if school districts adopted a choice model. Proposed school-choice systems include either public or private school choice. Public school choice includes open enrollment, magnet schools, and charter schools. Private or parochial school choice is more expansive and therefore preferable, because it provides vouchers for students to attend any certified school. The vouchers would be paid for by the state through property taxes. If states adopted school choice (as I describe in later chapters), families would be empowered, teachers and students could be innovative, schools would compete, and the poor would benefit because they could opt out of their current school and choose a new one, or they could stay at their current school and with more money, improve it dramatically.

My interest is specifically with the poor children. Education is undoubtedly the core building block, the essential currency, of today's society. With it, doors open; without it, doors close. Overwhelmingly, poor children attend poor schools. I counseled children in a poor school in Hopkins Park, Illinois. I looked into the eyes of children and I saw children whose eyes lacked hope. Gone from their eyes was any expectation of a bright future in which they'd move up the ladder or even the natural excitement of a third grader. They were eight-year-olds with the sadness of some eighty-year-olds.

School choice is the single most effective weapon at the disposal of today's policy makers to liberate the poor. If we believe that education is a fundamental right, then we ought not give more or less of it based on one's income. With choice, the doors to the finest schools will be opened to all children. No longer will poor children be condemned to failing schools operating on a bare minimum of funds within their own school districts. Now, the poor will be empowered; they will be able to sit alongside their peers from the proverbial "good side of the tracks." Indeed, if we can imagine a future in which the educational system will not add another barrier in the path of the poor, then certainly we can make it a reality. Justice requires that we evaluate a society based upon how it treats the least well off. Properly structured, school choice will be a more just system because it gives poor children a chance; it provides them with hope.

The evidence supports this claim. Students in choice programs in both Milwaukee and Cleveland have benefited from attending schools of choice. And even if student test scores had only remained equal to those in the traditional public school, we should still adopt a system of choice because the private schools the students attended were cheaper and parental satisfaction was higher. In poll after poll, the poor consistently favor school choice.

Nevertheless, most poor children still remain trapped in substandard schools. Clearly, getting a poor child into a good school will not solve all of the child's problems. It will not make up for malnutrition, poor parenting, or too much television watching. It will not magically transform a child into Einstein. It will not guarantee the child a future of prosperity. But it will help. And it will remove an unjust obstacle in her path, a system that sentences the child to a poor school. It will provide the child with an opportunity and that is what justice requires.

In this book, I make the case for school choice and cite the evidence showing that the poor have benefited from the choice programs in Milwaukee and in Cleveland. In chapter 1, I document how poorly disenfranchised students are performing in the current K–12 system. In chapter 2, I argue that justice requires that we consider the needs of the poor as we structure our educational system. In chapter 3, I show that the legal hurdles against school choice have been removed as the U.S. Supreme Court in 2002, building on a long history of jurisprudence, ruled that there is no violation of the separation of church and state with school choice. With that hurdle cleared, in chapter 4, I sketch the contours of a good school choice plan, offering a model that states could follow. In chapter 5, I describe what is already happening on a small scale with school vouchers in the United States. Finally, in chapter 6, I document how the poor have been helped by the school choice programs in both Milwaukee and Cleveland.

The time has come for all fifty states to adopt full systems of school choice in which every parent will receive a voucher to send her child to the school of her choice. Such a system will strengthen families, improve educational quality, and empower the poor. The time has come for school choice in the United States.

NOTES

1. National Commission on Excellence in Education, *A Nation at Risk* (Washington, D.C.: U.S. Department of Education, 1983); *A Special Report: School Choice* (Princeton, N.J.: Carnegie Foundation for the Advancement of Teaching, 1992), 1.

2. Sarah Lubman, "Breaking Away: Parents and Teachers Battle Public Schools by Starting Their Own," *Wall Street Journal*, May 19, 1994. Similarly, Rosemary Salomone said, "Sometimes to achieve equal educational opportunity, we have to provide different kinds of opportunity." Stacy A. Teicher, "The Case for Single-Sex Schools," *The Christian Science Monitor*, July 1, 2003, 15.

3. National Commission on Excellence in Education, *A Nation at Risk*. For a pithy summary of the lack of progress in education, see William Kristol and Jay Lefkowitz, "Our Students, Still at Risk," *New York Times*, May 3, 1993. In contrast to the NCEE's call for top-down reform, the following arguments call for bottom-up education reform: P. L. Boyer, *High School: A Report on Secondary Education in America* (New York: Harper & Row, 1984); J. I. Goodlad, *A Place Called School: Prospects for the Future* (New York: McGraw-Hill, 1984); T. R. Sizer, *Horace's Compromise: The Dilemma of the American High School* (Boston: Houghton Mifflin, 1984).

Chapter One

How Are the Poor Doing in Our Current System?

American elementary and secondary education is in a crisis. And we know it. While parents from around the world send their children to American colleges, few exhibit the same enthusiasm about our K–12 schools. Twenty years ago in 1983, a blue-ribbon panel entitled the National Commission on Excellence in Education published *A Nation at Risk* and described our nation's crisis of educational performance with these words: "The educational foundations of our society are presently being eroded by a rising tide of mediocrity that threatens our very future as a nation and a people."

Things haven't improved over the past two decades. A 1997 NBC News–*Wall Street Journal* survey found 58 percent of Americans agreed that "we need to make fundamental changes" in public education. Only 1 percent argued for "no changes at all."[1] Similarly, according to a Center for Education Reform survey, 78 percent of Americans feel that children are not receiving the education they need.[2] The Democratic Leadership Council found that only 3 percent of Americans graded our public schools with an A, while 43 percent chose a D or F.[3] The 33rd *Annual Phi Delta Kappa/Gallup Poll of the Public's Attitudes toward the Public Schools* found that only 25 percent of parents with a child in the public schools gave the schools an A or a B and 70 percent gave a C, D, or F.[4] Similarly, in the 32nd *Annual Phi Delta Kappa/Gallup Poll*, the top five problems in public schools were lack of financial support, lack of discipline, overcrowding, violence, and drugs.[5] Americans believe our overall system of public education is in trouble.

Frequently overlooked in both the surveys and the corresponding debates about educational reform are the children, especially children living in poverty.[6] And this is no small percentage of children. According to Richard

1

Kahlenberg, children from poor families are the majority in approximately 25 percent of the schools in America, and he says, "Those schools overwhelmingly fail to educate children to high levels of achievement."[7] A 1999 poll by the Joint Center for Political and Economic Studies found that 58 percent of African Americans rated their local school as "fair" or "poor."[8]

What is best for them? Those five words drove me to write this book. To get at that issue, let's examine how well the present system is serving poor children.

POOR SCHOOLS ARE FAILING TODAY'S POOR CHILDREN

Introduction: A Story

What's life like for poor children? In *Amazing Grace*, Jonathan Kozol paints a picture of what life is like for poor children in the United States:

> Many children in Mott Haven who, like Anthony, do not have a bedroom have a hard time finding quiet places to do homework. I ask him, "Where do you do your writing?" "In the closet of my brother's bedroom. With a flashlight," he replies.[9]

Kozol goes on to suggest that life is so challenging for poor American children that they don't just experience traumas; rather, their way of life is so characterized by one trauma after another that the children might be described as living with "traumatization."

> The notion of "trauma" as an individual event, he and other teachers say, does not really get at what they feel is taking place, because these things are happening so often. "'Traumatization' as an ordinary state of mind is closer to the fact of things for many children here," another teacher says. "They lead the life most people only read about. A little one speaks to me, and I have tears in my eyes."[10]

Structural/Systemic Issues

Today poor American children lack choice, attend substandard school buildings, and have less spent on them per year. Many people look to education as the answer for poor children. For example, Kahlenberg writes:

Abraham Lincoln noted that education is "the most important subject we as a people can be engaged in." In *Brown v. Board of Education*, the Supreme Court reiterated the importance of education: "In these days, it is doubtful that any child may reasonably be expected to succeed in life if he is denied the opportunity of an education"—a statement far more true now than it was in 1954. Today, education spending constitutes the single largest budget item in nearly every state budget; and yet we fail, miserably, to educate large segments of our population.[11]

Does our educational system offer hope to impoverished children? Is education really the "ticket out of poverty" for twenty-first-century poor children? Is education helping to end the cycle of poverty? In other words, how does the "rising tide of mediocrity" impact America's poorest children?

To get at this issue, ask yourself this question, what are the odds that an equally intelligent poor and rich five-year-old will get the same quality of education from kindergarten through high school? Put differently, one cannot simply make the blanket argument that poor children put forth less effort in school than their rich peers and therefore they themselves are responsible for their poor educational performance. Undoubtedly, some poor children do not try very hard. But is their lack of effort the only, or even the primary, reason for their underperformance? Here the answer is an unqualified no.

Poor children are condemned to their local public schools. They have no options; they have no chance to "opt out." Their parents have no choices. Parents' hopes and dreams are diminished by sending their children to schools at a severe competitive disadvantage due to a lack of funding. Their children might not live better lives than they did.

Much of this results from the way our system itself is set up. The first structural barrier poor children face is that they have no way out. The current American K–12 educational system is based on the location of one's house. Children attend the local school in their district. This seemingly benign idea has exerted negative consequences, especially for African Americans. Consider the following: Howell and Peterson have pointed out that African American families with two children have a median household income of $25,351 whereas white households have a median income of $40,912. Moreover, an African American family's median net worth was $7,000 whereas a white family's median net worth was nearly $50,000. Seventy-two percent of whites owned their own homes compared with 47 percent of African Americans, and African Americans were twice as likely as whites to be turned down for a home loan. Nineteen percent of African American families pay over 40 percent of their income in housing costs compared with 13 percent of white families. African Americans are far more likely to live in areas infested with crime and physical problems within their housing unit.

Howell and Peterson cite studies showing that African American loan applications with comparable financial statements as white loan applications were denied at a rate of 17 percent, compared to a rate of 11 percent for the white loan applications. They state, "The net result of economic factors and racial discrimination is a highly segregated housing market. Eight in ten African Americans live in neighborhoods where they are the majority, despite the fact that they constitute just 12 percent of the population nationwide." They conclude, "It should be no surprise, then, that public schools inherit the racial inequality that pervades the housing market . . . [and] the educational consequences can be devastating." Only 23 percent of students at urban high-poverty schools read at grade level and the historically high black–white test-score gap increased in the 1990s. Finally, they quote columnist William Raspberry: "Poor children desperately need better education. Yet the schools they attend—particularly in America's overwhelmingly black and brown inner cities—may be the least successful of all public schools."[12] The rich have a choice when it comes to schooling and the poor do not; this is a system aptly described as "socialism for the rich."

So, the quality of children's schooling is in large part related to their parent's income, since schools are funded largely by property taxes. In other words, the present system discriminates against the poor. John Coons described the plight of the poor over a decade ago, "They cannot afford formal education of their own choosing."[13] It's no wonder that poor children become caught in a cycle of poverty.

Contrast their situation with that of the rich. School choice is a common feature of American life for many except for the poor. *The Condition of Education* in 1999 showed that 73 percent of high-income families chose their child's preschool as compared with only 19 percent of low-income parents. The numbers are similar in terms of kindergarten choice (28 percent compared with 7 percent), elementary school choice (17 percent compared with 3 percent), and secondary school choice (13 percent compared with 3 percent).[14] At every level of school, the rich are four times more likely to exercise choice in schooling than the poor.[15] Similar conclusions were reached by Henig and Sugarman, who estimate that over one-half of all American families have exercised some type of choice: 36 percent select their home with the public school in mind, 11 percent use some form of public school choice, 10 percent send their children to private schools, 2 percent home school, and 1 percent send their children to charter schools.[16]

The consequence of this is summed up by Peter Cookson, director of educational outreach and extension at Teachers College, Columbia University: "The American education system reproduces class differences with eerie predictability. This is because race and class segregation are not based on law, but on residence."[17]

The poor cannot choose their school because they lack the money to do so. In 1997, the median cost of a private preschool was $1,358; kindergarten, $1,813; elementary school, $2,115; and secondary school, $4,116.[18] The poor cannot choose a school because the poor cannot afford to choose. A 1998 Center for Education Reform Manifesto stated the case accurately:

> But millions of Americans—mainly the children of the poor and minorities— don't enjoy those options. They are stuck with what "the system" dishes out to them, and all too often they are stuck with the least qualified teachers, the most rigid bureaucratic structures, the fewest choices and the shoddiest quality. Those parents who yearn for something better for their children lack the power to make it happen. They lack the power to shape their own lives and those of their children.[19]

Clearly, then, poor children cannot get out of their failing school in the same way that a rich child could. The poor lack options. Therefore, what Horace Mann did not want, we now have in the United States: one set of schools for the rich, and another set of schools for the poor. Society has lost the "common school," and the poor have lost the "great equalizer."[20]

The American educational system places barriers in the pathway of children from lower socioeconomic status in the United States. This is the system five-year-old children enter into. Without choices, poor children must attend the school in their district. From the start of their educational career, they are denied choices available to the wealthy, who may select a private school or move to a wealthy community with a good school system. For the poor, there is no such choice. Poor children get the luck of the draw and frequently their only luck is bad luck. American children are not treated equally in terms of educational opportunity. Don't the poor deserve the same quality of education as the rich? Jonathan Kozol writes about one who doesn't think so:

> "Some people are better than others," wrote conservative social scientist Charles Murray several years ago. "They deserve more of society's rewards." The coldness of this statement offended many people at the time that it was published. But Murray's views are not entirely different from what politicians, business leaders, and the school board of New York seem to believe and have embodied in providing the "best" kids with the best building and best vista not just of the harbor, but of their own future.[21]

The Center for Education Reform powerfully sums up the quality of education offered to today's poor children:

> In today's schools, far too many disadvantaged and minority students are not being challenged. Far too many are left to fend for themselves when they need instruction and direction from highly qualified teachers. Far too many are passed from grade to grade, left to sink or swim. Far too many are advanced without even learning to read, though proven methods of teaching reading are now well-known. *They are given shoddy imitations of real academic content, today's equivalent of Jim Crow math and back-of-the-bus science. When so little is expected and so little is done, such children are victims of failed public policy* [emphasis mine].[22]

The substandard condition of schools in poor districts is a second systemic barrier poor children face. In fact, the schools they enter into are frequently abysmal. According to the U.S. Department of Education, the average age of a public school is approximately forty years, and the average number of years since the last major renovation is sixteen; these numbers mean that approximately 60,000 schools nationwide need some type of renovation, which average $2.2 million each, with a total price tag of $127 billion.[23]

Some of the worst school buildings are those serving poor children. In *Amazing Grace*, Kozol provides some firsthand examples:

At one junior high school in the South Bronx, for example, in which money was so scarce in 1994 that girls were using pieces of TV cable as their jump ropes at the time I visited the area, only 15 teachers in a faculty of 54 were certified. The over-crowding of children in these schools compounds the chaos caused by staffing difficulties. At some schools in the South Bronx, in the same year, classes were taking place in settings like stair-landings, bathrooms, and coat closets, because the population of poor children was increasing but there was, according to the press, no money to build schools for them.[24]

Similarly, Kozol writes:

"I count the graduating class," writes City University Professor Michelle Fine, in speaking of one of these segregated high schools "a total of 200 in a school of approximately 3,200." Almost a thousand students out of these 3,200 are officially "discharged" for poor attendance or a number of other reasons, including violent behavior, every year. Studying the fate of 1,436 children enrolled in the ninth grade during one academic year, she finds that, six years later, a full 87 percent have been "discharged"—the term used by the school—and that 80 percent of the original ninth graders have yet to receive a degree from any other academic institution.[25]

In his *Just Generosity*, Ron Sider cites several other examples of substandard schools. At Pyne Point Junior High—98 percent black and Latino—the school has no money for computers and still uses the same typewriters as when the students' parents attended the school. At Woodrow Wilson High School, the chemistry lab has no equipment and 58 percent of all students drop out before graduation. Sider then adds:

A black principal from Camden High is more blunt. When she is invited to speak at places like Princeton and people try to argue that it makes little difference that Camden spends $4,000 and Princeton $8,000 per student, she retorts, "If you don't believe that money makes a difference, let your children go to school in Camden. *Trade* with our children. When I say this, people will not meet my eyes. They stare down at the floor."[26]

Summing up this point of two different systemic opportunities, Jesse Jackson said, "One child is programmed for Yale, one programmed for jail."[27]

These stories put a face upon the larger, broader points regarding the substandard condition of schooling for the economically disadvantaged in the United States. In this information age, the poor have much less access to computers in their classes. As Patricia Leigh writes, "What has not changed is the fact that the level of access to these tools correlates to race membership or socioeconomic status." She goes on to quote Becker and Sterling who, analyzing survey data, wrote, "Black elementary school students in 1985 were less likely to attend schools with computers, and blacks of all ages attend schools with fewer computer-using teachers than do whites." She sums up the issue in this way: "The results of this study strongly suggest that access to educational technologies are unequally distributed among schools of differing racial or socioeconomic makeups." She adds, "The higher the socioeconomic status of the student body, the more likely the school will have higher levels and faster types of Internet access."[28]

In addition to lacking choice and attending substandard school buildings, a third systemic problem is that poor students have less spent on them per year than students from richer districts. For example, the nation's richest school districts spend 36 percent more per pupil than the poorest school districts, according to the 1997 *Report on the Condition of Education* by the U.S. Education Department.[29] Moreover, the July 1998 U.S. Department of Education's *Inequalities in Public School District Revenues* reports that the schools with the most students from households with the lowest income spent $4,677 per student whereas the schools with the most students from households with the highest income spent $5,321 per student. So, the rich districts spend $644 more *per student per year*. Sider notes that in a district of 515 students, this amount of money would mean an extra $332,000 per year—or enough to pay for five or six more teachers and thirty-two new computers every year.[30]

These spending inequities translate tangibly into fewer opportunities for poor students. Poor students have a much higher likelihood of having an unqualified teacher. The National Commission on Teaching and America's Future reported that new teachers without proper certification are typically assigned to teach in low-income and high-minority areas.[31] Moreover, four times as many new teachers without a license begin teaching in schools where more than half the children are poor, and the schools with the most minority students have less than a 50 percent chance of having a math and science teacher who has both a degree in that field and a state teaching license. In fact, the 1997 *Report on the Condition of Edu-*

cation by the U.S. Department of Education found that in schools with a high concentration of minority students, more than 70 percent of the teachers lacked necessary classroom materials.[32] Similarly, *Education Week* reported in its "Quality Counts 2003" article that teacher quality was severely lagging in poorer schools. For example, 22 percent of students nationwide take at least one class from a teacher who neither majored nor minored in the subject, but 32 percent of students in high-poverty schools take at least one class with such a teacher (a number almost 50 percent higher). Moreover, in affluent areas, only 9 percent of teachers have fewer than three years of teaching experience, whereas in high-poverty areas, the number is almost fifty percent higher at 13 percent. Teachers in high-poverty areas reported more problems with atmosphere and morale. These teachers described more problems in terms of student disrespect, students who were ill prepared to learn, and a lack of parental involvement.[33]

These facts represent the reality of the situation for many poor students in America's schools. John Witte paints a picture of this reality:

I am seated in the basement of a sixty-year-old school in the spring of 1991. The room is painted graying green and it is clean, but clearly the space has been improvised for the music class I have been watching for twenty minutes. Twenty-three first-grade students sit on folding chairs. All are African American; there are nine boys and fourteen girls. The boys wear white dress shirts and blue pants. The teacher is a black woman who I have heard has had problems showing up for work. She is not having any problems today. The class is quiet as they listen to her sing and talk. They love this class. She begins by talking about a verse they have just sung. She says the song is a black spiritual: "Lord Help Me Lay My Burdens Down." She asks the class if they know what "burdens" are.

An overly eager boy shoots up his hand as his mouth opens: "Burdens are heavy things!"

"Well, yes, they are sort of, but in the song they refer to worries," responds the teacher. "Can anyone tell me about worries they want the Lord to help with?"

A compatriot of the first boy: "Like when I go home with my report card." (Laughter)

A tiny girl in the second row, hair in pigtails, with a voice so small it is hard to hear from ten feet away: "To make the shooting over my house stop."

Another girl, sitting next to her: "So the fighting will stop at home."

The first boy (laughter gone): "To keep the gangs and the druggers away."

The teacher looks at me, shakes her head, and says: "Let's try the second verse."[34]

These stories are representative of the general conditions poor children face. Aptly summing up the problem with where the United States is currently spending its money, Kozol writes regarding New York City:

> The city spends $58,000 yearly on each adult inmate, $70,000 on each juvenile—nearly ten times what it spends to educate a child in its public schools. "The cost is justified," says a woman who runs an education program on the island, "in terms that go beyond financial calculations. Without this island (Rikers), the attractive lives some of us lead in the nice sections of New York would simply not be possible. If you want to get your outcasts out of sight, first you need a ghetto and then you need a prison to take pressure off the ghetto. The fact that it doesn't make financial sense is not the point. Short-term terror and revulsion are more powerful than long-term wisdom or self-interest. That's why corrections is one of the few growth industries in New York City now."[35]

THE RESULTS: POOR CHILDREN ARE FAILING IN TODAY'S POOR SCHOOLS

Clearly, the present system does not provide equal educational opportunity to all American children. Poor children lack choice, attend substandard school buildings, and have less spent on them per year. It is not surprising, therefore, that poor children are not succeeding under the current system. The evidence regarding dropout rates, academic performance, and racial integration are all disturbing.

According to Jay Greene, senior fellow at the Manhattan Institute in New York, 79 percent of Asian students and 76 percent of white students graduate from high school—but only 55 percent of black students and 53 percent of Hispanic students graduate from high school. One might be encouraged by the fact that dropout rates for African American students has decreased from 21 percent in 1972 to 11 percent in 2001, until one finds out why the dropout rate has been reduced. Bruce Western, professor of sociology at Princeton University explains, "About half the fall in the dropout rate is due to the rise in imprisonment of young black males." Statistics don't include people as dropouts who are incarcerated. The incarceration rate for African American males aged twenty-two to thirty who haven't finished high school is 40 percent (1999), up from only 14 percent in 1980. And the problems start young. About 50 percent of Cleveland's students do not make it from the ninth to the tenth grade.[36]

Further information on dropouts is even more disconcerting. At least 50 percent of incoming high school students drop out in the high schools of the nation's thirty-five largest cities, according to a 2001 Johns Hopkins University report, and 12.6 percent of African Americans and 28.6 percent of Hispanic Americans aged sixteen to twenty-four are neither in school nor have a high school diploma.[37] Ron Sider reports that while one-third of African Americans live in the suburbs, thus sending their children to better schools, the national dropout rate for African Americans is twice as high as it is for whites, and for Latinos it's four times higher than it is for white children. The unemployment rate for high school dropouts is 20 percent, high school graduates 11 percent, and college graduates 2 percent.[38]

And the story doesn't get much better. According to research conducted by Sider, only 46 percent of urban students can read at a "basic level," and only 23 percent of children in urban high-poverty areas. The average seventeen-year-old African American or Latino child reads at the same level as the average thirteen-year-old white child and fewer than half as many black and Latino students graduate from college as white students.[39]

Overall, the disparities are even worse if one considers the economic extremes. Richard Kahlenberg points outs:

> Low-income twelfth-grade students read on average at the level of middle-class eighth-graders. Children whose families are in the bottom income quintile are twice as likely to drop out of high school as those from families in the top quintile. In the end, some 76 percent of high-income students complete bachelor's degrees, compared with a mere 4 percent of low-income students.[40]

And so poor children are increasingly left out of American society. The key to success in today's economy is education, including a variety of technological proficiencies. Lacking education or these proficiencies, some of the poor may be more "likely to engage in various social pathologies, including crime, bad parenting, and drug abuse."[41]

Former Secretary of Education William Bennett summarized the condition of the poor in today's schools in his five-year assessment of public education: "Good schools for the disadvantaged and minority children are much too rare, and the dropout rate among black and Hispanic youth in many of our inner cities is perilously high."[42] And the minority achievement gap is as much as 105 points lower on the SAT.[43] Moreover, 58 percent of Hispanic and 63 percent of African American fourth-grade students scored below the "basic" reading level according to the 2000 National Assessment of Educational Progress Reading Report Card.[44] Furthermore, the performance gap between advantaged and disadvantaged students increases throughout K–12. While this type of educational system does not guarantee failure, it does add significant hurdles; these are unjust hurdles since they are erected solely as a result of parents' financial status. The doors to the better schools are closed to the children who need them the most.

Many other studies have documented the ways in which inner-city schools are failing today's poor students. Paul Peterson sums this up writing:

> Cecilia Rouse reports in Milwaukee student test scores fall as students "progress" through the public schools. Also, when the *New York Times* compared the scores of New York city students with those of students statewide, controlling for the students' racial and income status, it found that the city students scored three percentile points behind the statewide average in third grade, six percentile points behind in sixth grade, and as much as fifteen points behind in high school.[45]

People of minority status are clustered in these failing schools: at least 88 percent of the students are of minority status in the public school systems in the cities of Chicago, Detroit, Houston, Los Angeles, and Washington, D.C. And according to the Harvard Civil Rights Project, the racial balance in many schools has *declined* from 1986 to 2000. The Harvard report found that the proportion of African Americans in white-majority schools dropped from 43.5 percent to 32.7 percent. The most segregated schools are in New York, California, Michigan, and Illinois. The most rapidly resegregating school districts are in the South. In fact, in the following ten school districts, the African Americans exposure to whites has declined anywhere from 30 to 45 percent: Clayton County, Georgia; Alief, Texas;

Gwinnett County, Georgia; Cobb County, Georgia; Irving, Texas; Arlington, Texas; Minneapolis; Aldine, Texas; Klein, Texas; and Fremont, California. And in Charlotte's Mecklenburg County, barely a quarter of the schools achieve the district's overall racial balance goal while some majority-black schools are just half-full and some majority-white schools are overcrowded.[46] Therefore, the evidence is overwhelming that today's public schools are not meeting the needs of today's poor students. Professor Lawrence Stedman sums up the crisis today's poor students are facing:

[Twelfth-] grade black students are performing at the level of middle school white students. These students are about to graduate, yet they lag four or more years behind in every area [including] reading, math, science, writing, history, and geography. Latino seniors do somewhat better . . . in math and writing but, in the other areas, are also four years behind white 12th graders. . . . Racial gaps in achievement . . . are as large or larger than they were a decade ago. . . . The conclusion is distressing but unavoidable. . . . A generation has passed and the achievement of educational equality remains an elusive dream. Schools and society remain divided into two different worlds, one black and white, separate and unequal.[47]

Similarly, the Center for Education Reform powerfully summarizes the current state of schools:

We are re-creating a dual school system, separate and unequal, almost half a century after it was declared unconstitutional. We face a widening and unacceptable chasm between good schools and bad, between those youngsters who get an adequate education and those who emerge from school barely able to read and write. Poor and minority children, by and large, go to worse schools, have less expected of them, are taught by less knowledgeable teachers, and have the least power to alter bad situations. Yet it's poor children who most need great schools.[48]

Sider concludes the sorry state of public education for poor children today: "While poor schools have a greater *negative* impact on disadvantaged kids than other children, good schools have a stronger *positive* impact on disadvantaged kids. Quality education is the best way to empower the poorest, most disadvantaged children. Educational opportunity is the new civil rights struggle."[49] Schools serving the poorest children simply aren't working. Summing this up, five Republican governors issued a joint statement in 1998 that said, "We believe every child, regardless of social or economic status, should have the same variety of educational opportunities, wonderful teachers, and safe schools as the most privileged children enjoy."[50] Richard Kahlenberg sums up the point, "Economically separate schools are the fountainhead of countless discrete inequalities."[51]

So, poor children may well enter kindergarten with bright hopes. Many fewer graduate high school. Even fewer graduate high school with bright hopes. Clint Bolick, agreeing with Sider, suggests that these systemwide injustices to children are so serious that they rise to the level of depriving poor children of their civil rights:

> In modern society, the pursuit of education is critically important in exercising fundamental rights. Thus, any arbitrary interference with the pursuit of education constitutes a deprivation of civil rights. Moreover, as the Supreme Court observed in *Brown v. Topeka Board of Education*, the principle of equality under the law requires that education, "where the state has undertaken to provide it, . . . must be available to all on equal terms."
>
> The denial of educational liberty stands as one of the most flagrant and crippling violations of civil rights today. The principal source of this deprivation is the monopoly of the public school system, which limits opportunities for alternative types of education on the one hand while allocating benefits unequally on the other.[52]

After *Brown v. Topeka Board of Education*, some public officials stood in school doorways barring certain children from entering. Today, we have a system that prevents children from exiting. Poor children are trapped: they are stuck in substandard schools and they can't get out. The parents of poor children are trapped: they have no options for better schooling for their children. Under the present system, the poor are the ones losing out.

Clearly, our system of schooling is not the "ticket out of poverty" for the poor; rather, our system accentuates the poverty of America's poor instead of offering poor children a way out. Muriel Newman writes: "Failing schools are the blight of a nation. They destroy children's futures. It is a crime to have children condemned, year after year, to attending schools that fail to give them the skills, habits and knowledge that they will need to succeed in later life."[53]

And the effects of this poor education will shape a child's life. According to the National Center for Education Statistics (NCES), young male adults with a college degree earn 58 percent more than their counterparts with only a high school degree, and young female adults with a college degree earn 92 percent more than their counterparts with only a high school degree. Moreover, the NCES reports that higher education correlates positively with increased civic engagement, more employable skills, and even a healthier living style.[54]

The final tragedy is that the poor are powerless to change the current system. Bruce Goldberg writes, "As things stand now, parents who are dissatisfied with a school policy are virtually powerless. When they try to act on behalf of their children against a school policy, they are regarded as a nuisance."[55] But under a system of vouchers, the poor would be empowered. Over thirty years ago, Christopher Jencks wrote that school choice would "give parents, and particularly disadvantaged parents, more control over the kind of education their children get."[56] As one who has studied the Milwaukee experiment in detail, John Witte writes:

> Choice can be a useful tool to aid families and educators in inner city and poor communities where education has been a struggle for several generations. If programs are devised correctly, they can provide meaningful educational choices to families that now do not have such choices. And it is not trivial that most people in America . . . already have those choices.[57]

Of all the people in society, children of poor parents will be helped the most by school choice. Howell and Peterson said, "New educational opportunities will most benefit those groups that cannot exercise choice in the residential market."[58] They go on to write, "Because vouchers can break the link between place of residence and schooling options, we should expect African American families, who fare worst in housing markets, to be the most pleased with and to receive the greatest benefits from school choice."[59] Lowell Weicker and Richard Kahlenberg sum the point up: "American children have returned to schools that are increasingly segregated by economic status. That central reality—that poor children and middle-class children increasingly attend separate schools—is at the heart of America's education problem. Poverty concentrations have a way of defeating even the best education programs."[60]

Despite the overwhelming evidence of the failure of the poor in our current system, some still argue that a new system of school choice will harm the poor by shaking up the public education system in the United States! But as Theodore Sizer and Phillip Whitten pointed out over two decades ago, and is now patently clear, the public educational system itself is already failing poor children:

> Those who would argue that our (school choice) proposal would destroy the public schools raise a false issue. A system of public education which destroys rather than develops positive human potential now exists. It is not in the public interest. And a system which blames its society while it quietly acquiesces in, and inadvertently perpetuates the very injustices it blames for its inefficiencies, is not in the public interest. If a system cannot fulfill its responsibilities, it does not deserve to survive. But if the public schools serve, they will prosper.[61]

THE OVERALL STATE OF PUBLIC SCHOOLS THAT POOR CHILDREN CANNOT GET OUT OF

Not only are today's public schools poorly serving poor students, but the overall quality is also quite poor. What might come as a surprise to many is just how horrible things really are.[62] Are the public schools in crisis?

There are many, many problems with America's schools, especially with its central-city public schools. In central-city public secondary schools, problems associated with preparedness, apathy, absence, and tardiness are ten times more common than they are in private schools. Similarly, verbal abuse of teachers and disrespect for teachers is also about ten times higher in large city public schools.[63] The ninth annual Bracey Report concludes with these words: "Public school teachers are more likely than private school teachers to perceive their students and their families as having problems that can interfere with learning."[64]

Many trends are disheartening. In 1998, for example: 10 million high school seniors could not read at a basic level, 20 million could not do basic math, 25 million did not know the basics of American history, and 6 million dropped out of school. The numbers are even more disturbing in the minority communities. In 1996, 13 percent of all African Americans ages sixteen to twenty-four were not in school, 17 percent of first-generation Hispanics had dropped out, and 44 percent of Hispanic immigrants ages sixteen to twenty-four had dropped out.[65]

Furthermore, if students have poor teachers for a couple of years in a row, they are much more likely to perform poorly on standardized tests. Gerald Bracey explains:

> Perhaps more interesting is the finding that the cumulative impact of a sequence of highly test-effective or highly test-ineffective teachers is large. Sanders examined an average district and a high-scoring district and found that students who had test-effective teachers three years in a row scored at the 83rd and 96th percentiles respectively; students who had test-ineffective teachers three years in a row scored at the 29th and 44th percentiles.[66]

There also remains a significant gap between the SAT scores of white and African American students. In the 1986–1987 school year, the average white and African American verbal scores were 524 and 428 respectively, compared with a comparable difference in 1999–2000 of 528 and 434 respectively. A similar gap exists in terms of SAT math scores, where in 1986–1987 the average white score was 514 and African American score was 411; in 1999–2000, the scores were 530 and 426 respectively.[67]

Compared with other industrialized country's students, the overall public education numbers leave one concerned. The Center for Education Reform reports the following:

> American 12th graders scored near the bottom of the recent Third International Mathematics and Science Study (TIMSS): U.S. students placed 19th out of 21 nations in math and 16th out of 21 in science. Our advanced students did even worse, scoring dead last in physics. This evidence suggests that, compared to the rest of the industrialized world, our students lag seriously in critical subjects vital to our future.[68]

And performance decreases the longer a student is in a public school. According to the Center for Education Reform, when U.S. fourth graders competed against students from Japan, Korea, Hong Kong, Singapore, and ten other countries they did well; but when they competed against them four years later, they "fell well below" the other students. The Center for Education Reform again reports, "Internationally, U.S. youngsters hold their own at the elementary level but falter in the middle years and drop far behind in high school. We seem to be the only country in the world whose children fall farther behind the longer they stay in school."[69]

There are also some disturbing long-term trends. Since 1967, SAT verbal scores have dropped 37 points while grade inflation is up: 41 percent of college bound students reported As in 2001 compared with only 28 percent in 1991.

In fact, across the board, in almost every subject, American students perform poorly. Sixty-four percent of high school students did less than one hour of homework per day, 30 percent worked more than five hours a day, 21 percent watched television five hours or more per day, and they performed worse on the TIMSS test than did students from Hungary and Slovenia.[70] According to the 2001 *Reality Check*, little more than one-third of college professors and employers ranked graduates' basic math skills as good or excellent and little more than a fourth were satisfied with college graduates' ability to write clearly.[71]

In terms of reading and writing, 37 percent of fourth-grade students scored below the "basic" reading level, and only 32 percent were reading at the "proficient" level, according to the 2000 National Assessment of Educational Progress (NAEP) Reading Report Card.[72] Only 25 percent of high school juniors in Washington, D.C., scored at or above "basic" in reading, and only 23 percent of fourth graders in Washington state passed all four subjects in the state's standardized tests.[73]

The reading proficiency gap between white, Hispanic American, and African American students is alarming. According to the NAEP test, white students ages nine, thirteen, and seventeen scored an average reading proficiency score of 221, 267, and 295; Hispanic students at the same age levels scored 193, 244, and 271; and African American students at the same age levels scored 186, 238, and 264. The average thirteen-year-old white student scored higher than the average seventeen-year-old African American student.[74] In terms of math, American student performance is equally dismal. In international math testing, American seniors came in nineteenth out of twenty countries and were significantly below the first fourteen countries. On the advanced math assessment, our students came in twelfth out of fifteen.[75] In a 1996 national science test, 40 percent of eighth graders and 43 percent of high school students scored "below basic"—the lowest possible grade—and in a 2000 national math assessment, 35 percent of seniors scored "below basic."[76] These scores reflect challenges across the board.

According to the 2000 NAEP Math Report Card, 31 percent of fourth graders, 34 percent of eighth graders, and 35 percent of seniors were "below basic" in math testing.[77]

In terms of science, public schools are also failing our students. According to the Third International Mathematics and Science Study (TIMSS), American seniors scored far below students from eleven other countries and ahead of students from only two countries. According to the 1996 NAEP Science Report Card, 3 percent of students developed advanced skills, while 33 percent of fourth graders, 39 percent of eighth graders, and 43 percent of seniors performed at the lowest level, below basic skills.[78]

When these numbers are put into an international context, they do not look quite as bad. According to the 2000 Program for International Student Assessment of Fifteen-Year-Olds (PISA), a study comparing students in most of the twenty-seven countries in the Organization for Economic Cooperation and Development (OECD), American students performed about as well as students from the other countries in reading, math, and science.[79] Similarly, according to the Third International Mathematics and Science Study, American students did well in international comparisons:

> In 1999, U.S. students on average scored higher in both mathematics and science than the international average of the 38 countries. In mathematics, the average U.S. score was higher than the score in 17 countries, similar to the score in 6 countries, and lower than the score in 14 countries. In science, the average U.S. score for 8th-graders was higher than the score in 18 countries, similar to the score in 5 countries, and lower than the score in 14 countries in 1999.[80]

When we focus just on math, students seem to recede the longer they remain in the U.S. educational system. According to the TIMSS, "On average 4th-grade students in the United States scored above the international average in mathematics; students in the 8th and 12th grades scored below the international average."[81] It appears, though, overall, that the longer a U.S. student is in school, the further behind she becomes. The National Center for Education Statistics writes about the 1999 TIMSS-R in which eighth graders were compared after being compared four years earlier as fourth graders:

> The results from TIMSS-R are mixed. Eighth-grade students in the United States exceeded the international average of the 38 countries that participated in the mathematics and science studies in 1999. Similar to most other

countries participating in both assessments, there was no significant improvement, however, in the average scores of U.S. 8th-graders in either subject between 1995 and 1999. By permitting a comparison of 4th-graders in 1995 and the same cohort 4 years later in 8th grade, TIMSS-R shows that U.S. 4th-graders in 1995 performed at about the international average of the 17 countries participating in both assessments in mathematics but that by 1999 U.S. 8th-graders had fallen behind the international average. In science, U.S. 4th-graders performed above the international average of the 17 participating countries in 1995, while U.S. 8th-graders' performance was similar to the international average in 1999.[82]

Perhaps even more important than international comparisons are issues of equity in education in the United States itself. According to the National Center for Education Statistics, comparing scores from the National Assessment of Educational Progress, a test taken since the 1970s to assess long-term student performance:

> As was the case in reading, white students outperformed black students in each assessment in both mathematics and science. In mathematics, the gap decreased from 1973 until 1990 for 17-year-olds and from 1973 until 1986 for 13-year-olds. The gaps have widened since then. In 1999, the gaps were greater for both 13-year-olds and 17-year-olds than in 1990 and 1986, respectively. In science, there has been no significant change from 1969 to 1999 among 17-year-olds. Among 13-year-olds, the gap decreased from 1977 to 1982, and has remained stable since.[83]

In terms of history, the story is equally disturbing. A survey of college seniors at America's top fifty colleges demonstrated some troubling findings: More seniors thought Ulysses S. Grant was the American general at Yorktown than thought he had been a president of the United States, more than one-third couldn't identify the Constitution as the document that established separation of powers, only 22 percent could identify the Gettysburg Address as the document containing the line "government of the people, by the people, for the people," but 98 percent could identify rapper Snoop Doggy Dogg.[84] According to the 1994 NAEP assessment of U.S. history, 57 percent of high school seniors scored below basic skills level, and according to the 1998 Department of Education's Civic Report Card, less than three-quarters of students demonstrated proficiency in civics.[85]

Such challenges ought not to surprise us. According to the National Center for Education Statistics (where level 1 is the lowest and level 5 is the highest in terms of adult literacy levels), "Compared to most other countries assessed, the United States showed a greater concentration of adults scoring at the lowest literacy level . . . [and] one of the highest concentrations of adults scoring at or above level four."[86] Such literacy is associated with overall quality of life. The higher one's education, the more one is likely to read a magazine or newspaper and at least one book in the past six months.[87]

CONCLUSION

In "A Nation Still at Risk," the Center for Education Reform states, "America today faces a profound test of its commitment to equal educational opportunity. This is a test of whether we truly intend to educate all of our children or merely keep everyone in school for a certain number of years."[88]

The goal throughout this book is to demonstrate that a just system of education will benefit poor children—children like this one, who started attending a school of her choice: "'As soon as I came here it was a big change. Here, teachers care about you. . . . In public school the teachers were too busy to help.' Worst of all, she said, were the fights: 'You really can't avoid it. They'll think you are scared.'"[89]

Will poor children be better served in a system of school choice? At this point one thing is very clear: they cannot be served any worse than they are under the current system. Today's public educational system is failing the most desperately poor of America's children.[90]

What is clear from the evidence presented in this chapter is what the poor don't need: the status quo. As the Center for Education Reform put it, "What truly threatens public education is clinging to an ineffective status quo."[91]

And the poor don't just need more money thrown into a failed system. We've tried throwing more money into the system for the past few decades and it hasn't resulted in a better system. Much of the money never gets to students and teachers who need that money in the classroom. Newark Councilman Cory Booker explains the futility of throwing money at the problem:

In Newark, per capita expenditure is about $10,000, over $10,000 if we include capital costs. I try to speak in one public school a week, talk to teachers, work with them. I found some creative ways to help them. But before I go into a classroom, I will always ask the teacher, "What can I do for you?" And inevitably, he or she always says, "Can you help me get some books? Can you help me get some school supplies?"[92]

Councilman Booker goes on to tell how Newark school students organized a penny drive to buy pencils, pens, and basic school supplies.

What the poor need, what they want, what they demand, is a system in which they are empowered. That's what they're lacking in the current system. As the Center for Education Reform puts it, "Only those children whose parents have power end up with an excellent education."[93] And empowerment is precisely what school choice offers, for it is precisely these poor students that choice programs are targeting. According to research conducted by Brian Gill, students entering the choice programs in the United States averaged scoring between the 17th and 37th percentiles on standardized tests.[94] School choice is the answer for today's poor, not a tweaking of the current system. As one mom who received a voucher to send her child to a parochial school put it, the school "worked miracles on him."[95]

Columnist William Raspberry has summed up the situation of poor children in today's inner-city schools: "Poor children desperately need better education. Yet the schools they attend—particularly in America's overwhelmingly black and brown inner cities—may be the least successful of all public schools."[96] Today's schools are failing the poor. Getting them out may well be the civil rights issue of the day.

NOTES

1. Richard Kahlenberg, *All Together Now* (Washington, D.C.: Brookings Institution Press, 2001), 4.

2. American Council of Trustees and Alumni, "The American Education Diet: Can U.S. Students Survive on Junk Food?" *Center for Education Reform* (2001) at www.edreform.com/pubs/junkfood.htm.

3. American Council, "The American Education Diet."

4. American Council, "The American Education Diet."

5. Lowell Rose, "The 32nd Annual Phi Delta Kappa/Gallup Poll of the Public's Attitudes toward the Public Schools," *Phi Delta Kappan* 82 (September 2000): 41–58.

6. Great attention must be placed on the education of poor children from kindergarten on, since the U.S. Department of Education reports that gaps in student performance upon entering kindergarten continue through the end of the first grade. See U.S. Department of Education, *The Condition of Education 2001*, (Washington, D.C.: Office of Educational Research and Improvement), 15, 19, 116, and 238.

7. Kahlenberg, *All Together Now*, 2.

8. American Council, "The American Education Diet."

9. Jonathan Kozol, *Amazing Grace: The Lives of Children and the Conscience of a Nation* (New York: Crown, 1995), 216.

10. Kobol, *Amazing Grace*, 124.

11. Kahlenberg, *All Together Now*, 3.

12. William Howell and Paul Peterson, *The Education Gap: Vouchers and Urban Schools* (Washington, D.C.: Brookings Institution Press, 2002), 23–26.

13. John Coons, "The Healthy Burden of Choice: An Opportunity to Empower the Poor," *ESA Advocate* (January/February 1991): 12.

14. *The Condition of Education 1999*, Section II, 58 (Washington, D.C.: U.S. Dept. of Commerce, Bureau of the Census). "October Current Population Surveys," quoted in Black Alliance for Educational Options, *The Continuing Struggle against Unequal Educational Opportunity*, August 24, 2000.

15. According to education policy professor Charles Glenn, 72 percent of families making over $50,000 had opted for some form of choice, either private school, magnet school, or public school selected by their choice of residence. He goes on to note that public schools in affluent areas and not private schools are really the elite option for many since it's less expensive to send a child to the prestigious Phillips Andover Academy in Massachusetts than it is to buy a house in the upscale city of Andover and send your children to its well-regarded public schools. And then the problems become cyclical as well-to-do families leave poorer areas, encouraging more well-to-do families to leave. See Lawrence Hardy, "Public School Choice," *American School Board Journal* (February 2000): 23, 24.

16. Henig and Sugarman, 1999, table 1-1, 29, quoted in Brian Gill et al., *Rhetoric versus Reality: What We Know and What We Need to Know about Vouchers and Charter Schools* (New York: Rand Education, 2001), 118.

17. Cookson quoted in Gill, *Rhetoric versus Reality*, 24. Summing up the hope for poor children Lawrence Hardy (2000) writes, "Of course, without school choice, disadvantaged children stuck in neighborhood schools that are failing have no alternatives. An inadequate choice program may give them few options, but with no choice program, they have none at all."

18. *The Condition of Education 1999*, Section II, 58.

19. "A Nation Still at Risk: An Education Manifesto," *Center for Education Reform* (April 30, 1998) at www.edreform.com/pubs/manifest.htm.

20. Kahlenberg, *All Together Now*, 1.

21. Kozol, *Amazing Grace*, 154.

22. "A Nation Still at Risk: An Education Manifesto."

23. Clara Vangen, "Condemned: America's Public Schools," *Buildings* 95 (January 2001): 62–66.

24. Kozol, *Amazing Grace*, 155.

25. Kozol, *Amazing Grace*, 150–51.

26. Sider, Ron. *Just Generosity: A New Vision for Overcoming Poverty in America* (Grand Rapids, Mich.: Baker Books, 1999), 153–55.

27. Sider, *Just Generosity*, 153.

28. Patricia Leigh, "Electronic Connections and Equal Opportunities: An Analysis of Telecommunications Distribution in Public Schools," *Journal of Research on Computing in Education* 32, no. 1 (Fall 1999): 108–27. See H. J. Becker and C. W. Sterling, "Equity in School Computer Use: National Data and Neglected Considerations," *Journal of Educational Computing Research* 3 (1998): 289–311.

29. Sider, *Just Generosity*, 159.

30. Sider, *Just Generosity*, 159. According to figures for the 2001 school year released in March 2003 by the U.S. Census Bureau, the average state spends $7,284 per pupil in elementary/secondary school per year. See U.S. Census Bureau, "Public Education Finances: 2001," quoted in "The Notebook," *The Christian Science Monitor* (March 28, 2003): 12.

31. Sider, *Just Generosity*, 160.

32. Sider, *Just Generosity*, 160.

33. "Quality Counts 2003," *Education Week* quoted in Marjorie Coeyman, "Teacher Quality Lags in Poorer Schools," *Christian Science Monitor* (January 7, 2003): 19.

34. John Witte, *The Market Approach to Education: An Analysis of America's First Voucher Program* (Princeton, N.J.: Princeton University Press, 2000), 1.

35. Kozol, *Amazing Grace*, 142

36. All citations in this paragraph are from Marjorie Coeyman, "The Story behind Dropout Rates," *Christian Science Monitor* (July 1, 2003): 13, 14, including the statistics on graduation rates which are from the Jay P. Greene Civic Report 31. Overall, the states with the highest graduation rates are Vermont 92.1 percent, Connecticut 87.6 percent, Nebraska 85.9 percent, Minnesota 85.3 percent, and North Dakota 85.1 percent. The states with the lowest graduation rates are Louisiana and Tennessee 62.5 percent, Mississippi 60.4 percent, South Carolina

60.1 percent, Georgia 58.5 percent, and Arizona 55.8 percent. See *Christian Science Monitor* (June 2, 2003): 24.

37. American Council, "The American Education Diet."

38. Sider, *Just Generosity*, 155.

39. Sider, *Just Generosity*, 155.

40. Kahlenberg, *All Together Now*, 3.

41. Kahlenberg, *All Together Now*, 13.

42. William Bennett, *American Education: Making It Work* (Washington, D.C.: U.S. Government Printing Office, 1988), 30.

43. "Back-to-School Bulletin #1," *Center for Education Reform* (August 28, 2001) at www.edreform.com/update/2001/010828.html.

44. American Council, "The American Education Diet."

45. Paul Peterson, "School Choice: A Report Card," *Virginia Journal of Social Policy and the Law* 6 (Fall 1998): 47–80. See Pam Belluck, "Learning Gap Tied to Time in the System: As School Stay Grows, Scores on Tests Worsen," *New York Times* (January 5, 1997): A-5.

46. The Harvard Civil Rights Project quoted in *The Christian Science Monitor* (January 7, 2003): 14, 16.

47. Lawrence Stedman, "An Assessment of the Contemporary Debate over U.S. Achievement," School of Education and Human Development, State University of New York at Binghamton, presented in May 1997, at the Brookings Institution, quoted in Black Alliance for Educational Options, *The Continuing Struggle against Unequal Educational Opportunity*.

48. "A Nation Still at Risk: An Education Manifesto."

49. Sider, *Just Generosity*, 155–56.

50. Kahlenberg, *All Together Now*, 4.

51. Kahlenberg, *All Together Now*, 4.

52. Clint Bolick, *Changing Course* (New Brunswick, N.J.: Transaction, 1988), 104–5.

53. Muriel Newman, "Choice of School Is a Fundamental Freedom" (February 13, 2002) at www.scoop.co.nz/mason/stories/PO0202/S00052.htm.

54. "Learner Outcomes," *National Center for Education Statistics* (2001) at http://nces.ed.gov/programs/coe/2001/section2/indicator14.html.

55. Bruce Goldberg, "A Liberal Argument for School Choice," *American Enterprise* 7 (September 1996): 27.

56. Quoted in Gill et al., *Rhetoric versus Reality*, 117.

57. Witte, *The Market Approach to Education*, 6.

58. Howell and Peterson, *The Education Gap*, 22.

59. Howell and Peterson, *The Education Gap*, 27.

60. Lowell Weicker and Richard Kahlenberg, "The New Educational Divide," *The Christian Science Monitor* (October 9, 2002): 9.

61. Theodore Sizer and Phillip Whitten, "A Proposal for a Poor Children's Bill of Rights," *Psychology Today* (August 1968): 34.

62. In fact, even scholars who argue that there is no crisis in American schools admit there are troubles in inner-city schools. Good and Braden write, "Although it is true that in some American schools (especially in some inner-city schools) students are performing abysmally, more generally, our schools appear not to be in crisis." See chapter 3 "Student Performance in American Schools: An Empirical Report Card," in Thomas Good and Jennifer Braden, *The Great School Debate: Choice, Vouchers, and Charters* (Mahwah, N.J.: Lawrence Erlbaum, 2000).

63. Gerald Bracey, "Public and Private Schools Compared," *Phi Delta Kappan* 81 (April 2000): 633–34.

64. Bracey, "Public and Private Schools Compared," 633–34. The quote is taken from "Public and Private Schools: How Do They Differ?" *Findings from the Condition of Education 1997* at http://nces.ed.gov/pubs97/97983.

65. "A Nation Still at Risk: An Education Manifesto."

66. Bracey, "The Ninth Bracey Report on the Condition of Public Education," *Phi Delta Kappan* 81 (October 1999): 147–48. Bracey cites Sanders. See William L. Sanders, "Value-Added Assessment," *School Administrator* (December 1998): 24–29.

67. "Scholastic Assessment Test (SAT) Scores," *National Center for Education Statistics* (2000) at http://nces.ed.gov/fastfacts/display.asp?id=53.

68. "A Nation Still at Risk: An Education Manifesto."

69. "A Nation Still at Risk: An Education Manifesto." See also "Back-to-School Bulletin #1," *Center for Education Reform*.

70. American Council, "The American Education Diet."

71. American Council, "The American Education Diet."

72. American Council, "The American Education Diet."

73. American Council, "The American Education Diet."

74. "Reading," *The National Center for Education Statistics* (2001) at http://nces.ed.gov/fastfacts/display.asp?id=35.

75. The Third International Mathematics and Science Study (TIMSS) scores released in February 1998, quoted in American Council, "The American Education Diet."

76. The 1996 National Assessment of Educational Progress science tests and the 2000 Math NAEP tests quoted in American Council, "The American Education Diet."

77. American Council, "The American Education Diet."

78. American Council, "The American Education Diet."

79. "International Comparisons (student achievement)," *National Center for Education Statistics* at http://nces.ed.gov/fastfacts/display.asp?id=1. See also "Student Achievement (National)," *National Center for Education Statistics* at http://nces.ed.gov/fastfacts/display.asp?id=38.

80. "Indicator 14 (2001) International Comparisons of 8th-Graders Performance in Mathematics and Science" at http://nces.ed.gov/programs/coe/2001/section2/indicator14.html.

81. "Indicator 14 (2001) International Comparisons."

82. "Learner Outcomes," *National Center for Education Statistics* (2001) at http://nces.ed.gov/programs/coe/2001/sections2/index.html.

83. "Learner Outcomes," *National Center for Education Statistics*.

84. American Council, "The American Education Diet."

85. American Council, "The American Education Diet."

86. "Adult Literacy," *National Center for Education Statistics* (2001) at http://nces.ed.gov/fastfacts/display.asp?id=69.

87. "Learner Outcomes: Summary," *National Center for Education Statistics*, http://nces.ed.gov/programs/coe/2001/section2/index.html.

88. "A Nation Still at Risk: An Education Manifesto."

89. Paul Peterson and Jay Greene, "Race Relations and Central City Schools: It's Time for an Experiment with Vouchers," *Brookings Review* 16 (Spring 1998): 3307.

90. Some argue that we don't know enough about the effects of school choice; see for example, Dan Goldhaber, "School Choice: Do We Know Enough?" *Educational Researcher* 29 (2000): 21–22. However, what we do know is that the current system is not working for today's students, especially the poor ones.

91. "A Nation Still at Risk: An Education Manifesto." .

92. Cory Booker, "School Choice and Government Reform: Pillars of an Urban Renaissance," *Manhattan Institute Civic Bulletin* 25 (February 2001): 6.

93. "A Nation Still at Risk: An Education Manifesto."

94. Gill et al., *Rhetoric versus Reality*, 147, 148.

95. Virginia Walden, quoted in Bracey, "The Ninth Bracey Report on the Condition of Public Education," 147–48.

96. William Raspberry, "A Reluctant Convert to School Choice," *Washington Post* (May 30, 1997): A-25, quoted in Peterson, "School Choice: A Report Card," 47–80.

Chapter Two

Justice: A Philosophy
of Empowering All Parents

A theory of justice requires that societies be judged by how they treat the least well off. As we have seen in the previous chapter, the poor are not faring well in the current system. In this chapter I explain why the current system should be changed to a system of vouchers—*a just educational system is one in which the poor have equal access to quality education.* For if education is a fundamental right, then it ought not be distributed based upon one's family income. If a government is to act justly, it should treat all schools equally, preferring none.

Justice requires three things: 1) parents should have the power to educate their children, 2) all perspectives should be treated equitably by the government, and 3) special concern should be paid to the poor. How well is our system doing according to these criteria? Is our current system just? I first describe the injustice in our current system and then the principles of a just educational system.

INJUSTICE IN OUR CURRENT SYSTEM

A Monopoly: Only One Perspective Is Financially Supported

Obviously, many of the family's and the poor's problems are not caused by the American system of education. However, that point begs the central question: Does the educational system contribute to the challenges faced by poor children and by all children? If it does, then, justice requires Americans to reform the system so that it will provide opportunities for all children, including the poor.

Today, parents may select one of four types of schooling for their children: 1) public, 2) private, 3) parochial, or 4) home school. However, parents may only select a public school without incurring any additional costs. While the United States offers varying types of education, many parents only have one practical choice: public school.

Injustice occurs in our present system because the government only supports children who make the "right" choice, public education. Those who choose private, religious, or home schooling must pay twice for their education, and many others who wish to exercise one of these options cannot.[1] Stephen Gilles powerfully makes this point:

> But as Stephen Arons has long argued, for many nonaffluent families the financial coercion associated with selective funding is practically as irresistible as the penal coercion in *Pierce*. Selective funding forces many parents to act against their better judgment about what kind of education their children need, and forces many others to pay heavily for the privilege of differing with the majority about their children's educational best interests. In that way it runs directly counter to the parentalist axiom that government should defer to and facilitate parents' reasonable educational judgments.[2]

This is certainly true for the poor. If one's school is funded by the dollars from a relatively impoverished district, the school will likely be substandard. In our system, then, the poor do not have the option to have the doors to the finest schools opened to them. For today's poor children, the best chance to break free from the cycle of poverty by getting into finer schools is not available to them. The poor can't afford the extra money to fund a private school education; even if they could, it would still be unfair, argues Myron Lieberman, because they'd still be paying twice for their education.

> The political argument for vouchers is also based on a concept of equity. All citizens are taxed to support education. Arguably, it is unfair to subject parents to "double taxation" because they choose one type of school over another for reasons of conscience. The alleged inequity gives rise to political conflict as those excluded from the benefits seek redress. Presumably, a voucher system would eliminate this inequity.[3]

The question is this: If all four types of schooling are valid, legal, and public, then, why shouldn't all four types receive funding? The United

States offers equal educational opportunity (four types of schooling), but many parents do not get to exercise equal educational opportunity (only one of the four is funded).

Therefore, the major challenge to the U.S. educational system is that the system itself constitutes a monopoly. All of the money goes to the public school. This constitutes the root problem—or, as Quentin Quade used to say, the North Star of educational reform. Charles Glenn clearly explains the problem:

> American parents who want schooling for their children based upon a secular worldview receive it free, while those who want a religious schooling must provide it at their own expense, if indeed they can do so. While with respect to daycare and to higher education government operates on the basis of strict neutrality, "evenhandedness among people of all faiths and of none," this is far from being the case when it comes to K–12 schooling.[4]

Similarly, Clifford Cobb writes: "The Bill of Rights attests to the idea that protecting the minority from abuse of power by the majority is a central feature of a democratic society. Yet government schools are founded on the opposite view: namely, that majorities have the right to impose their will and their brand of truth on minorities."[5]

Until parents are empowered to select their child's school, then not only is their right to control their child's education a mere theory, but the children, especially the poor, have the finest schools unavailable to them. To provide genuine educational opportunity to all Americans, every parent should have fair access to any of the four valid types of schooling.

In other words, the problems principally aren't with teachers not trying, textbooks being outdated, students learning from incorrect theories such as whole language instead of learn and recall (or vice versa), teachers focusing too much on students in the middle of the class instead of the gifted, and so forth; rather, the principal problem is systemic, in the very structure of the American educational system itself. That is the roadblock.

The primary barrier to the educational achievement of the poor is our educational system itself. The primary liberator of poor children is school choice. Rosemary Salomone writes, "To that end, a growing number of reformers are seeking to break the state's monopoly over the operation of schooling and to use public funds to offer a variety of educational options within the public and private sectors."[6]

Such a monopolistic system, to a large degree, contradicts the very fiber of our being as Americans. We believe in equal opportunity for all. William Howell and Paul Peterson explain:

> When Americans speak of equality, they speak mainly of *equal opportunity*. Each citizen has a right to the pursuit of happiness, not a guarantee of its realization. As long as the starting line in the economic race is clearly drawn, those who can run fast or are lucky enough to find shortcuts may dash unrestrained to the finish line, well ahead of their competitors.[7]

This Injustice Is Reflected in Our Definitions of Public and Private

Part of this injustice is reflected in our very definitions of public and private. Today we define public as governmental and private as nongovernmental. So, public schools are those paid for by the state and private schools are those paid through private funds.

Furthermore, we have come to associate public with secular and private with religious. We understand public schools as dealing with the things of this world and those things that are religiously neutral or value-free while private schools are those that may wish to be explicitly religious, if they so desire.

These definitions of public and private are only one way of defining public and private. What if we *began* our thinking with the fact that all children are part of the public served by many educational institutions and that all families contribute to the public through their tax dollars. Then, we could say that all schools were public and that the four different types of public schools were: government-run, private, parochial, and home school.

Certainly private, parochial, and home schools serve many public and secular purposes. These schools are public in the sense that they are contributing to the common good by graduating students who will take their place as responsible members of society. They are secular in the sense that they deal with things and life in this world. Biology, chemistry, foreign language, history, and so forth are taught in all these schools.

Furthermore, public schools can be described as religious, in the following sense: throughout the curriculum are choices as to which subjects will be taught and for how many years. These choices reflect answers (i.e., prior commitments) to some of life's biggest questions, such as who or what is God, human nature, society, nature itself, what's the basic problem, and what's the basic answer. When answering these questions, public school officials are making belief statements as to what they think is important. In that sense, public schools are religious. Clifford Cobb makes this point powerfully:

The use of the word "public" to characterize government schools is part of the propaganda that has been internalized by most Americans. It is highly misleading. If public means nonexclusive, then 80 to 90 percent of non-government schools are more public than the government schools in elite suburbs where the price of admission is the down payment on an expensive house. If public means paid for out of public revenues, then vouchers would make almost all schools public (the exceptions being some elitist schools for the very rich that probably would not accept vouchers). If public means accessible to the public or serving a public purpose (as in the case of a privately owned but publicly accessible restroom within a department store, a privately owned intercity bus line, or a privately owned "public" golf course), then most nongovernment schools already qualify as public.[8]

Cobb goes on to describe the history of the successful attempt to monopolize the term "public" as synonymous with "governmental":

Before the common school movement of the 1840s, no one would have imposed the terms public or private on schools. The schools were simply voluntary. The rich attended academies and the poor attended either the same schools on scholarship or "free schools" operated by charitable agencies. When tax support for schools expanded in the 1830s in Massachusetts (the most urbanized state at the time), voluntarism could have been maintained by providing state support for attendance at any school. Instead, reformers such as Horace Mann, the first secretary of the State Board of Education, insisted on channeling taxes into government-run schools over which the state had authority. Rather than increasing total school enrollment, the common schools displaced most of the voluntary schools.

As a result of the policy, only the rich could afford to attend a voluntary school by paying a double price: a school tax plus tuition. Mann then set

about attacking the remaining institutions as elitist. He repeatedly insinu-
ated that there was a *moral* distinction between public and private schools.

Yet what was really at stake was a political power struggle over who would
control the schools. Mann pitted state compulsion against voluntarism and
parental control. Since the context was over elementary schools where children learned only the bare rudiments of literacy, and since most employment
at the time was not dependent on education, it is important not to read modern concerns about equal educational opportunity into the debates of that time.

When Mann complained that some students attended schools outside the
state's control, this reflected less a concern for the quality of instruction than
his desire to inculcate a uniform set of ideas and nonsectarian religious beliefs. For Mann and many other reformers, public school was a conscious
means of removing children from the influence of their parents. Their attacks on independent schools were a disguised attack on religious diversity
and working-class solidarity. Because history has been written by the winners, compulsory government schools came to be viewed as guardians of
the moral order, whereas nongovernment education is still regarded with
suspicion by millions of Americans.

The question before us now in the debate over vouchers is whether private institutions can serve public ends better than government institutions
can. We should judge the institutions in each sector on the basis of their actual performance rather than experiencing a Pavlovian reaction to the words
"public" and "private." The question of whether vouchers or a government
school monopoly will better serve the public interest is one that should be
decided by debate, not according to terminology.[9]

Therefore, to be most precise, what we presently have is a governmental policy that supports children who attend government schools and a
governmental policy that fails to support children who attend nongovernmental schools. The problem is now clear: the government does not support equal educational opportunity for all children. Educational reform
must be clear in pinpointing its main goal: *equal educational opportunity
for all children in any of the four types of public schooling*. If all four
types of schools are seen as public, then the rationale for supporting only
government run schools evaporates. As the former superintendent of Milwaukee Public Schools Howard Fuller said, "A school does not need to be
run by government in order to be public."[10]

The consequences of these ill-defined definitions of public and private
have been pointed out by Supreme Court justices. Supreme Court Justices

Stewart, dissenting in *Schempp*, and Douglas, in *Lemon*, both argued the following: many students and parents who disagree with the moral/religious perspective taught in the public schools, whatever that perspective might be, are nevertheless subjected to it without alternatives. The government ends up supporting whatever perspective is dominant in the government schools at any given time. The moral perspective of the government schools is imposed on all students regardless of the student's religious perspective.[11] Since it's the public school—defined as the only one that receives funding—parents are left without a choice.

The problem then is not so much what is being taught in the schools as it is that one perspective is taught and many children have no option but to be subjected to it. The issue isn't that one or the other of the perspectives of Christianity, humanism, or postmodernism is being taught in the public schools; from the vantage point of my argument, the issue is that any one of those perspectives becomes a monopoly where everyone's tax dollars are used to support it and then it is imposed on all the students. Homogeneity at any cost, even if the perspective being imposed is "good," is not worth the price of the infringement on parental prerogatives. To say anything else is to deny justice to all parents. To do anything else is to subject children to a blatantly undemocratic system. The U.S. Supreme Court supported this line of thinking in a decision handed down on May 15, 1972. In *Wisconsin v. Yoder*, the Court exempted the Amish from compulsory school attendance until age sixteen:

> The State's claim that it is empowered . . . to extend the benefit of secondary education to children regardless of the wishes of their parents cannot be sustained against a free exercise claim of the nature revealed by this record, for the Amish have introduced convincing evidence that accommodating their religious objections by foregoing one or two additional years of compulsory education will not impair the physical or mental health of the child, or result in an inability to be self-supporting or to discharge the duties and responsibilities of citizenship, or in any other way materially detract from the welfare of society.[12]

Ultimately, then, our current system leaves parents in a bind. Society expects them to raise well-adjusted children yet strips them of the ability to educate them according with their preferences. Since *Pierce*, the UN Universal Declaration of Human Rights, Article 26, and the UN Declaration of the

Rights of a Child, Principle 7, all declare that parents have a prior right to educate their children, then it is simply unjust for the U.S. government to preempt those rights by mandating governmental school education. James Skillen skillfully makes this point:

> Parents clearly do not have equitable freedom to train their children within the framework of their own convictions, because at a very early age in the life of children the government steps in with its preemptive claim to determine the structural framework of education within which parents must fulfill their responsibilities. Those parents who believe that the local government schools are not compatible with their own moral, intellectual, and religious outlook are dealt a severe blow of financial discrimination by the government itself—especially in the case of the poor. The social contradiction is that government expects parents to fulfill their responsibilities, but it turns around and takes away an essential part of parental freedom which is necessary for the fulfillment of those responsibilities. *It is a modern day picture of Pharaoh demanding that the Israelites make bricks while taking away the straw that makes brick production possible* [emphasis added].[13]

Elsewhere, Skillen ties this line of thinking together by asking this question: "But why do we assume that governments have an original right to establish and operate schools when we reject their right to establish churches and to control the major economic enterprises of our society?"[14] We should alter our definition of public to include all four types of schools that serve the common good.

Historically, Why Was This Injustice Built into Our Educational System?

How did the U.S. educational system come to be monopolistic, supporting only government-run schools? The American system is built upon the assumptions of one perspective—the Enlightenment worldview. At the heart of this worldview is the fact/value dichotomy: All of life can be divided into two camps—things we know and things we believe. The first is the domain of the natural sciences, the second of religion. The first is public; the second is private. The first is worthy of being taught in schools, the second is the proper domain of the church or the home. Therefore, appropriate subjects in school are the "value-neutral" ones of reading, writing, arithmetic; inappropriate subjects are "value-ladened," those existing in the realm of belief or religion. Public schools embodied knowledge, all other schools embodied religion.

This is the perspective then that has shaped our system of education. The public school movement in the United States grew out of the nineteenth-century crusade for the common school. The idea was that common schools could provide the next generation with a common perspective on life through a common language, political culture, and set of values. The next generation of good Americans would be shaped in the common school. And such a school system was deemed necessary given the large masses of newly arriving immigrants in the mid-nineteenth century. The common school could homogenize children of the immigrants (and, in fact, all Americans) into the American way of life.

Who was the intellectual father of this monopolistic, homogenized idea? Rockne McCarthy, James Skillen, and William Harper, in *Disestablishment a Second Time*, suggest that this monopolistic homogenization idea finds its origins in the thinking of Thomas Jefferson. To get at Jefferson's educational thinking, one must first examine his political thinking because Jefferson's political philosophy forms the foundation for his educational theory.

The heart of Jefferson's political philosophy was that all individuals find their identity in the universal law but that universal law defines nothing more than sovereign, free, and independent individuals. Jefferson assumed the universality of this idea to such an extent that McCarthy et al. draw a parallel between Jefferson's proposal of shipping Negroes to foreign islands with shipping away unenlightened people, that is, anyone who disagrees with him. After all, Jefferson believed his ideas were self-evident ideals— that is, from Jefferson's perspective anyone who disagreed was controlled by strange and peculiar opinions (read *religion*). Affirming sense experience as the primary method of achieving knowledge (thereby agreeing with Locke but disagreeing with Descartes), Jefferson concluded that anyone who preferred supernatural revelation to the concrete facts provided by the senses would only be led "in to the fathomless abyss of dreams and phantasms."[15] Or perhaps a few of the unenlightened could be shown the light, as Jefferson told William Bache in 1800; the majority would have to "inculcate on minorities the duty of acquiescence in the will of the majority."[16]

It's within this context that Jefferson defined religion: that very narrow area related to the supernatural, to opinion, uncommon dogmas, in short, to the irrelevant side issues of life outside of the significant ideas of reason. Religion relates to the minor issues of life where there might be some small differences, even among the enlightened (we are, after all, still human). Americans should have the freedom to attend churches but only with the consent of keeping religious beliefs on the private side of life. But religion must never leave its box to challenge the rational, significant public ideas which for Jefferson were, according to McCarthy et al., "1) the autonomy and sovereignty of rational/moral individuals, and 2) the sovereignty of their majority in a homogeneous republic."[17] When it comes to public, legal, and political affairs, check your religion at the door. The United States will have a homogenous public (as any enlightened individual will agree with the basic principles) and we will then leave some tiny room for opinion off to the side.

How could Americans come to see the superiority of the rationalist view of the Enlightenment? How could Jefferson's view come to be the dominant one accepted by all Americans? How could his perspective win out against all the others? Public education. All American students would be trained from the perspective of republican virtues through the common school. Homogeneity (i.e., all believing in this one perspective) would be shaped through a common, universal education paid for by the government.

This Jeffersonian perspective (buttressed by Horace Mann) has become the controlling paradigm for education in America over the past two centuries. Jefferson and Mann believed that public schools were common schools whose primary purpose was to educate and socialize all Americans into the American way of life to be good citizens. Compulsory education governed by the state would shape future generations of citizens by minimizing differences in the interest of national cohesion. Only in the most extreme case, such as the imminent disintegration of a minority community, could compulsory education be trumped.[18]

Jefferson believed that certain moral and scientific truths were "self-evident," and that through reason all individuals could agree on the "self-evident" truths that could hold together the common good. These truths he identified as the virtues of enlightened republicanism. The state should teach individual liberty and rationality to prevent citizens from becoming subject to tyranny. Rationality should form the basis of society, in order to achieve unity around moral precepts in the public square.[19]

Similarly, Horace Mann began the common school to bring together a variety of people into a single sustaining unity. Whatever one's background, one could become American through the "melting pot" of public education. Anyone could be made into an enlightened citizen, since "it was the common school . . . that molded citizens to produce an enlightened and tolerant attitude."[20] The twofold purpose of the public schools was to be the symbolic expression of American identity and the vehicle for national unity. Nation-building meant bridging religious, economic, and ethnic differences and forming one great people. The common school agenda was to foster in youth a set of attitudes, loyalties, and values under the central direction of the state. Mann's goal was to engender a civic faith, related to liberal, low Protestantism, in which people would grow up‎ with a love for the state. Social cohesion would result from students learning to agree about "self-evident" truths.

It is important to note that the substance of the paradigm has changed from White-Anglo-Saxon-Protestantism to various attempts at a "neutral" view of education: an effort to educate for equal opportunity and multiculturalism for increased understanding, or an effort to educate for America's economic interest so students will be able to participate in a modern economy. However, few challenge the old notion that government should unify citizens around some common principle through education.

Is the Enlightenment Worldview Really Neutral or Universal?

But is this worldview, itself, just a given? Has Jefferson defined things the way that things really are? What if his way of looking at things and defining things is only one way of looking at and defining life—one among many? What if this Enlightenment perspective is just another philosophical perspective? Does the U.S. system of education then give all of its money to one form of schooling that teaches one perspective? Do we have, in this sense, state-sponsored religion?

Even more directly, are Americans really just carbon copies of one another able to be formed into one homogenous whole? Don't deep, genuine differences really exist even among Americans? Rosemary Salomone explains these deep differences:

> American society obviously has not remained static since the early days of the common school movement, and neither has the field of knowledge that informs educational policy and practice. . . . Social and political transformations of the past four decades, from the civil rights and women's movements of the

sixties, to the religious revivalism and political mobilization of the seventies and eighties, to the racial and ethnic backlash, religious conciliation, and public school failures of the nineties, have further altered the context for examining the purpose, process, and substance of education in America.[21]

The basic problem with the Jefferson/Mann perspective enshrined into our educational system is that Thomas Jefferson never adequately accounts for the genuine diversity among Americans. He assumes that all Americans will agree with his one rationalistic perspective. While Jefferson thought that his religion of public morality was common and universal, it is really only one faith, one perspective, among many. So, what did Jefferson do to convince the masses to agree with him? Jefferson saw public schools as a means of converting children to his perspective. McCarthy et al. write:

> Nor was Jefferson entirely unconscious of this. In private letters he confessed his hope that the changes brought about by a public school system would include "a quiet euthanasia of the heresies of bigotry and fanaticism which have so long triumphed over human reason."[22] And by bringing the various sects together at the University of Virginia without allowing any single one to have a special position, he hoped that it would be possible to "liberalize and neutralize their prejudices, and make the general religion a religion of peace, reason, and morality."[23] But is this anything more than a restatement of Constantine's hope that a newly enforced public religion would be able to snuff out older enforced religions? Is this anything more than a plan to use political power for the support of a new faith in reason than for the support of an old faith in Christ? *Jefferson's plan did not really exclude dogmas from the public schools after all; it merely substituted the dogma of rationalistic empiricism and moralism for those dogmas belonging to the super-naturalistic revelation of Christianity* [emphasis added].[24]

Benjamin Rush, a friend of Jefferson and an early advocate of a public educational system, supported Jefferson in his quest: "Our schools of learning, by producing one general and uniform system of education, will render the mass of the people more homogeneous."[25] With what goal in mind? Rush echoes Jefferson's conception of conversion: "From the observations that have been made it is plain that I consider it as possible to convert men into republican machines. This must be done if we expect them to perform their parts properly in the great machines of the government of the state."[26] The point now becomes clear: from their earliest conception, public schools were dedicated to converting America's children to the one true perspective of the Enlightenment with the end result being a sense of homogeneity in the United States. The foundation for the triumph of one perspective among many was established. American civil religion was born. Public schooling, therefore, has never been unreligious or merely value free; it has always been religious, as Sidney Mead makes clear: "Must it not be said that prominent among the reasons was a desire to make possible and to guarantee the dissemination and inculcation among the embryo citizens of the beliefs essential to the existence and well-being of the democratic society?"[27]

What were the results? By the middle of the nineteenth century, the American government came to support Jefferson's idea in public education: governmental support for republican commonness instead of religious pluralism. The government came to support financially one perspective. Today, then, the government supports this one particular, religious perspective at the expense of all others. Today's children continue to be socialized into one particular vision. The bottom line is this: regardless of which perspective dominates public education (the Enlightenment, Christianity, humanism, positivism, postmodernism, etc.), the Jeffersonian vision of one perspective dominating and receiving all of the money continues. Jefferson declared that a plurality of visions may not live in the public arena; that vision continues unchecked today. Only one school system may exist to promote homogeneity amongst all Americans. As a result, everyone, including the poor, is trapped in that one system today.[28]

Neither Jefferson nor Mann envisioned that problems of diversity would arise, since they believed that every parent would agree with the self-evident or neutral beliefs taught in the public schools. McCarthy et al. explain Jefferson's perspective:

> While Jefferson argued that sectarian religion must be privatized lest it disrupt society, he maintained that society must be undergirded by a common nonsectarian morality. This public morality was essentially a rational view of life which Jefferson assumed everyone could accept because he believed its truthfulness was self-evident. Jefferson identified this public morality with the very principles of republicanism. And in his mind one

of the primary purposes of public schools was to spread Enlightenment-republican principles throughout society.[29]

The problem is that Jefferson's view that one worldview is somehow value-free or neutral is a myth. The systemic inequities of supporting only governmental schools that emerge in today's educational system occur because Jefferson and Mann believed in philosophical neutrality and set up a system based on that belief. But such neutrality is mythical. No self-evident "Archimedean point" of pure objectivity and neutrality exists. Jefferson and Mann accepted the Enlightenment worldview, one belief system among many. To believe that Enlightenment rationality, rather than Marxism, Islam, or Christianity, can unite people is not to hold a neutral worldview—rather, it is to believe in one worldview among many. The Enlightenment worldview rests as much on "religious" beliefs as does any worldview. The Enlightenment worldview holds specific beliefs regarding the nature of humanity, the nature of God, the role of progress in history, and the nature of rationality. Justice, rationality, freedom, equality, and patriotism are all "essentially contested concepts," and the debate about them did not end with the Enlightenment.[30] It is as "religious" to believe that God has *no* value in history or science as it is to believe that God plays a central role in history and science.

Richard Baer relates this myth of neutrality to the context of a school curriculum:

> Every curriculum . . . rests on fundamental understandings and commitments regarding the nature of reality itself, the nature of the good life and the good society, and how one ought to live. These commitments are not neutral. Whenever either secular education or religious education deals with what I call the "Big Questions"—Who are we? What is reality like? How ought we to live? What is worthy of our deepest loyalty and commitment?—it will not be neutral in terms of religion and nonreligion. There are no neutral answers to the Big Questions.[31]

The implications of an educational system's answers to the "Big Questions" extends beyond courses on values, self-esteem, or ethics, as Baer goes on to explain: "On what basis does a school decide that it is more important to emphasize math and science than say, poetry and music? Or how should the school accommodate those parents who wish their children to learn to be less competitive, less oriented toward the consumption of natural resources and the exploitation of nature?"[32]

Phillip Johnson further claims that the "myth of neutrality" masks a bias in the public schools against religion:

> The schools of today try to teach children everything they really need to know—not just the three R's, but subjects such as automobile driving, values clarification, and how to have sex without getting AIDS. The clear premise of the system is that what is excluded from the curriculum—God, for example—is either pernicious or unnecessary. The schools do not teach that God created us, but they emphatically teach what did, namely, naturalistic evolution, which got along just fine without God's help. The same schools that would not dream of having Bible readings present as "science" the lavish Cosmos series that begins with astronomer Carl Sagan's raging metaphysical claim that "the Cosmos is all that is, or ever was, or ever will be." Whether this kind of education is good or bad may be debatable, but it certainly is not neutral.[33]

In short, public education never was neutral, nor could it ever be. Since the perspective taught in public schools is just one religious worldview among many, then in effect, public schooling has established one religion at the expense of others (i.e., whatever worldview is being taught and paid for), despite government's claims to be opposed to the establishment of religion. *If the neutral philosophy advocated by Jefferson and Mann is a myth, then the rationale for funding only one system of public education evaporates.*

The great consequence of this mythical value-free perspective is this: in our present system we have denied full religious freedom to most Americans. By relegating religion to the private sphere, we have prevented religious pluralism from entering into the public sphere. As Richard John Neuhaus has put it, we have created the "naked public square." Put differently, not every one agrees with Jefferson and his excessively narrow definition of religion. Myron Lieberman powerfully makes this point:

> The First Amendment prohibits government from establishing a religion or interfering with its free exercise. What, however, is a "religion" or a "reli-

gious belief" from a constitutional point of view? The Supreme Court has already held that a "religious" belief need not be based on belief in a Supreme Being or on belief in a supernatural realm; Confucianism illustrates the kind of nontheistic belief system that can neither be established nor prohibited by the First Amendment. The difficulty lies in distinguishing which nontheistic views are religious and which ones are not.[34]

Religion, then, refers not just to one's belief in God; rather, it refers to what one holds to be ultimate, or as Roy Clouser has argued, what has "nondependent status." And that can be anything from God to an individual to nature itself. Whatever we hold to exist autonomously (as a law unto itself) may be considered as one's (G)god.

Therefore, even among the country's leading supporters of a separation between church and state, many end up supporting state-sponsored religion—that is, the one perspective of the Enlightenment, or whatever the perspective of the majority is at a given time. Stephen Arons makes this point in his *Compelling Belief* (1983) where he suggests that the separation of school and state is even more critical than the separation of church and state. In *On Liberty*, John Stuart Mill points out the problem that some one or some belief will shape the state-sponsored education:

A general State education is a mere contrivance for moulding people to be exactly like one another; and as the mould in which it casts them is that which pleases the predominant power of the government, whether this be a monarch, a priesthood, an aristocrat, or the majority of the existing generation; in proportion as it is efficient and successful, it establishes a despotism over the mind, leading by natural tendency to one over the body.[35]

Mill went on to argue that:

All attempts by the State to bias the conclusions of its citizens on disputed subjects, are evil. . . . If the government would make up its mind to require for every child a good education, it might save itself the trouble of providing one. It might . . . content itself with helping to pay the school fees of the poorer classes of children, and defraying the entire school expenses of those who have no one else to pay for them.[36]

Similarly, Associate Justice Robert H. Jackson wrote in *West Virginia Board of Education v. Barnette* (1943):

> As governmental pressure toward unity becomes greater, so strife becomes more bitter as to whose unity it shall be. Probably no deeper division of our people could proceed from any provocation than from finding it necessary to choose what doctrine and whose program public educational officials shall compel youth to unite in embracing. Ultimate futility of such attempts to compel coherence is the lesson of every such effort.[37]

Sadly, what Mill and Jackson wrote about long ago has become our present reality. Since all the money goes to support one particular type of worldview, we can therefore conclude that the United States today has state-sponsored religion.[38]

What Advocates of the System Claim: Public Education Supports Civic Education

Advocates of public schooling believe that public education safeguards democracy. Democracies need good citizens, and good citizens need to be educated. As John Dewey argued in *Democracy and Education*, without citizens who are prepared to participate effectively and intelligently in an open political system as law-abiding, competent, and active individuals, democracy will slowly die. This preparation can be accomplished through a standard curriculum that trains citizens how to rationally assess issues and options in public policy from a standpoint of justice and the common good.[39] Thus, the government has society's best interests in mind when it mandates criteria for a national curriculum that prepares citizens for effective and self-reliant adult life and social participation.[40] No other social institution can match the school in fulfilling this important social function.

Preparing citizens for society involves more than teaching skills and providing information; it requires the formation of character and the inculcation of virtue, and paramount among these virtues is public-spiritedness. Two of the most eloquent advocates of civic education, Thomas and Lorraine Pangle, argue: "A strictly practical education . . . is not enough to infuse this valiant spirit. . . . Those who will eventually set the tone for society need to be given the leisure to ponder, and be touched by, the examples of Achilles and Socrates, of Abraham and David, of Joan of Arc and

Napoleon."[41] The Pangles argue that the purpose of civic education is to form democratic character, and to infuse souls with a robust passion for public-spiritedness and democratic participation. This formation can be achieved by integrating "moral and political lessons into the entire curriculum . . . [through] continual practice in orations, debate, and journalistic writing—all focused on momentous moral and political issues of the day."[42]

William Bennett is another advocate of the inculcation of civic virtue through education. In his bestseller *The Book of Virtues*, he offers a program of moral education through exemplary poems and stories. He has also argued for a comprehensive core curriculum:

> The classical and Jewish-Christian heritage, the facts of American and European history/the political organization of Western societies, the great works of Western art and literature, and the major achievements of the scientific developments. Indeed, the core of the American college curriculum—its heart and soul—should be the civilization of the West, source of the most powerful and pervasive influences on America and its people.[43]

Moral and political lessons and examples should inspire individuals toward public-spiritedness; when that happens, democracy will be strong.

This philosophy of education is rooted in the very origins of democracy. Five centuries before Christ, Pericles declared, "We do not say that a man who takes no interest in politics is a man who minds his own business; we say that he has no business here at all." Similarly, Aristotle argued that a human being is essentially a political being, a *"zoon politikon."* Benjamin Barber argues that the American founding fathers, such as Thomas Jefferson, revived the classical ideal. By training the character of the individual soul, they believed, society would never again fall under the rule of a tyrant. Enlightened, free individuals, who were bonded to others of like character, would never submit to another King George III. Barber thus concludes that, according to Jefferson, education served to better both the individual and society. Jefferson linked education with democracy, since education not only supports democracy but also forms its vital foundation. Further, education contributes to a sense of the unity in community necessary for civilization. Echoing Jefferson, Barber says, "Participatory democratic communities permit an identification with others that is compatible with political liberty and that unites instead of divides." Enlightened self-interest is responsible public service.[44]

Proponents of civic education posit that the telos of education is the formation of character in citizens, which builds the inherent capacities of a person to engage in the public sphere.[45] The role of education is to equip the leaders of tomorrow with the philosophical, historical, and psychological capacities that enable them to participate in a rational manner in public life. Education should "engender civic competence" for a "common understanding" to prevent societal divisiveness and fragmentation.[46] This is a task so noble, and confronted by obstacles so daunting, that it can be accomplished only by government itself.

Civic Education: It Isn't Worth the Price

Civic education is a noble aim. But should social unity be achieved at the cost of parental responsibility? Have the advocates of democratic citizenship been so zealous to create national unity and respect for democracy that they have usurped parental prerogatives? Coons and Sugarman believe so:

> Society's general presumption that parents should speak on behalf of their children is simply abandoned with respect to education. With respect to food, clothing, and shelter, all families are fit to choose; in matters respecting basic loyalties, intellect, and fundamental values—in short, where the child's humanity is implicated—the state must dominate the prime hours of the average child's day. Whether a distinction of this sort among economic classes is good public policy is the basic issue.[47]

The champions of democratic citizenship hold unexamined premises about the role of education in a democracy and about the kind of loyalty citizens owe the state. Many parents in a democracy hold deep loyalties to such nongovernmental institutions as churches, families, and private schools.[48] These parents argue that social cohesion and democratic participation cannot be the only criteria of the common good, especially when parents are forced to sacrifice their most cherished loyalties on these public altars. Today, there is little room for the exercise of parental responsibility in choosing a school consistent with values taught in the home. Although lower courts have been reluctant to widen the "burden"

on parents that they attributed to the Amish.in *Yoder,* many parents claim
that burden today.

This high price of compromising parental responsibility is manifest in
two concrete ways. First, religious liberty is denied. Parents are only
able to exercise religious liberty if they can afford to send their children
to a private or parochial school. Otherwise, parents are forced to send
their children to the public school, which may teach a philosophy that
counters lessons taught in the home.[49] A child might be taught in public
schools to "think for one's self," "find one's own answers," or "make up
one's own mind." Whether or not one agrees with this philosophy of education, one must acknowledge it is not neutral. By valuing indifference
to questions of truth or by advocating a general sense of relativity regarding questions of truth, the current system makes a sectarian argument. Establishing "autonomous" reason or one's own "feelings" as the
standard of truth is merely one sectarian argument among many. Poor
parents are forced to send their children to schools that profess a sectarian argument.

Second, the present system fails to distribute justice equitably. While
the right to "opt out" is guaranteed, poor parents have fewer opportunities
to exercise this right by sending their children to good public, private, or
parochial schools. No system of ethics justifies granting fair access to educational opportunities based solely on one's financial status. As Stephen
Carter put it: "Of course, it is in a sense unfair that my children attend a
school where there is organized prayer because my wife and I are able to
afford it, and other children whose parents want the same for them cannot,
because it is too expensive."[50]

PRINCIPLES OF A JUST EDUCATIONAL SYSTEM

Why Parents Should Choose Instead of the Government

This discussion brings us to the central issue: Should the government or parents decide which school a child will attend? Our current system is built upon
the premise that the government should decide. Summing up the battle between the two sides, *Education Week* noted in 1996, "Some see it as no less
than a battle between parents and the state for the control of a child's mind."[51]

Chubb and Moe in *Politics, Markets and America's Schools* argue that the "core academic mission" of schools lies in the teaching of core competencies in "math, science and foreign language" which is "so crucial to a future of sophisticated technology and international competition."[52] Good education, in other words, equips students with the skills so that they can help America gain a competitive edge in the global market.

But what if education is more than the mere acquisition of skills (*techne*)? What if education also includes principles, values, virtues, in short, ways of life, ways of living in the world (*arête*)? On this question there is widespread agreement amongst diverse thinkers. Significant modern philosophers support the idea that education should shape the development of virtuous character in children. John Locke, the single most significant thinker for the founding fathers' views on revolution, wrote: "It is virtue then, direct virtue, which is the hard and valuable part to be aimed at in education; and not a forward pertness, or any little arts of shifting. All other considerations and accomplishments should give way and be postponed to this."[53]

If the proper domain of education includes inculcating virtues in addition to acquiring competencies, then, one might ask, should educational systems support the primary source of moral education for children, the parents?

As we have seen, some say no. Horace Mann, typically referred to as the founder of American public education, argued that the government should select a child's school instead of the parents. Concerned over the papists' superstitious beliefs of some immigrants arriving in the United States, Mann turned to the public school. A Congregationalist journal, the *New Englander*, gave him high praise, writing, "These schools draw in the children of alien parentage with others, and assimilate them to the native born. . . . So they grow up with the state, of the state and for the state."[54]

Some say that the government knows better than parents which school their child should attend. This governmental assumption is rooted in the idea, in part, that all children are basically the same, with the same needs, the same learning styles, the same family backgrounds, and so forth. But what if children entering schools are diverse with different needs, different learning styles, and a variety of backgrounds?

What will happen then to these children who have been turned over to the educational experts? Bruce Goldberg quotes one English educator who said: "I'm not sure that parents know what is best educationally for their children. They know what's best for them to eat. They know the best environment they can provide at home. But we've been trained to ascertain the problems of children, to detect their weaknesses, to put right those things that need putting right, and we want to do this freely, with the cooperation of parents and not under undue strains."[55] Hopefully, this idea is running its last lap.

But what if many disagree that children should grow up of, by, and for the state? After all, few doubt that families form the indispensable building blocks for society. Replacing the contemporary system, in which a child is assigned a school by the state, with a system in which a parent chooses a child's school would represent an extraordinary shift in decision making from the state to the family. To some, this proposed shift may sound idealistic given what has been reported about the American family. Some parents are not interested, do not attend PTA meetings, and do more to discourage than encourage their children's education. But failures on the part of some parents do not negate the general principle that parenting deserves honor and distinction.

Because families are the indispensable foundation for healthy societies, they should be kept strong. The family should be the unit that forms a child's character, emotions, and worldview. The family can provide a child with a sense of value, meaning, and purpose. The family should be the place where the child can be free to be himself or herself with his or her joys or tears because the child is loved unconditionally without the fear of guilt or shame. The family should give children what all human beings need—unconditional love and acceptance. The family should be the place where many adults can make their greatest social contribution by preparing their children for society. The family should demonstrate passionate concern for the life and well-being of the child.

Since parents know their children better than the state does, parents should control the choice of their children's education. In the words of John Coons:

> The right to form families and to determine the scope of their children's practical liberty is for most men and women the primary occasion for choice and responsibility. One does not have to be rich or well placed to experience the family. The opportunity over a span of fifteen or twenty years to attempt

the transmission of one's deepest values to a beloved child provides a unique arena for the creative impulse. Here is the communication of ideas in its most elemental mode.[56]

Richard Neuhaus and Peter Berger have highlighted the failure of the current system to recognize the importance of parental responsibility:

Most modern societies have in large part disfranchised the family in the key area of education. The family becomes, at best, an auxiliary agency to the state, which at age five or six coercively (compulsory school laws) and monopolistically (for the most part) takes over the child's education. Of course there are private schools, but here class becomes a powerful factor. Disfranchisements fall most heavily on lower-income parents who have little to say in what happens to their children in school. This discrimination violates a fundamental human right, perhaps the most fundamental human right— the right to make a world for one's children.[57]

Our anger at parents who abuse their children reflects the degree to which we depend on parents to raise their children responsibly. Hence the fundamental question: Should a school be an opponent to or a teammate of parents? On this question, there can be little doubt: schools should support parents. And the government should support parents by empowering them to select a school that corresponds with the values taught at home.

If a free and democratic society is to be truly free and democratic, then parents should not be coerced into sending their children to a school that undermines the principles taught at home. Choice in a democracy cannot be limited to Coke or Pepsi if that democracy is to live up to the values to which it purports to adhere. Powerfully making this point, former Supreme Court Justice Jackson writes: "Freedom to differ is not limited to things that do not matter much. That would be a mere shadow of freedom. That test of its substance is the right to differ as to things that touch the heart of the existing order."[58] Parents should be allowed to send their children to schools that are compatible with their worldview. The Catholic philosopher Jacques Maritain said, "No teaching deprived of conviction can engender conviction."[59] Stephen Gilles makes this point with conviction:

Moreover, we have every reason to think that stable, loving, responsible parenting makes a huge difference in helping children to become stable, loving, responsible adults. This parental nurturing encompasses the whole of a child's life; it cannot be arbitrarily confined to the sphere of home education as distinguished from democratically controlled formal schooling. That is why parents seek schooling that meshes with and reinforces what they are trying to do at home. To require parents to accept schooling that contradicts and undermines their own values, teaching and example would jeopardize the foundational, paradigmatic loving relationships in a child's life. In a society in which it is increasingly obvious that both good parents and good substitutes are in short supply, undermining parental authority is an exceedingly peculiar strategy for advancing the well-being of children.[60]

Gilles echoes the sentiments of the English philosopher John Stuart Mill, who in the nineteenth century wrote:

Is it not almost a self-evident axiom, that the State should require and compel the education . ... of every human being who is born its citizen? . . . Were the duty of enforcing universal education once admitted, there would be no end to the difficulties about what the State should teach, and how it should teach, which now convert the subject into a mere battlefield for sects and parties, causing the time and labor which should have been spent in educating, to be wasted in quarreling about education. . . . It might leave to parents to obtain the education where and how they pleased, and content itself with helping to pay the school fees.[61]

Parents had this freedom for much of America's history. David Kirkpatrick writes:

It needs to be recalled that for most of our history there was no public school system. It began to emerge 150 years ago, and compulsory attendance was extensively established only at the end of the nineteenth century.

Most citizens prior to that time—including the Founding Fathers responsible for the creation of the nation and the writing of its constitution—were educated either at home, in nonpublic schools, or by a tutor. There is even evidence that literacy was higher in the nineteenth century than today.[62]

Similarly, Howell and Peterson write:

The word "public" simply implied communal instruction outside the home. Benjamin Rush, an early advocate of public education, made that explicit claim when he proposed that "free, public" schools, funded in part by parental fees, be organized so that "children of the same religious sect and nation may be educated as much as possible together." Thomas Paine went further. In *The Rights of Man*, Paine proposed compulsory, publicly financed education but recommended vouchers so that parents would have a choice of schools. To ensure compliance, "the ministers of every . . . denomination [would] certify . . . that the duty is performed." As late as the 1830s, state-funded schools in Connecticut still charged tuition.[63]

Howell and Peterson go on to point out that it was mid-nineteenth century before there was a significant push for universal public education taught from one particular perspective, and even then public schooling became synonymous with state-run and state-funded:

Not until the 1840s did public schools become synonymous with state-funded and state-operated schools. The man usually credited with founding public education as we now know it in the United States, Horace Mann, a Massachusetts secretary of education and practicing Unitarian, expressed great concern about the papist superstitions of immigrants pouring into American cities. "How shall the rising generation be brought under purer moral influences," he asked, so that "when they become men, they will surpass their predecessors, both in the soundness of their speculations and in the rectitude of their practice?" His answer, the public school, won praise in, the *New Englander:* "These schools draw in the children of alien parentage with others, and assimilate them to the native born. . . . *So they grow up with the state, of the state and for the state* [emphasis added]."[64]

If societies require healthy families, then educational systems should support the creation and maintenance of strong families. Parents should choose a child's school and the government should assist parents by enabling them to select freely from the four types of public schools.

Religious Tradition, the United Nations, and the Supreme Court Support Parental Responsibility

Religious tradition, the UN, and the U.S. Supreme Court have all supported the right of parents to choose their child's school. Catholics, Protestants, and Jews have all supported parental primacy in education.[65]

In 1987 Pope John Paul II made this point clearly:

Permit me, brothers and sisters, to mention briefly something that is of special concern to the Church. I refer to the rights and duties of parents in the education of their children. The Second Vatican Council clearly enunciated the Church's position: "Since parents have conferred life on their children, they have a most solemn obligation to educate their offspring." Hence, parents must be acknowledged as the first and foremost educators of their children (Gravissimum Educationis, 3). In comparison with the educational role of all others, their role is primary; it is also irreplaceable and inalienable. It would be wrong for anyone to attempt to usurp that unique responsibility (cf. Familiaris Consortio, 36). Nor should parents in any way be penalized for choosing for their children an education according to their beliefs.[66]

The Catholic Church has been one of the clearest advocates of parental rights. In 1995 the U.S. Catholic Conference made the claim that "parents are the first and foremost educators of their children," and that the parents have a fundamental "right to choose the kind of education best suited to the needs of their children."[67] Parents hold the primary responsibility for a child's moral and academic development. Translating that responsibility into public policy is the goal of school choice. The greatest likelihood of childhood success results from parental involvement as the lead advocates for their children.[68]

In other words, many see educating one's child as a religious mandate. Many Christian and Jewish parents believe that they are commanded to teach their children about God's faithfulness in history: "When in the future your child asks you, 'What does this mean?' you shall answer, 'With strength of hand the Lord brought us out of Egypt, from the house of slavery'" (Exodus 13:14). The Bible also encourages parents to nurture a moral fiber in their children: "Train children in the right way, and when old, they will not stray" (Proverbs 22:6). Children are told to obey their parents, in Exodus 20:12, Ephesians 6:1, and Colossians 3:20. James Skillen has succinctly captured the seriousness with which the church has taken this command throughout history:

In the biblical tradition . . . Judaism and Christianity . . . recognize the primacy of parental authority in the education of children. Some governmental responsibility for schooling may be legitimate, according to this tradition, and a variety of agencies outside of the home may be required for the education of young people, but laws governing schooling must be built on respect for the primacy of the parental role in the education of children.[69]

The primacy of the parental role in the education of children has been recognized in a variety of major documents. The United Nations has declared that parents have a right to choose their child's education. According to the UN's "Universal Declaration on Human Rights" (1948), Article 26, "Parents have a prior right to choose the kind of education that shall be given to their children."[70] Principle 7 of the UN's "Declaration of the Rights of the Child" (1959) states, "The best interests of the child shall be the guiding principle of those responsible for his education and guidance; that responsibility lies in the first place with his parents."[71] The nations that signed the International Covenant on Economic, Social and Cultural Rights in 1966 agreed "to have respect for the liberty of parents . . . to choose for their children schools, other than those established by public authorities, which conform to such minimum educational standards as may be laid down or approved by the State and to ensure the religious and moral education of their children in conformity with their own convictions."[72]

The landmark report *A Nation at Risk* calls a parent a child's "first and most influential teacher" who should be "a living example of what you expect your children to honor and emulate."[73] Societies expect parents to raise responsible, civically minded children. The seminal *Education by Choice* by John Coons and Stephen Sugarman argued that educational decisions should be made by families regardless of their economic circumstances.[74]

Even before the 2002 Supreme Court decision ruling that parents have a right to choose their child's education (I elaborate on this in the next chapter), the Court had ruled in favor of parental primacy in opposition to state-mandated uniform education in three different cases. In *Meyer v. Nebraska* (1923), the Court declared that public education should be restricted from fostering "a homogenous people with American ideals." In *Pierce v. Society of Sisters* (1925), the Court ruled that public education should not "standardize its children." In *West Virginia Board of Education v. Barnette* (1943), the Court decided that public education cannot institute an "officially disciplined uniformity."[75] The Court's clearest support for parental primacy came in the *Pierce* decision, in which the Court ruled that Americans have a right to private or parochial education, since the Constitution protects

> the liberty of parents and guardians to direct the upbringing and education of children under their control. . . . The fundamental theory of liberty upon which all governments in the Union repose excludes any general power of the state to standardize its children by forcing them to accept instruction from public teachers only. The child is not the mere creature of the state; those who nurture him and direct his destiny have the right, coupled with the high duty, to recognize and prepare him for additional obligations.[76]

This series of cases culminated with *Wisconsin v. Yoder* (1972), in which the Supreme Court granted Amish students an exemption from a Wisconsin state law for compulsory education beyond the eighth grade.

The Supreme Court has supported the freedom for parents to choose their children's school. In *Pierce v. Society of Sisters* (1925) the Court held that it is within the province of parents to select the appropriate form of education for their children. The highest court in the land confirmed this fundamental parental prerogative three-quarters of a century ago. In *Pierce*, the Court ruled that an Oregon initiative requiring compulsory public education was unconstitutional. William Guthrie, defending Pierce, argued:

> Private and religious schools have existed in this country from the earliest times. . . . For generations all Americans—including those who fought for liberty and independence in the eighteenth century, and who drafted the Declaration of Independence, the Northwest Ordinance of 1787, and the Constitution of the United States—were educated in private or religious schools, and mostly the latter.[77]

Guthrie continued:

> The rights of the parents and guardians who desire to send their children to such (private and religious) schools, and the rights of the children themselves . . . those rights . . . are the very essence of personal liberty and free-

dom. In this day and under our civilization, *the child of man is his parent's child and not the State's* [emphasis added]. It is not seriously debatable that the parental right to guide one's child intellectually and religiously is a most substantial part of the liberty and freedom of the parent.[78]

The Supreme Court agreed with Guthrie. Associate Justice James Clark McReynolds, writing for the Court, argued:

The fundamental theory of liberty upon which all governments in this Union repose excludes any general power of the State to standardize its children by forcing them to accept instruction from public teachers only. *The child is not the mere creature of the state* [emphasis added]; those who nurture him and direct his destiny have the right, coupled with the high duty, to recognize and prepare him for additional obligations.[79]

Similarly, Associate Justice Jackson, in *West Virginia Board of Education v. Barnette* wrote eighteen years later:

Struggles to coerce uniformity of sentiment in support of some end thought essential to their time and country have been waged by many good as well as by evil men. . . . Those who begin coercive elimination of dissent soon find themselves exterminating dissenters. Compulsory unification of opinion achieves only the unanimity of the graveyard. . . . *If there is any fixed star in our constitutional constellation, it is that no official, high or petty, can prescribe what shall be orthodox in politics, nationalism, religion, or other matters of opinion or force citizens to confess by word or act their faith therein. If there are any circumstances which present an exception, they do not now occur to us* [emphasis added].[80]

In 2002, the Supreme Court of the United States ruled that a system of educational vouchers does not violate the separation of church and state. The Supreme Court has clearly supported the idea that parents should have the freedom to control their child's education. But without legislators approving a system of funding for all four types of schools, this right is still distributed according to wealth. Distributing a right based on wealth violates every tenet in the canon of Western ethics. As John Rawls, the Harvard philosopher, wrote, "Each person is to have an equal right to the most extensive basic liberty compatible with a similar liberty for others."[81]

Shifting to a just educational system in which parents control their children's schooling instead of the state will not only strengthen the family
but it will also strengthen American communities. Clifford Cobb writes:

> The fundamental question should be how communities can be organized
> and strengthened so that people need not feel powerless or dependent on
> large, distant institutions. . . . Education vouchers provide an opportunity to
> develop an alternative, communitarian model of government policy: one
> that gives power back to ordinary people and community groups in tangible
> forms.[82]

Similarly, Howell and Peterson write:

> Social capital is generally understood as consisting of the resources gener-
> ated by the routine interaction among people in a well-functioning commu-
> nity. . . . If declining social capital is the problem, then school choice may
> provide a solution. If private school communities are voluntarily con-
> structed as parents and schools choose each other, then a commonality of in-
> terest may provide a basis for mutual support and continuing interaction. In-
> deed, the very term "social capital" was coined in a study that found private
> schools to be more effective than public schools. University of Chicago so-
> ciologist James Coleman and his colleagues accounted for the higher per-
> formance of students in Catholic schools by nothing the social capital gen-
> erated when parents gather at religious services, bingo parties, Knights of
> Columbus meetings, fund-raising events, and other gatherings. Although
> those communal occasions had no ostensible educational content, they pro-
> vided a positive foundation for student learning.[83]

The indispensability of the parental role in education is thus supported
by the Judeo-Christian tradition, international law, and the Supreme
Court. Society generally and children specifically are best served when
parents are given the right to direct and control their children's education.
Parents should no longer be subjected to the financial coercion of select-
ing the public school. It is time to free children and their parents from that
stranglehold.[84] Ron Sider sums up the point well: "To promote the common good, society must use government's powers of taxation to ensure
that every child has access to the necessary funds for a quality education.
. . . Equal access to quality education for all is both morally right and also
in the long-term interest of everyone."[85]

CONCLUSION

If the current system is monopolistic both in terms of money and per-spective, then the issue becomes, what might replace it? Clearly, a system that supports equal educational opportunities for all children regardless of which of the four options they select. The government must cease sup-porting one particular perspective and offer real opportunities to all Amer-icans. Here Terry Moe writes with precision: "The point is not just to give parents and students better schools in some technical academic sense, but also to give them the *kind* of education they want—and in the process, to shift power from government to parents in deciding what values the schools will pursue."[86]

The goal, then, is a just system—one which handles its responsibility to-ward education equitably without penalty or advantage to any group or in-dividual in society. The current U.S. system is a far cry from this ideal. Only when the government has adopted a system of full school choice with every parent empowered with a voucher will we say that our government has adopted a just educational policy. Only when the U.S. government shifts its tax money to becoming inclusive of all children will we cease our demand for justice for all. Only that system can offer justice for poor chil-dren. Only that system can promote freedom and pluralism instead of con-finement to the local district school. And only when that system has be-come a reality will our country appear favorably when we are asked to judge ourselves according to how the poorest in our society are treated.[87]

NOTES

1. By offering this philosophical foundation for school choice, I differ from many school-choice advocates who support a foundation rooted in free-market competition.

2. Stephen Gilles, "Why Parents Should Choose," *Learning from School Choice*, edited by Paul Peterson and Bryan Hassel (Washington, D.C.: Brookings Institution Press, 1998), 399.

3. Myron Lieberman, *Privatization and Educational Choice* (New York: St. Martin's Press, 1989), 216.

4. Charles Glenn, *The Ambiguous Embrace: Government and Faith-Based School and Social Agencies* (Princeton, N.J.: Princeton University Press, 2000), 99.

5. Clifford Cobb, *Responsive Schools, Renewed Communities* (San Francisco: ICS Press, 1992), 33.

6. Rosemary Salomone, *Visions of Schooling: Conscience, Community, and Common Education* (New Haven, Conn.: Yale University Press, 2000), 7.

7. William Howell and Paul Peterson, *The Education Gap: Vouchers and Urban Schools* (Washington, D.C.: Brookings Institution Press, 2002), 2.

8. Cobb, *Responsive Schools, Renewed Communities*, 34.

9. Cobb, *Responsive Schools, Renewed Communities*, 34–35.

10. Nina Rees, "Public School Benefits of Private School Vouchers," *Policy Review* 93 (January/February 1999): 16–19.

11. See Stewart's dissent in *Abington School District v. Schempp* 374 U.S. 203 at p. 313, and Douglas in *Lemon v. Kurtzman* 403 U.S. 602 at 630, quoted in James Skillen, *Justice for Education* (Washington, D.C.: Association for Public Justice, 1981), 10.

12. Quoted in David Kirkpatrick, *Choice in Schooling: A Case for Tuition Vouchers* (Chicago: Loyola University Press, 1990), 89, 90.

13. Skillen, *Justice for Education*, 12.

14. Skillen, *Justice for Education*, 8.

15. Letter to John Adams, August 15, 1820, in Koch and Peden, *Life and Writings*, 701, quoted in Rockne McCarthy, James Skillen, and William Harper, *Disestablishment a Second Time: Genuine Pluralism for American Schools* (Grand Rapids, Mich.: Christian University Press, 1982), 42.

16. McCarthy, Skillen, and Harper, *Disestablishment a Second Time*, 34.

17. McCarthy, Skillen, and Harper, *Disestablishment a Second Time*, 36.

18. *Wisconsin v. Yoder*, 406 U.S. 205 (1972).

19. James Copple argues this well: "Thomas Jefferson advocated the creation of a tax-supported public school system in order to prevent the control of education by sectarian interests such as religion or business." James Copple, "When Choice Is Not a Good Choice: Reform on the Backs of the Poor," *ESA Advocate* (January/February 1991): 8.

20. Charles Glenn, *The Myth of the Common School* (Amherst: University of Massachusetts Press, 1988), 10.

21. Salomone, *Visions of Schooling*, 267–68.

22. Letter to William Short, October 31, 1819, in Koch and Peden, *Life and Writings*, 694, quoted in McCarthy, Skillen, and Harper, *Disestablishment a Second Time*, 43.

23. Letter to Thomas Cooper, November 2, 1822, in Gordon Lee, ed., *Crusade against Ignorance*, 79, quoted in McCarthy, Skillen, and Harper, *Disestablishment a Second Time*, 43.

24. McCarthy, Skillen, and Harper, *Disestablishment a Second Time*, 43.

25. Frederich Rudolph, ed., *Essays on Education in the Early Republic* (Cambridge, Mass.: Harvard University Press, 1965), 10, quoted in McCarthy, Skillen, and Harper, *Disestablishment a Second Time*, 45.

26. Rudolph, *Essays on Education in the Early Republic*, 17, quoted in McCarthy, Skillen, and Harper, *Disestablishment a Second Time*, 46.

27. Sidney Mead, *The Lively Experiment: The Shaping of Christianity in America* (New York: Harper & Row, 1963), 66–67, quoted in McCarthy, Skillen, and Harper, *Disestablishment a Second Time*, 48.

28. It should be pointed out that Jefferson defines religion in the narrowest way possible. Furthermore, Jefferson's thought leaves him trapped in a paradox: he's attempting to achieve individual liberty through universal education.

29. Rockne McCarthy et al., *Society, State and Schools: A Case for Structural and Confessional Pluralism* (Grand Rapids, Mich.: Eerdmans, 1981), 83.

30. Despite profound differences, some of the twentieth century's most important thinkers (Richard Rorty's postmodernism, Feyerabend's and Polanyi's philosophies of science, and Herman Dooyeweerd's and Eric Voegelin's critiques of theoretical thought) came to the same epistemological conclusion: there is no such thing as purely objective rationality. Amy Gutmann has applied this insight to education: "Every educational system now in existence closes children's minds to some potentially desirable conceptions of the good life and the good society." See her "Children, Paternalism, and Education," *Philosophy and Public Affairs* 9 (Summer 1980): 350. For more on the "myth of neutrality," see Roy Clouser, *The Myth of Neutrality* (South Bend, Ind.: University of Notre Dame Press, 1993); Richard Baer, "American Public Schools and the Myth of Value Neutrality," in *Democracy and the Renewal of Public Education* (Grand Rapids, Mich.: Eerdmans, 1987); and Stephen Arons, "The Myth of Value-Neutral Schools," *Education Week*, 7 November 1984. Furthermore, the debate over these concepts is ongoing within the American public school system. For the battles over "values" in Western civilization, see Alasdair MacIntyre, *Whose Justice? Which Rationality?* (South Bend, Ind.: University of Notre Dame Press, 1989); James Hunter, *Culture Wars: The Struggle to Define America* (New York: Basic Books, 1991); David Walsh, *After Ideology: Recovering the Spiritual Foundations of Freedom* (San Francisco: Harper, 1990); and Dante Germino, *Political Philosophy and the Open Society* (Baton Rouge: Louisiana State University Press, 1982).

31. Richard Baer, "'Strict Neutrality' and Our Monopoly System," in *School Choice: What Is Constitutional?* (Grand Rapids, Mich.: Baker Books, 1993), 15–16. Herman Dooyeweerd and Eric Voegelin provided much of the philosophical foundations for this point, arguing that there is no neutrality and that religious presuppositions or human experiences always undergird everyone's thinking and approaches to life. See, for example, Dooyeweerd's *A New Critique of Theoretical*

Thought (Ontario: Paideia Press, 1984), 1–165, and Voegelin's *Autobiographical Reflections* (Baton Rouge: Louisiana State University Press, 1989), 67–68.

32. Baer, "Strict Neutrality," 20.

33. "School Vouchers and the United States Constitution" in *The School Choice Controversy: What Is Constitutional?* edited by James W. Skillen (Grand Rapids, Mich.: Baker Books, 1993), 62.

34. Lieberman, *Privatization and Educational Choice*, 197.

35. John Stuart Mill, *On Liberty*, 130, quoted in Kirkpatrick, *Choice in Schooling*, 35.

36. John Stuart Mill, *On Liberty*, 129, quoted in Kirkpatrick, *Choice in Schooling*, 36.

37. Paul Peterson powerfully summed up the fights against this attempt to create uniformity with the following words, declaring that voucher supporters "are a small band of Jedi attackers, using their intellectual powers to fight the unified might of Death Star forces led by Darth Vader, whose intellectual capacity has been corrupted by the urge for complete hegemony." Paul Peterson, "Money and Competition in American Schools," *Choice and Control in American Education*, edited by William Clune and John Witte (London: Falmer Press, 1990), 73.

38. Clifford Cobb passionately makes this point: "The cultural image of schools as a secularized church that unites us in our differences is the oldest and most powerful source of inspiration for those who oppose changes in the structure of schooling in the United States. The fact that unity under one banner has always meant the suppression of dissenting voices has never troubled liberal Protestants too deeply, for the simple reason that the schools have reflected their biases. It is all too easy for those whose truth is represented officially as a universal truth to regard dissenters as mere troublemakers." Clifford Cobb, *Responsive Schools, Renewed Communities*, 36.

39. William Bennett, *James Madison Elementary School: A Curriculum for American Students* (Washington, D.C.: Department of Education, 1988).

40. Jesse Goodman, *Elementary Schooling for Critical Democracy* (New York: University of New York Press, 1992).

41. Lorraine Pangle and Thomas Pangle, *The Learning of Liberty: The Educational Ideas of the American Founders* (Kansas City: University of Kansas Press, 1993), 11.

42. Pangle and Pangle, *The Learning of Liberty*, 286.

43. William Bennett, *Education and the Public Trust: The Imperative for Common Purposes*, edited by Edwin Delattre (Washington, D.C.: Ethics and Public Policy Center, 1988), xi, xii; see also William Bennett, *The Book of Virtues: A Treasury of Great Moral Stories* (New York: Simon & Schuster, 1993).

44. Benjamin Barber, *An Aristocracy of Everyone* (New York: Oxford University, 1992), 226–28.

45. See David Steiner, *Rethinking Democratic Education: The Politics of Reform* (Baltimore, Md.: Johns Hopkins University Press, 1994).

46. Benjamin Barber, *Strong Democracy: Participatory Politics for a New Age* (Berkeley: University of California Press, 1984), 270.

47. John Coons and Stephen Sugarman, *Education by Choice: The Case for Family Control* (Berkeley: University of California Press, 1978), 27.

48. Jeremy Waldron has argued that these differences are so significant that it is impossible for the state to unify its citizens effectively through any program of national cohesion. "The Trouble with Compossibility," paper prepared for the American Political Science Association (August 1992): 63–66.

49. For an account of one parent's frustration when forced to send children to a school that contradicts values taught at home, see Stephen Bates, *Battleground: One Mother's Crusade, the Religious Right, and the Struggle for Control of Our Classrooms* (New York: Poseidon Press, 1993), especially 76–94.

50. Stephen L. Carter, *The Culture of Disbelief: How American Law and Politics Trivialize Religious Devotion* (New York: Basic Books, 1993), 192.

51. Quoted in Salomone, *Visions of Schooling*, 5.

52. John E. Chubb and Terry M. Moe, *Politics, Markets and America's Schools* (Washington, D.C.: Brookings Institutions, 1990), 2.

53. J. Roger Lee, *Education in a Free Society*, edited by Tibor R. Machan (Stanford, Calif.: Hoover Institution Press, 2000), 5. John Locke, *Some Thoughts Concerning Education* (1693), section 70; Lee quotes Kant, "Moral culture must be based upon maxims, not upon discipline. The first endeavor in moral education is to establish a character. Character consists in the readiness to act according to maxims. . . . He can therefore become morally good only through virtues. . . . Everything in education depends upon one thing: that good principles be established and be made intelligible and acceptable to children." Immanuel Kant, *The Educational Theory of Immanuel Kant*, edited and translated by E. F. Buchner (Philadelphia: Lippincott, 1904), paragraphs 77, 78, 102, 103, 185, 186, 210, 211.

54. Quoted in Howell and Peterson, *The Education Gap*, 6.

55. Bruce Goldberg, "A Liberal Argument for School Choice," *American Enterprise* 7 (September 1996): 28, 29.

56. John Coons, "Intellectual Liberty and the Schools," *Journal of Law, Ethics, and Public Policy* 1 (1985): 511. See Charles Glenn and Joshua Glenn, "Making Room for Religious Conviction in Democracy's Schools" in *Schooling Christians: "Holy Experiments" in American Education*, edited by Stanley Hauerwas and John H. Westerhoff (Grand Rapids, Mich.: Eerdmans, 1992);

Charles Glenn, "Putting Choice to Work in Public Education," *Equity and Choice* 2 (May 1986): 5ff; and Coons and Sugarman, *Education by Choice*.

57. Richard Neuhaus and Peter Berger, *To Empower the People: The Role of Mediating Structures in Public Policy* (Washington, D.C.: American Enterprise Institute for Public Policy Research, 1977), 21.

58. Justice Jackson in the 1943 Supreme Court case *West Virginia Board of Education v. Barnette*, a case involving a West Virginia law related to saluting the flag and the pledge of allegiance, quoted in Kirkpatrick, *Choice in Schooling*, 28.

59. Anthony S. Bryk et al., *Catholic Schools and the Common Good* 39 (1993), quoted in Paul Peterson, "School Choice: A Report Card," *Virginia Journal of Social Policy and the Law* 6 (Fall 1998): 47–80.

60. Gilles, "Why Parents Should Choose," 397–98.

61. Quoted in Howell and Peterson, *The Education Gap*, 13–14.

62. Kirkpatrick, *Choice in Schooling*, 28.

63. Quoted in Howell and Peterson, *The Education Gap*, 6.

64. Howell and Peterson, *The Education Gap*, 6.

65. See Stephen L. Carter, "Virtue via Vouchers: The Supreme Court's Recent Decision Can Help Prevent More Corporate Scandals," *Christianity Today* (November 18, 2002): 82.

66. John Paul II, *Catholic Education: Gift to the Church, Gift to the Nation* (Washington, D.C.: National Catholic Educational Association, 1987), 14, quoted in Michael Guerra, "A Tale of One City and Two Families," *Momentum* (Washington, D.C.) 32, no. 2 (April/May 2001): 34–37.

67. Principles for Education Reform in the United States, U.S. Catholic Conference 1995, quoted in Mary Ellen Russell, "Parent Advocacy Spurs School Choice Decisions," *Momentum* (Washington, D.C.) 32, no. 2 (April/May 2001): 30.

68. The Christian philosopher Herman Dooyeweerd wrote: "The cultural education of children is as a rule completely concentrated in the inner family in the first years of life of the infants. . . . The family is the only natural community able to give the first and foundational cultural molding to the disposition and character of the infant. . . . The integral character of the education in the family sphere is irreplaceable and in many respects decisive for the entire further life of the children. They belong to the parents in a personal sense as long as they have not reached the state of maturity, necessary for them to be considered as responsible persons in human society. . . . Parental cultural shaping of a child in the inner family sphere retains its irreducible and irreplaceable nature. This is why the ancient and modern totalitarian ideas of state education of the children contradict the divine world order and are indeed inhuman and destructive to human society." Dooyeweerd, *A New Critique of Theoretical Thought*, vol. 3, 286–88.

69. James W. Skillen, "Changing Assumptions in the Public Governance of Education: What Has Changed and What Ought to Change," in *Democracy and the Renewal of Public Education*, edited by Richard J. Neuhaus (Grand Rapids, Mich.: Eerdmans, 1987), 86–87.

70. *Human Rights: A Compilation of International Instruments*, part 1, 6, proclaimed by the General Assembly on 10 December 1948.

71. *Human Rights: A Compilation of International Installments*, vol. 1, declared by the General Assembly on 20 November 1959.

72. Charles Glenn, "What's Really at Stake in the School Choice Debate," *Clearing House* 66 (November/December 1992): 75.

73. National Commission on Excellence in Education, *A Nation at Risk* (Washington, D.C.: U.S. Department of Education, 1983), 35.

74. John Coons and Stephen Sugarman, *Education by Choice: The Case for Family Control* (Berkeley: University of California Press, 1978). Similarly, Stephen Gilles argues that parents should be under a sort of Rawlsian veil of ignorance and should be encouraged to select a fair system without knowing precisely where their child will end up, writing: "A selectively funded system inflicts real hardship on both those who exit and those who dissent but cannot afford to exit. Parents of comfortably mainstream views are unlikely to give that hardship due weight, because they know it is unlikely the tables will ever be turned. It would be otherwise in an impartial referendum on selective funding—one in which parents could not know in advance whose views on the content of public education were likely to prevail." Gilles, "Why Parents Should Choose."

75. See *Meyer v. Nebraska* 262 U.S. 390 (1923), *Pierce v. Society of Sisters* 268 U.S. (1925), and *West Virginia Board of Education v. Barnette* 319 U.S. 624 (1943). Particularly important is the Court's unanimous ruling in *Pierce* that an Oregon law requiring all children to attend public schools was unconstitutional, and that parents have a constitutional right to educate their children in private schools. In *Barnette,* the Court declared, "If there is any fixed star in our constitutional constellation, it is that no official, high or petty, can prescribe what shall be orthodox in politics, nationalism, religion, or other matters of religion." It should be noted that even if the Supreme Court recognized parental primacy as a fundamental right, it does not necessarily follow that the Court will also find a governmental duty to pay for the exercise of that right, since Court has recognized other rights without correspondingly finding a governmental duty to pay. Abortion is one example. See *San Antonio v. Rodriguez*, 411 U.S. 1 (1973) and *Norwood v. Harrison* 413 U.S. 455 (1973). The Supreme Court has also routinely distinguished between college students and primary/secondary school students in its treatment of parental primacy.

76. The Supreme Court has implied a limited degree of parental responsibility in *Farrington v. Tokushiga* 273 U.S. 284 (1927) and in *Prince v. Massachusetts*

321 U.S. 158 (1944). Parental responsibility has also been recognized by Congress to a limited degree. For example, in the Serviceman's Readjustment Act of 1944 (the GI Bill), Congress recognized no church–state conflict in permitting public money to follow the student for the school of his or her choice.

77. Kirkpatrick, *Choice in Schooling*, 38.

78. Kirkpatrick, *Choice in Schooling*, 39.

79. Kirkpatrick, *Choice in Schooling*, 39.

80. Kirkpatrick, *Choice in Schooling*, 43–44.

81. Quoted in Howell and Peterson, *The Education Gap*, 1.

82. Cobb, *Responsive Schools, Renewed Communities*, 41–42.

83. Howell and Peterson, *The Education Gap*, 14–15.

84. And they are beginning to demand it. As Rosemary Salomone writes: "While the common school concept may have proven significant and perhaps even essential to that cause through the early years of nation building, a curiously diverse group of advocates for family choice—from religious conservatives, to libertarians, to inner-city minorities and their clergy—are now joining forces in an effort to regain a meaningful voice for families in the education of their children that was lost more than a century ago in the common school movement." Salomone, *Visions of Schooling*, 269–70.

85. Ron Sider, *Just Generosity: A New Vision for Overcoming Poverty in America* (Grand Rapids, Mich.: Baker Books, 1999), 161.

86. Terry Moe, *Schools, Vouchers, and the American Public* (Washington, D.C.: Brookings Institution Press, 2001), 18.

87. The issue of educational choice is then an issue of justice. It is a far deeper issue than merely a balancing act between the common good and individual freedom as some suggest. On this see, Sheila Suess Kennedy, "Privatizing Education: The Politics of Vouchers," *Phi Delta Kappan* 82 (February 2001): 455–56; Moe, *Schools, Vouchers, and the American Public*, 1, 2, 17, 21–23; and Kirkpatrick, *Choice in Schooling*, 31. As an issue of justice, school choice can be seen as a means of strengthening American democracy. Myron Lieberman points out that vouchers will help reduce social conflict and will help to improve America's social capital; Lieberman, *Privatization and Educational Choice*, 204–206 and 215. Americans will likely rally to support such a system. See also Witte, *The Market Approach to Education*, 11–15.

Chapter Three

The Supreme Court Aids the Poor

THE BASIC LEGAL POINT

For many years, opponents of school choice argued that tuition vouchers would violate the Establishment Clause's separation of church and state. In June 2002, the U.S. Supreme Court disagreed, ruling that there is no constitutional violation of the Establishment Clause in a system of choice in which the voucher goes to a parent and then the parent uses that voucher at a school of the parent's own choosing. In so ruling, the Supreme Court removed one of the major obstacles in the path to a system of school choice.

As we have seen in chapter 1, poor children are not faring well in the current K–12 system. And as I argued in the previous chapter, justice requires that all parents, including poor ones, be granted the right to control their children's education. Now the proverbial ball lies in the hands of the public and legislators as the legal barriers have been removed.

As I have argued, many factors impact the educational success of poor children in the United States, including the system itself. Over thirty years ago, Rodger Hurley observed, "Although the system of public education in America is certainly not solely responsible for the failure of the poor to learn and for their over-representation in special education classes for the mentally retarded, it is more responsible than any other single institution in our society."[1] And while individual parents with a voucher may make a mistake, the incompetence of the government to make decisions is far worse, as David Kirkpatrick explains:

> Whether a tuition voucher system or family choice would involve some mistakes is not the real question. The essential point is whether individual

incompetence is greater than governmental incompetence. Mistakes by parents are individual mistakes, affecting only their children. Mistakes made by school officials may involve entire schools, districts, states, or the nation. Those by any government agency may be massive indeed.

Individual mistakes are also more easily corrected, not only because they are smaller in scale but because they are private mistakes. Governmental mistakes, being public, are rarely admitted or corrected. Should this actually occur in some instances, the length of time required to alter the system is so long that the correction would come too late for vast numbers of students.[2]

Entering into a discussion of the constitutionality of school choice and the separation of church and state brings us into an incredibly complex area of the law. Alan Brownstein writes, "The Establishment Clause doctrine is an area of constitutional law where nothing is settled."[3] Charles Glenn explains this ambiguity in American law:

> As we have seen, there are deep ambiguities in the American jurisprudence that determine what activities with a religious character government may and may not fund. Services for small children and for adolescents, and college-level education, receive public funding without discrimination based on the religious character of the institutions that provide them, but faith-based schools have been denied such assistance. This distinction is a peculiarly American phenomenon; other Western democracies do not share this reluctance to provide public funds for faith-based schools.[4]

As we discovered in chapter 2, part of the debate centers around one's definition of religion. As we learn in this chapter, part of the legal debate centers around the Supreme Court's approach to questions of religion. Certainly, none will disagree that the issues are incredibly complex and defy simplistic answers. Nevertheless, it is into these waters that we now enter and what we find—when we look from the vantage point of the poor—is incredibly encouraging.

THE U.S. SUPREME COURT WEIGHS IN
WITH ITS DECISION

The Supreme Court has weighed in on the constitutionality of vouchers. On June 27, 2002, the United States Supreme Court issued its major school-choice decision in *Zelman v. Simmons-Harris*, 536 U.S. 639. In a 5–4 decision (the Justices in the majority were Chief Justice Rehnquist, who authored the decision, and Justices O'Connor, Kennedy, Scalia, and Thomas), the Court voted for school choice. The Court ruled that it is constitutionally permissible for parents to use public tax money to send their children to parochial and other nongovernmental schools. The main criteria for such a program to pass constitutional muster is that it must offer parents choices from governmental and nongovernmental schools. For the majority, Chief Justice William Rehnquist wrote:

> There is no dispute that the program challenged here was enacted for the valid secular purpose of providing educational assistance to poor children in a demonstrably failing public school system. . . . In sum, the Ohio program is entirely neutral with respect to religion. It provides benefits to a wide spectrum of individuals, defined only by financial need and residence in a particular school district. It permits such individuals to exercise genuine choice among options public and private, secular and religious. The program is therefore a program of true private choice. In keeping with an unbroken line of decisions rejecting challenges to similar programs, we hold that the program does not offend the Establishment Clause.

The number one argument against vouchers has been rendered mute.

The facts of the case are the following: Cleveland has one of the country's worst-rated public school systems; as Ohio Chief Justice Frank Battisti said over a decade ago, "Every voice laments the unsatisfactory condition of the school district."[5] Similarly, Diane Ravitch wrote that the Cleveland Central School District (CCSD) is renowned as the country's greatest educational failure "because of the confluence of poverty, poor management, and low educational achievement."[6] And the schools were racially segregated. "Public schools in the Cleveland area are remarkably segregated. Most students attend schools that are almost all white or almost all minority and very few students attend schools that resemble the racial proportion in the whole community. Families wishing to attend a racially integrated school in the public system in Cleveland have very few opportunities to do so."[7]

On June 29, 1995, in order to provide adequate educational opportunities for Cleveland's children and respond to an "academic emergency," the Ohio General Assembly passed the Cleveland Scholarship and Tutoring

Grant Program. Poor students trapped in the Cleveland system now had options—funded options. They were now empowered with the right to "opt out." They were given hope. And it was concrete hope in the form of real choices; now, poor children could

> remain in their neighborhood school, transfer within the CCSD, attend a magnet school within CCSD, enroll in one of Ohio's charter "community" schools, use the scholarship for supplemental services such as tutoring, use the scholarship to pay a portion of private school tuition, or enroll at full public expense in any public school district in the State that has agreed by resolution to admit them under Ohio Rev. Code Ann. 3313.98.[8]

Joseph Viteritti explains the options, the choices, and the opportunities that economically disadvantaged parents now had for their children this way: "The purpose of the program was to avail poor parents of an opportunity that they did not previously enjoy. Of course, this would motivate some parents to transfer their children to private or parochial schools, especially if these children previously attended public schools they found unsatisfactory. Why else do this if not to give parents something that would be expected to benefit their children?"[9]

Similarly, Jay Greene points out:

> If a family wants to live in the Cleveland area and wants to send their children to a racially integrated school at public expense, they are more likely to do so by choosing a private school with a voucher than they are by attending a public school. Despite court orders and political pressure to improve integration in the public schools, the Cleveland Scholarship Program offers families a better opportunity for a racially integrated school experience.[10]

Prior to the adoption of this bill, the city had tried, according to the Center for Education Reform, "virtually everything. The desegregation plan opened up school assignments, implemented non-discriminatory testing and tracking procedures, required significant efforts to improve reading scores, added magnet, charter, and vocational opportunities, upgraded and reorganized transportation, implemented stronger financial and management practices, desegregated teacher and professional staff assignments, and provided extra State funding."[11]

Despite these efforts, the status of the Cleveland schools remained abysmal. In 1997 the Ohio State Supreme Court declared that "school districts were starved for funds, lacked teachers, buildings, and equipment, and had inferior educational programs, and that their pupils were being deprived of educational opportunity."[12]

Nevertheless, opponents of Cleveland's choice program went to court. They won a lower court victory when a three-judge panel from the Sixth Circuit Court struck down Cleveland's program that provided scholarships for 4,000 poor children, ruling the program unconstitutional on the grounds that it constituted an establishment of religion, thereby violating the separation of church and state, and thus overturning the trial court decision authored by Judge Lisa Sadler. The main argument in the Circuit Court's decision was that since most of the schools were sectarian, they could not separate their religious and educational functions, and therefore such a program could not be funded with public tax dollars.[13] Using the standard of neutrality, the Circuit Court argued that the Cleveland program was not neutral because suburban schools were not involved and that children who participated in the program received special tuition grants thus creating an "impermissible incentive for parents to send their children to sectarian schools."[14]

In May 1999, the Ohio Supreme Court upheld the Sixth Circuit Court's decision on the basis of a technicality. The court ruled that the CCSD school-choice plan was unconstitutional for it violated the Ohio constitution's "one subject rule" since the law was passed as a rider to an appropriation's bill. However, significantly, the Court also declared that the plan neither violated the Establishment Clause of the First Amendment nor the religion clause of the Ohio constitution because "no money flows directly from the state to a sectarian school and no money can reach a sectarian school based solely on its own efforts or the efforts of the state. . . . Sectarian schools receive money . . . only as the result of independent decisions of parents and students."[15] In other words, the State Supreme Court did not strike down the plan based on its merits; rather, it struck it down based on a technicality: the method by which the program was adopted in the first place.

The U.S. Supreme Court reversed the decision of the Ohio State Supreme Court and endorsed the six-year-old Cleveland plan that allows parents to use the voucher money to get their child out of the assigned inner-city school and send their child to a school of their choice. Even though more than 95 percent of the vouchers are used to support parochial education, the Court ruled that the government is not in the unconstitutional position of sponsoring religious indoctrination.[16] As a result, the Supreme Court has removed one of the most significant roadblocks in the way of school choice: its constitutionality. The Court has settled the issue: vouchers are constitutional.

This decision represents a major victory for religious and educational freedom in the United States. Now, states are free to move ahead with their choice plans. The choice plans in Cleveland, Milwaukee, and Florida will continue.

This decision could open the door for the most significant reform in educational policy since *Brown v. Topeka Board of Education*. The Supreme Court has essentially redefined public education to include all community-serving schools—whether they are run by the government or not. In essence, the Court has substantiated the argument I made in chapter 2. The Court effectively ended the privileged status government-run schools have had for years. Legally, the monopoly is over. Now, all community-serving schools may have access to public tax dollars. The new definition of "public" now appears to be any of the four types of community-serving schools, instead of whether the school is operated by the government. The stage is set for public policymakers to walk through this opening and implement school-choice programs in their respective states.

Moreover, this case represents a hopeful sign about a new direction in the Court's understanding of the relationship of religion to public life: The Court ruled that it is not an establishment of religion to have educational programs that allow parents to choose schools that square with their own religious convictions. For years, religious discrimination has been done to those parents who haven't been able to choose a school consistent with their religious convictions. In effect, the Court has ruled that avoiding religious discrimination outweighs any "separation of church and state" argument. In other words, the Court supports a just sense of religious freedom in which all parents may now choose freely among many educational options for their children. The U.S. government may not favor any particular type of school; that is, no longer can the educational system only allow public funding for some community-serving schools, those run by the government. Religious discrimination in educational policy must end: There will be no law prohibiting parochial schools from using vouchers to educate children in government, private, parochial, or home schools.

Therefore, the Court made a wise decision consistent with the line of argumentation in the previous chapter. The Cleveland system does not support any faith above another or grant any preferential treatment. The program allowed any student whose family income was 200 percent of the poverty line or less to select any school involved in the program.

The Court's decision means that the real religious establishment lies in the thinking of the minority justices who argued that only one type of school should receive federal funding: government-run schools that promote only one perspective. However, as we saw in the last chapter, not all Americans agree with that definition of religion—that religion is a private matter, of "sectarian" concern.[17] Many other Americans believe religion is a way of life that shapes public concerns, including education. The minority, in this case, are the ones who seek to establish religion by enshrining into law one particular view of religion to the exclusion of all other definitions. This should not be allowed.[18] This was not allowed.

Stephen Lazarus has made a compelling case that the dissenting opinions of the Justices fail to promote the religious freedom of all Americans. First, Justice Souter, in his dissent, argued that unless a religious school can separate its religious and secular functions, then such a school does not deserve federal funding. But, as Lazarus points out, "This is not religious freedom. This is religious discrimination. Such reasoning divides Americans into first- and second-class citizens based on how religious they are."[19] Moreover, Souter's line of argumentation contradicts the fact that the government already supports many religious institutions that support the public, such as colleges, hospitals, and social service groups.

Second, Lazarus notes that Justice Stevens, in his dissent, argued that the government can't fund a child's education at a religious school because that's indoctrination, not education. But, as Lazarus points out, Stevens's argument: 1) is bigoted against the quality of religious education, 2) supports a monopoly in which government-run schools that promote secular values should be favored in law over schools that reflect Muslim, Christian, or Hindu values even though children educated in these schools are indoctrinated no more than students in government-run schools are indoctrinated into secular values, and 3) fails to support the decisions of all parents to choose their children's schools thereby opposing the idea that the government's job is to be neutral and protect the religious freedom of all its citizens.

Third, Lazarus notes that Justice Breyer, in his dissent, argued that the wall of separation of church and state needs to be of mythological proportions or else the United States will descend into religious and political chaos. But, Breyer cites no evidence that this strife occurred either in Cleveland or throughout Europe where countries have adopted systems of school choice.[20]

June 27, 2002, has the potential to go down in history as the most significant, pro-poor educational decision since *Brown v. Topeka Board of Education*. President Bush eloquently made this point to a Cleveland audience saying:

> The Supreme Court of the United States gave a great victory to parents and students throughout the nation by upholding the decisions made by local folks here in the city of Cleveland, Ohio.
>
> The Supreme Court in 1954 declared that our nation cannot have two education systems. . . . And that was the right decision. Can't have two systems, one for African Americans and one for whites.
>
> Last week, what's notable and important is that the court declared that our nation will not accept one education system for those who can afford to send their children to a school of their choice and for those who can't. And that's just as historic.[21]

The constitutional barrier barring the poor from getting into quality schools has been dismantled. The potential of this date will be fulfilled when every state adopts a statewide system of school choice.

THIS CASE BUILDS UPON A LONG LINE OF SUPREME COURT DECISIONS

The Shift in the Court's Focus

The Supreme Court's decision on June 27, 2002, should not have come as a surprise to any close follower of the Supreme Court. The decision that the Court made that day drew upon a long line of Supreme Court adjudication. To get at that line of thinking, we must analyze the past fifty years of Supreme Court religious decision making.

Over the past one-half century, the Supreme Court has shifted its approach to religion cases. The Court no longer focuses on the *nature* of the aid itself to religious institutions, but instead now focuses on the *way* aid gets to religious institutions. From the 1940s through the early 1980s the Court focused on the nature of the aid, asking whether the aid will promote a religious or secular purpose. Early on in this period the Court approved secular aid but struck down religious aid. Later in this period the Court became wary of any aid to religious schools, arguing that even secular aid could indirectly "advance religion" or create the appearance of government support of religion. However, from the mid-1980s up to the present, the Supreme Court has shifted its approach to focusing on the way in which the aid will reach religious institutions. Nathan Lewis writes:

> In a line of cases beginning half a century ago, the Supreme Court has interpreted the "Establishment Clause" of the First Amendment to strike down various attempts to provide financial assistance to students in religious schools. More recent Supreme Court decisions, however, suggest that a majority of today's Court is more sympathetic to the needs and rights of such students.[22]

In other words, over the past twenty years, the Court has come to deem public aid neutrally given to parents who could then spend it on the governmental or nongovernmental institutions of their choice as permissible if it met the criteria of neutrality. Any benefit to a religious institution would pass constitutional muster if it is the result of independent and private choice. There is no constitutional violation if the money goes to the parent instead of the school. This is the trend that the Court upheld in the Cleveland decision.[23]

The main principle that the Court has established over the past quarter of a century has been that the government fulfills its public purpose of providing schooling to all children when it allows the recipients of governmental funds to decide where to spend those funds, whether at religious or government-run institutions. The Court has ruled that no governmental establishment of religion occurs when the government acts in this manner. The government should therefore ensure an education where the parents select what type of an education their children will receive.

The other central principle has been the following: There is no "excessive entanglement"—that is, no establishment of religion or violation of the principle of separation of church and state—if the money goes to the parents who then have the freedom to select their child's school. The government's interest ends at granting the money and ensuring adequate schooling. The government may not select the child's school for the parent. Summing this up, Lewis wrote three years before the Supreme Court's Cleveland decision:

> How . . . public aid is directed to religious institutions has become the decisive issue. . . . Programs that provide unrestricted public funding to private religious schools as a result of designations by private individuals have proved increasingly successful in the Supreme Court in recent years. Today's school-voucher programs naturally fall into the latter category, and there are positive signs that they would be upheld by the Supreme Court.[24]

The Supreme Court from the 1940s through the Early 1980s

These cases reflect a shift in the Court's approach to aid to religious institutions generally and to school choice specifically. From 1947 until the early 1980s, the Supreme Court focused on the nature of the public aid to private schools, asking if the aid was principally religious or secular. If the aid was secular in nature, the court would uphold the aid, but if the aid was essentially religious, the court would strike the aid down.[25]

In *Everson v. Board of Education* in 1947, Arch Everson brought suit against the state of New Jersey for using tax monies to pay for the transportation of students to a Catholic school. In this case, Justice Black discussed the "high wall of separation" between church and state. All the Justices agreed that "the clause against establishment of religion by law was intended to erect a wall of separation between church and state."[26] However, even in this case, the Court held that publicly financed transportation for parochial school children as part of a program for all school-age children does not violate the federal constitution. The Court reasoned that it was principally the students and the parents who benefited from the program, and not the parochial school itself. This case set the tone for many subsequent cases given its ambiguity: arguing for a strict separation while at the same time upholding the transportation program.[27]

In the seventies and early eighties, the Court, though still focusing on the nature of the aid, became less likely to approve any aid to sectarian schools, suggesting that even secular aid might advance religion or appear as an endorsement of religion itself. In *Lemon v. Kurtzman*, 403 U.S. 602 (1971), the Court developed the famous "Lemon Standard." On June 28, 1971, the Supreme Court struck down a Pennsylvania law that allowed direct aid to religious schools and a Rhode Island law that provided salary supplements to parochial school teachers. The Court ruled that that governmental aid to nonpublic schools was unconstitutional since the Pennsylvania nonpublic schools were predominantly denominational and that a majority of them were associated with just one church. The Court decided that states may not pay salary supplements to religious schoolteachers or reimburse religious schools for teacher salaries. Writing for the Court, Chief Justice Warren Burger established the now infamous three-pronged approach the Court has taken and would now take in deciding funding for religious institutions: "First, the statute must have a secular legislative purpose; second, its principal or primary effect must be one that neither advances nor inhibits religion; finally, the statute must not foster 'an excessive entanglement with religion.'"

In *Committee for Public Education and Religious Liberty v. Nyquist*, 413 U.S. 756 (1973), the Court ruled that public aid to private sectarian schools violates the Establishment Clause of the First Amendment. States were prevented from giving grants to repair religious schools, giving grants to low-income parents to send their children to religious schools, and giving income tax benefits to parents who sent their children to private schools. The decision read, "We know from long experience with both Federal and State Governments that aid programs of any kind tend to become entrenched, to escalate in cost, and to generate their own aggressive constituencies."[28] In its decision, the Court focused on the second prong of the *Lemon* test, arguing that the New York statute advanced religion. Repairing religious schools advanced religion because the repairs were not limited to nonsectarian parts of the building, thus, the money could go to repairing parts of the building where religion was taught. Furthermore, the tuition grants could be used to expand the sectarian mission of the school and the grant could be interpreted as an incentive for sending one's child to a religious school that would have the substantive impact of advancing religion thus violating the Establishment Clause. Justice Lewis F. Powell explains:

> If the grants are offered as an incentive to parents to send their children to sectarian schools by making unrestricted cash payments to them, the

Establishment Clause is violated whether or not the actual dollars given eventually find their way into the sectarian institutions. Whether the grant is labeled a reimbursement, a reward, or a subsidy, its substantive impact is still the same.[29]

Finally, the tax deduction is substantively similar to a grant so it too would violate the Establishment Clause. Nathan Lewis explains the thinking of the Court during this time period: "The Court based its decisions in each of these cases not on the nature of the aid itself, but on the potential for indirect advancement of religion, indoctrination by the teachers of secular subjects, 'political divisiveness,' and 'entanglement.'"[30]

However, the seeds of change in the thinking of the Court are already found in a footnote in this important decision. Justice Powell writes that the court was not deciding "whether the significantly religious character of the statute's beneficiaries might differentiate the present cases from a case involving some form of public assistance (e.g., scholarships) made available generally without regard to the sectarian–nonsectarian, or public–nonpublic nature of the institution benefited."[31]

Frank Kemerer explains the significance of this footnote:

For this reason, Powell observed, the Nyquist ruling did not lead to the conclusion that the G.I. Bill impermissibly advanced religion in violation of the Establishment Clause. This observation carries immense design implications, a point not lost on the Minnesota Legislature, which developed a tax deduction program in 1982 similar to the discredited program in Nyquist but allowing parents a deduction for expenses occurred in providing tuition, textbooks, and transportation for children in either public or private schools.[32]

The Supreme Court from the Mid-1980s to the Present

Three recent Supreme Court decisions highlight the Court's shift to this position: *Mueller v. Allen*, *Witters v. Washington*, and *Zobrest v. Catalina Foothills School District*. In *Mueller v. Allen* (1983), the Court, in a 5–4 decision, upheld a Minnesota law that allowed for a deduction of state income tax for texts, transportation to public or nonpublic elementary or secondary schools, and even tuition at private schools:

A State's decision to defray the cost of educational expenses incurred by parents—regardless of the type of schools their children attend—evidences a purpose that is both secular and understandable. An educated populace is essential to the political and economic health of any community, and a State's efforts to assist parents in meeting the rising costs of educational expenses plainly serves this secular purpose of ensuring that the state's citizenry is well educated.[33]

The Supreme Court concluded that the Minnesota law did not have the primary effect of advancing religion even though most of the funds went to support "sectarian" school parents. The Court refused to judge the constitutionality of a facially neutral law based upon the number of parents (i.e., conduits) who used it.[34] The Court decided to uphold the constitutionality of the Minnesota law since it was equally available to all parents, and its use was based on the individual choices of the parents. Deductions could be made without reference to religion.[35]

The Court ruled that the Minnesota state law did not violate any of three prongs of *Lemon*: 1) the law had a secular purpose based upon the statute itself, 2) the law neither advanced nor inhibited religion because the tax deduction was available to all parents and the Court has typically deferred to legislatures in determining tax deductions, and since money never flowed directly to the schools themselves, and 3) the law does not "excessively entangle" government with religion since a tax deduction to an individual does not rise to the level of "excessive entanglement."[36] In fact, Joseph Viteritti suggests that Rehnquist began to move in a new legal direction departing from *Everson*'s strict separation and the *Lemon* test: "Writing for the majority, Justice Rehnquist suggested a relaxation of the primary effect prong of the *Lemon* test, which he declared to be no more than a "helpful signpost" rather than a hard and fast rule in reviewing Establishment Clause challenges."[37] Viteritti continues:

Two years later Chief Justice Rehnquist responded directly to the *Everson* edict when he opined, "There is simply no historical foundation for the proposition that the Framers intended to build the 'wall of separation' that was constitutionalized in *Everson*." Once again addressing the *Lemon* test, he noted that the *Lemon* standard merely repeated the historical error and promotes a body of case law that "has no basis in the history of the amendment it seeks to interpret."[38]

This decision strengthened the case for school choice in two ways. First, it clarified the responsibility of the state in supporting parents by allowing them to choose their child's school, regardless of its type, as long as it was equally available to all parents. The Court thereby ruled that parents are not mere "conduits." Second, the Court upheld the constitutionality of a subsidy to parents through tax deductions.

In other words, *Mueller* demonstrates the significant shift in the thinking of the Court that ultimately comes to fruition in the Cleveland cases of 2002. The Court ruled that no establishment violation occurs if the money goes to parents instead of to schools. For the majority Rehnquist wrote: "The historic purposes of the Establishment Clause simply do not encompass the sort of attenuated financial benefits, ultimately controlled by the private choices of individual parents, that eventually flows to parochial schools from the neutrally available tax benefit at issue in this case."[39]

Put differently, *Mueller* signaled the shift in the Court's approach to religious schools by indicating that if aid went to parents instead of directly to schools that no constitutional violation would occur. Rehnquist summed this up, writing, "Aid to parochial schools is [made] available only as a result of decisions of individual parents."[40]

The Supreme Court also upheld these principles in *Witters v. Washington Department of Services for the Blind* (1986) that held that vocational rehabilitation funds may be used for clergy education. The Washington State Supreme Court had denied Larry Witters funding from the State Commission for the Blind to attend a Christian college on federal constitutional grounds. The Court used the three-part test established in the 1971 *Lemon v. Kurtzman* case to assess a given statute's consistency with the Establishment Clause: "First, the statute must have a secular legislative purpose; second, its principal or primary effect must be one that neither advances nor inhibits religion . . . ; finally, the statute must not foster an excessive government entanglement with religion."[41] The State Supreme Court had found that providing assistance to a blind person studying for Christian ministry would violate the second prong of the test by advancing religion.

The U.S. Supreme Court then overturned the state's ruling in a 9–0 decision, contending that the more pertinent question related to discrimination rather than to government support for religion. Here the Supreme Court not only decided that Witters could study for the ministry but it ruled that a general program of vocational assistance could be used by any visually handicapped person seeking an education. The Court extended aid to the petitioner from the Washington State Commission for the Blind for training at Christian colleges (Whitworth College and Inland Empire School of the Bible) under the Washington vocational rehabilitation program.

The U.S. Supreme Court, however, decided that Witters' request would not advance religion (i.e., the second prong of *Lemon*) in a manner inconsistent with the Establishment Clause of the First Amendment. The Court ruled that the question is more one of not discriminating against anyone than a question of the government supporting religion. The Court ruled that "state programs that are wholly neutral in offering educational assistance to a class defined without reference to religion do not violate the second part of the *Lemon v. Kurtzman* test, because any aid to religion results from the private choices of individual beneficiaries."[42]

The Court found this use of public funds constitutional because it was part of a neutral program that provides benefits to a wide range of beneficiaries.

The Court decided it would be "inhibiting" religion, thereby supporting unequal treatment, if it assisted anyone pursuing any course of study except "religion." The Court decided that the *Lemon* test supports individuals choosing whatever career they might desire.[43]

Therefore, in *Witters* the Court decided that an individual can spend his or her money on whatever school desired. As in *Mueller*, the Court ruled that any aid going to sectarian institutions was only a result of the decisions made by individual recipients. In a concurring decision, Justice Powell clearly articulated these principles:

> State programs that are wholly neutral in offering educational assistance to a class defined without reference to religion do not violate the [primary effect] test, because any aid to religion results from the private choices of individual beneficiaries. Thus, in *Mueller* we sustained a tax deduction for certain educational expenses, even though the great majority of beneficiaries were parents of children attending sectarian schools. We noted the State's traditionally broad taxing authority, but the decision rested principally on two other factors. First, the deduction was equally available to parents of public school children and parents of children attending private schools. Second, any benefit to religion resulted from the "numerous private choices of individual parents of school-age children."[44]

The Court's decision in *Witters* is important because it provides a precedent for upholding a school-choice proposal by ruling that it is constitutionally permissible for an individual to spend his or her money at a religious institution. When the state gives a tax benefit or voucher to a parent, it becomes their money. The parent can choose to spend that money on any type of school they desire. All schools are free to compete for their dollars.

The *Witters* decision clarifies that the First Amendment guarantees equal consideration to both secular and religious schools. The First Amendment does not mean that only secular schools should receive federal funds. The First Amendment does not allow for an "establishment" of secular schools at the expense of religious schools.[45] The important consequence of *Witters* is that the Court decided that there must be equal treatment of religion and nonreligion, and that neither can be supported at the expense of the other.[46]

The Supreme Court upheld these principles a third time on June 18, 1993, in *Zobrest v. Catalina Foothills School District* (509 U.S. 1 1993). In a 5–4 decision, the Court ruled that James Zobrest should have been allowed to enjoy the benefit of a sign-language interpreter when he transferred to a Catholic school.[47] Zobrest had an interpreter when he attended a public school in Tucson (required by the Education of the Handicapped Act of 1991), but the school district, backed by Arizona's Attorney General, decided that he could not have the interpreter in the parochial school because it would violate the Establishment Clause of the First Amendment to the U.S. Constitution.

Once again, the Supreme Court ruled in favor of the petitioner. The Court decided that this type of assistance is similar to fire and police protection to churches, protection that is granted to all citizens regardless of their religious beliefs.[48] The Court ruled that the Establishment Clause does not bar a school district from providing a sign language interpreter under the Individuals with Disabilities Education Act to James Zobrest, a student at a parochial school. The decision read in part: "When the government offers a neutral service on the premises of a sectarian school as part of a general program that 'is no way skewed towards religion,'. . . it follows that under our previous decisions the provision of that service does not offend the Establishment Clause."[49] Since Zobrest and not the school was the primary beneficiary of the program, the Court ruled that there was no constitutional violation.

Even the dissenting Justices Blackmun and Souter wrote, "When government dispenses public funds to individuals who employ them to finance private choices it is difficult to argue that government is actually endorsing religion."[50]

This important case provides precedent for allowing federal funds to go to secondary schools, not just to postsecondary colleges and universities. Since the First Amendment guarantees religious freedom, the Court ruled that citizens should not have to compromise their religious convictions in order to receive a public service paid for through general tax dollars. The guarantee of religious freedom prevents the state from discriminating against a person.[51]

In these three cases the Supreme Court has ruled that tuition aid to parochial schools is permissible as long as the aid is administrated on a religiously neutral basis and the aid goes to the parents instead of directly to the schools.[52] In the following cases, the Court has ruled that religious institutions and the students who attend them are guaranteed the same benefits as secular institutions and the benefits those students receive under the First and Fourteenth Amendments.

In *Rosenberger v. Rector and Visitors of the University of Virginia* 515 U.S. 830 (1995), the Supreme Court ruled that a public university violates the free speech clause of the First Amendment when it prohibits student activity fees from going to an outside printer publishing a student religious newspaper. The Court decided, "We have held that the guarantee of neutrality is respected, not offended, when the government, following neutral criteria and evenhanded policies, extends benefits to recipients whose ideologies and viewpoints, including religious ones, are broad and diverse."[53] The Court distinguished between government speech and individual speech: "government speech endorsing religion which the Establishment Clause forbids, and private speech endorsing religion, which the Free Speech and Free Exercise Clauses protect."[54] In a concurring opinion Justice Thomas wrote, "The Clause does not compel the exclusion of religious groups from government benefit programs that are generally available to a broad class of participants."[55]

Similarly, in *Agostini v. Felton*, 521 U.S. 203 (1997), the Court, in a 5–4 vote, ruled that public school teachers could provide Title I educational services in parochial schools without violating the principle of separation of church and state.[56] The Court ruled that providing education to special-needs students does not advance religion nor create an excessive entanglement between church and state. Paul Peterson and Jay Greene explain the Court's logic:

> The Court conditioned its decision on policies that made instruction "available generally without regard to the sectarian-nonsectarian or public-non-public nature of the institution benefited," further justifying its decision on the grounds that no religion was aided except as the result of "private choices of individuals." Most school-choice programs can easily pass such a test.[57]

This decision is further indication that the Court's position regarding the Establishment Clause has been changing. Lisa Larson notes: "The Court's emphasis on neutrality arguably loosens the restraints of the Establishment Clause on public aid benefiting sectarian schools and broadens the public aid that a state can provide to sectarian schools."[58]

Finally, in 2000, the Supreme Court in *Mitchell v. Helms* 120 S.Ct. 2530 ruled that Chapter 2 federal funds could be used for computers, computer software, and other instructional materials in sectarian schools. The majority wrote:

> If numerous private choices, rather than the single choice of a government, determine the distribution of aid pursuant to neutral eligibility criteria, then a government cannot, or at least cannot easily, grant special favors that might lead to a religious establishment. . . . Private choice also helps guarantee neutrality by mitigating the preference for pre-existing recipients that is arguably inherent in any government aid program and that could lead to a program inadvertently favoring one religion or favoring religious schools in general over nonreligious ones. . . . If aid to schools, even direct aid, is neutrally available and, before reaching or benefiting any religious school, first passes through the hands (literally or figuratively) of numerous private citizens who are free to direct the aid elsewhere, the government has not provided any "support of religion."[59]

In a concurring opinion, Justice Sandra Day O'Connor, writing for herself and Justice Stephen Breyer, wrote:

> When the government provides aid directly to the student beneficiary, that student can attend a religious school and yet retain control over whether the secular government aid will be applied toward the religious education. The

fact that aid flows to the religious school and is used for the advancement of religion is therefore wholly dependent on the student's private decision.[60]

Rosenberger, Agostini, and *Mitchell* make the following point clearly: There is an enormous constitutional difference between direct aid to sectarian schools and indirect aid that reaches sectarian institutions as the result of many private choices. The prior would not pass constitutional muster, the latter would. If a school-choice plan offers parents many decisions from which to choose, the indirect nature of the assistance to sectarian schools moots any constitutional concerns related to direct aid. This is the trend that was upheld in the Cleveland decision of 2002. If money goes to individuals instead of schools, there is no Establishment Clause violation.[61]

As a result of the line established in these six Supreme Court decisions, it was not surprising that the Court upheld the constitutionality of a well-designed school-choice plan—that is, one that contained the following elements: it allowed for parent or student decision making, it was neutral in terms of religion, and it provided parents and students with more than one option.[62] The constitutional foundation is so firm that even a liberal such as constitutional scholar Lawrence Tribe predicted almost a decade ago: "One would have to be awfully clumsy to write voucher legislation that could not pass constitutional scrutiny. . . . Any objection that anyone would have to a voucher program would have to be policy based, and could not rest on legal doctrine."[63] Tribe turned out to be correct.

State Court Decisions

Consistent with our tradition of federalism, there is a tremendous amount of diversity in state action related to school choice. Given the fact that there are fifty state constitutions, fifty different sets of statutory requirements, and fifty different histories of judicial interpretation, it is no wonder that there exists tremendous diversity when it comes to state supreme court action relating to school choice. The issue of school choice and the law at the state level is therefore convoluted and messy.[64] Joseph Viteritti explains:

> The chaotic condition of state level jurisprudence has all the makings of a severe constitutional crisis: highlighting the widespread inconsistency that prevails among fifty distinct jurisdictions, the powerful role that state judiciaries will play in both interpreting their own constitutions and reconciling them

with existing federal standards, and—most troubling of all—the vulnerable position in which the fundamental liberty of religious freedom has been placed under the crunch of American federalism.[65]

Despite setbacks to school choice in Vermont and Maine, the Wisconsin State Supreme Court provide voucher supporters with a significant victory. Since 1869, Vermont has allowed students who do not have public schools in their own town to attend a public, private, or parochial school of their choice elsewhere at the state's expense. Consistent with that tradition, the Chittenden school board approved funds for fifteen students to attend a local Catholic high school.[66] In 1995, the state commissioner of education issued a statement to local school boards declaring that reimbursement for education at sectarian schools was not constitutional and that from now on, all private school tuition reimbursements must go directly to the schools. The Chittenden school board challenged the commissioner's legal opinion. A Vermont trial court upheld the commissioner's position, thereby opposing the school board's decision. Viteritti explains the significance of this decision, "Its significance was unmistakable: direct payments to the schools would make the program more vulnerable to judicial scrutiny even under the terms of the child benefit concept."[67] So, in the trial court decision, Rutland County judge Alden Bryan upheld the commissioner's policy, arguing that state payments should not go to religious institutions.

The Vermont State Supreme Court upheld *Chittenden* in June 1999. The State high court ruled that the Chittenden school district had violated the state constitution by failing to guarantee that public funds were not used for "religious worship" in the Catholic schools.

Similarly, Maine has enjoyed a long history of school choice, in which students could attend private or religious schools at public expense when there was no local public school available to them. In 1981 the state legislature passed a law excluding religious schools. In July 1997, five families from Raymond sued in state court, arguing that their freedom of religion and equal protection rights had been violated. In April 1998, the trial court upheld the exclusion of religious schools arguing that tuition payments to sectarian schools violate the Establishment Clause because it would "subsidize and advance religion."[68] In 1999, the Maine Supreme Court upheld the decision, agreeing that tuition payments to sectarian schools violate the Establishment Clause.

Explaining this decision, Viteritti wrote, "It was as though more than fifteen years of federal case law from the U.S. Supreme Court had been deemed irrelevant to the Maine proceedings."[69] Given the recent trend in U.S. Supreme Court cases, there is every reason to believe that future state court action will be shaped by the high court's decisions. The U.S. Supreme Court has now decided that a state may pay the costs of a parochial school education when the parents choose it and that the state may not discriminate against parochial schools in an otherwise open and competitive system. Laws will now have to conform to the Court's rulings.

Despite these setbacks, the U.S. Supreme Court's favorable trend in approaching school choice was clearly seen in its refusal to hear the Wisconsin State Supreme Court case *Jackson v. Benson*, 213 Wis.2d 1, 570 N.W.2d 407 (1998),[70] on Milwaukee's Program, thereby, in effect, upholding that state supreme court decision to allow the Milwaukee voucher program to continue. The Milwaukee program, entitled the Milwaukee Parental Choice Program (MPCP), was established in 1989. In *Davis v. Grover* (166 Wis.2d 501, 480 N.W.2d 460 [1992]), the state supreme court upheld the MPCP, ruling that the program did not violate any aspect of the state constitution. Religion was not an issue in the suit since only nonsectarian schools could participate in the program.

The program was amended in 1993 to allow 15 percent of Milwaukee's poor parents (those at 175 percent of the poverty line or lower) to select a private, nonsectarian school. The parents would be randomly chosen. The checks would be payable to the parents but sent to the schools where the parents could sign the check over to the schools, and the parents could opt out of the religious school if they so desired.

By 1995–1996, approximately 1,600 students attended seventeen different private schools. These schools could not discriminate, had to comply with state health and safety requirements, had to demonstrate annual performance criteria, and had to submit financial audits to the states. The schools were also under the scrutiny of the state superintendent who was directed to monitor curricular and financial issues related to the schools.

In 1995, the Wisconsin legislature amended the program to allow religious schools to participate in the program and to increase the percentage of students who could participate to 15 percent. The legislature deleted the superintendent's responsibilities to audit and report and now sent the aid directly to the parents (who would then send the voucher to the school) instead of sending the check directly to the schools. The legislature also set the amount of the voucher at the private school's tuition or the district's state aid per child, whichever was less, and removed a provision that said that the cap on MPCP students in a private school would be 65 percent. The legislature also added an "opt out" provision which enable students to "opt out" of specifically religious practices at certain schools.

Arguing that these changes were a violation of the Establishment Clause and the Equal Protection Clause, as well as the local bill provision, and the public purpose doctrine of the Wisconsin constitution, Warner Jackson, the Milwaukee Teachers Education Association, the NAACP, and several others filed suit against Wisconsin Superintendent of Public Instruction John T. Benson in the Wisconsin Circuit Court. The Institute for Justice defended the MPCP arguing the Wisconsin state actions were legal for the following three reasons: "that its purpose in founding the MPCP was to equalize educational opportunity for all; that the state assured adequate institutional accountability; and that it provided direct aid to parents rather than to educational institutions."[71] Viteritti explains what happened next:

> On petition from Governor Thompson, the Wisconsin Supreme Court accepted original jurisdiction over the proceedings, and in August 1995 it issued a preliminary injunction against the expansion of the program. In March 1996 the court deadlocked in a 3–3 vote, with one member removing herself from the case. The case was then remanded back to the Dane County Circuit Court, where Judge Paul B. Higginbotham partially lifted the injunction against the enrollment expansion but, citing provisions in the state constitution, kept in place the prohibition against participation by religious schools.[72]

In other words, the circuit court ruled that the MPCP violated some aspects of the Wisconsin and U.S. Constitutions. In the decision Higginbotham handed down, he wrote, "It can hardly be said that this does not constitute direct aid to sectarian schools. Although the U.S. Supreme Court has chosen to turn its head and ignore the real impact of such aid, this court refuses to accept the myth."[73] Subsequently, the court of appeals upheld the circuit court decision by a 2–1 decision in August 1997.

However, in a landmark decision handed down on July 10, 1998, the Wisconsin state supreme court reversed and upheld the constitutionality of MPCP in a 4–2 vote. The state supreme court ruled that low-income Milwaukee students may use publicly funded vouchers to attend private religious schools. Lisa Larson sums up the court's decision:

> The state supreme court concluded that the program: served the state's secular interest in providing educational opportunities to low-income children; avoided either advancing or inhibiting religion by basing student eligibility on neutral, secular criteria and selecting private schools to participate on a neutral, nonreligious basis; and avoided excessive state entanglement by foreclosing state involvement in matters affecting private religious schools' governance, curriculum, and daily operation.[74]

Morken and Formicola note, "Basing its decision on the principles established in *Everson*, the Court held that the expanded Milwaukee Parental Choice Program provided public funds for the benefit of children, rather than for the benefit of religious institutions. And, in essence it held that mere reimbursement is not aid."[75]

The Wisconsin state supreme court ruled that the MPCP did not violate the three-part test established in *Lemon v. Kurtzman* (1971) in which a government program does not violate the Establishment Clause if 1) it has a secular purpose, 2) it neither enhances nor prohibits religion as its primary purpose, and 3) it does not create excessive entanglement between the government and religion. On the first prong of the *Lemon* test, the court ruled that the MPCP's secular purpose was to provide educational opportunities to poor children; as Viteritti explains, "The program is neutral regarding the religious and secular options that were made available."[76] In other words, the program's goal of providing low-income parents with the opportunity to educate their children outside of the Milwaukee public schools was enough to meet the secular purpose prong of the *Lemon* test.

On the second prong, the court ruled that the MPCP did not enhance or prohibit religion as its primary purpose since the way to determine this is according to two principles: a) if aid is given to parochial schools based upon neutral, secular criteria, and b) if aid goes to parochial schools based on private individual choices. The court found that the MPCP met both of these criteria—a) since students must live in Milwaukee, meet income requirements, and are chosen randomly, and b) since parents are those choosing where the money goes, not the state—hence there was no problem with a violation of the second prong. Viteritti sums it up: "The funds were appropriated to parents and children rather than schools."[77] In other words, the court ruled that the MPCP would not have the primary effect of advancing religion because the program gave equal weight to private and public schools and placed the power of choice in the hands of the parents.

On the third prong, the court ruled that the MPCP does not rise to the level of excessive entanglement since that would include things like the government's involvement in running private schools, establishing curriculum, overseeing day-to-day activities, establishing a particular religious doctrine to be taught, detailed monitoring of the school, and close administrative contact between the government and the school. Viteritti sums it up saying, "Funds were directed to parochial schools only as a result of individual choices made by parents."[78] In other words, there was no "excessive entanglement" between the government and religion because the MPCP did not require additional state surveillance or supervision and because the day-to-day governmental interaction with the schools was minimal. Summing up the state court's reasoning, Elizabeth Lugg writes:

> In its conclusion, the Wisconsin high court held that the amended MPCP did not violate any of the prongs of the Lemon Test. The court gave as its summarized reasoning the MPCP was a state aid program that provided a neutral benefit directly to economically disadvantaged families, without regard to either their religion or the religion of the institution that they wished to attend, and therefore, was not invalid under the Establishment Clause of the United States Constitution.[79]

Responding to the decision, Morken and Formicola note, "With Clint Bolick immediately declaring the decision to be 'a total, unconditional victory for school choice' the Institute declared that 'David has beaten Goliath on a very important one.'"[80] Therefore, the state supreme court declared that economically deprived parents and children were the primary beneficiaries of the program, not religious schools. The court declared, "The purpose of the program is to provide low-income parents with an opportunity to have their children educated outside the embattled Milwaukee public school system."[81] Summing up the case, the court declared, "Not all entanglements have the effect of advancing or inhibiting religion. The Court's prior holdings illustrate that total separation between church and state is not possible in an absolute sense."[82]

And the poor benefited.

CONCLUSION

Future Considerations

Now that school choice has cleared the constitutional hurdle, the burden falls upon public policymakers to develop systems of choice. The task will be to develop state choice plans that will be consistent with the criteria outlined by the Supreme Court in its Cleveland decision. (I suggest what these criteria should be in the next chapter.) State legislators must make sure that parents have multiple educational choices, that the money goes to the parents and not to the schools, and that the plans square with the state's constitutional provisions. Moreover, any government action that specifically excludes religious institutions will raise the issue of religious discrimination.

Those general principles are clear. But public policymakers will also have to weave their way through multiple, murky, secondary questions as well. Policymakers must ensure that all schools, even small schools, are treated fairly and have an equal shot at attracting children. They must also design a plan in which they carefully balance freedom of religion issues along with care not to violate the Establishment Clause, say, for example, in the case of a religious school's hiring practices. They must watch the certification of each school carefully to ensure that no aid reaches schools that engage in racist education.[83] And they must carefully track the success of the program to demonstrate that all children are benefiting from a system of choices.[84]

The Supreme Court has interpreted the Constitution to support a fully orbed system of school choice. Now legislators, with pressure from voters, must develop plans that bring the promise of vouchers to "the least of these." There is no constitutional obligation on them to do so. The obligation falls on all of us to encourage them to do so for the benefit of those without a voice. There will be many voices opposing the creation of schools of choice. How many will there be championing the cause of the poor?

Where Do We Go from Here?

America's poor families are the big winners from the June 2002 Supreme Court decision. No longer will the law provide a barrier to the poorest children gaining access to the finest schools. No longer will the separation of church and state force a family to send a child to a school that challenges the values taught at home. No longer will children suffer as a result of the law supporting an educational monopoly. Now that the legal challenges to school choice have been eliminated, the question is up to legislators to design school-choice plans that will allow opportunities for all of society's children. Will the public put the pressure on them to design fair plans that will do justice to all of the people in society including the poor and families of all stripes? Only time will tell.[85]

What we can say with certainty is this: Americans have more opportunities to enjoy their freedom of religion than they did before the Court's ruling on the Cleveland program. Americans will now have the opportunity to exercise their public religious freedom in addition to their private religious freedom. In contrast to the current public school monopoly enjoyed by the public school system, the Supreme Court ruled that Americans may exercise their religious freedom in public when it comes to choosing a school of their liking. The monopoly of one view described in chapter 2 may be soon coming to an end. If education is one key to the future success of the poor, then the Supreme Court has helped more poor children in one decision than in any other Supreme Court educational decision since *Brown v. Topeka Board of Education*.

What the Supreme Court has determined means that poor children and all families in the United States will now have access to better education. The poor will now have options. No longer will they be condemned to their local public school. They will now have the opportunity to opt out. They will now have an opportunity to get a quality education. Justice now can be done to the poor.

The Supreme Court has signaled that all children now have the opportunity to have equal protection apply to them. The Court has decided that all parents may now receive equal treatment. Regardless of where they live or how much they make, every parent and child may now have the opportunity to receive funding for a good, quality education. State public policy can now begin to ensure that all children receive access to quality education.

What the Court has done is to match up the criterion established for justice in chapter 2 with our current educational policies. The Supreme Court
has now declared that there is no constitutional violation when governments
provide equal educational opportunities for all children. Legislators may
now set up educational plans that treat all educational institutions fairly and
that don't discriminate against any based solely on religion. The poor have
won, families have won, and most significantly, the children have won.

The benefits to families are potentially enormous. No longer will families be forced to choose between education and some other family expense. No longer will many families be forced to choose between education and a legitimate family need. And no longer will poor families be
without even that choice. Now the poor will have the opportunity for a
quality education—if public policymakers will act to design a system consistent with the Supreme Court's decision. Clearly, to provide justice to all
in society, they should. Hopefully, they will.

Those championing the cause of justice in America in the first decade
of the new century have cause for great rejoicing. Principles that help
shape a just society have been enacted in the Supreme Court's Cleveland
decision. The Court has signaled that all people in society should have an
equal opportunity to quality schooling, not just those fortunate enough to
live in wealthy school districts. The Court ruled that schooling should be
offered to all from a perspective of parity and that a fundamental right like
education should not be distributed based upon wealth. The Supreme
Court ruled that schooling should actually encourage family control and
provide equal access to the poor. If state and federal legislators follow
through on these principles by establishing just educational systems, poor
children will benefit for years to come. Our hope then is that we will continue the fight by taking the next step and pressuring our legislators to design educational systems that provide justice to all of America's children,
including her poor children. In the next chapter, I describe the elements of
a just educational system.

NOTES

1. Rodger Hurley, 1969, 91, cited in David Kirkpatrick, *Choice in Schooling:
A Case for Tuition Vouchers* (Chicago: Loyola University Press, 1990).

2. Kirkpatrick, *Choice in Schooling*, 49.

3. Alan Brownstein, "Constitutional Questions about Vouchers," *NYU Annual Survey of American Law* 57 (2000): 119.

4. Charles Glenn, *The Ambiguous Embrace: Government and Faith-Based Schools and Social Agencies* (Princeton, N.J.: Princeton University Press, 2000), 99.

5. *Reed v. Rhodes*, No. C73-1300, 1992 WL 80626 at *1 (N.D. Ohio, Apr. 2, 1992) quoted in *Amici Curia Brief for the Center for Education Reform, et al. in Support of Petitioners*, 8–9.

6. Diane Ravitch, *School Reform, Past, Present, and Future*, 51 Case West. L. Rev. 187, 189 (2001), quoted in *Amici Curia Brief for the Center for Education Reform et al. in Support of Petitioners*, 10.

7. Appendix 2, Jay P. Greene, *The Racial, Economic, and Religious Context of Parental Choice in Cleveland* (1999), quoted in *Amici Curia Brief for the Center for Education Reform et al. in Support of Petitioners*, 11.

8. *Amici Curia Brief for the Center for Education Reform et al. in Support of Petitioners*, 13.

9. Joseph Viteritti, *Choosing Equality* (Washington, D.C.: Brookings Institution Press, 1999), 175.

10. Jay Greene, *Context of Parental Choice*, J.A. at 213a-214a, quoted in *Amici Curia Brief for the Center for Education Reform et al. in Support of Petitioners*, 12.

11. *Amici Curia Brief for the Center for Education Reform et al. in Support of Petitioners*, 9.

12. *DeRolfe v. State*, 677 N.E.2d 733, 742 (Ohio 1997) (*DeRolfe I*), reh'g and clarification, 678 N.E.2d 886 (Ohio 1997), clarification, 699 N.E.2d 518 (Ohio 1998), quoted in *Amici Curia Brief for the Center for Education Reform et al. in Support of Petitioners*, 9.

13. For background, see Joseph Viteritti, "School Choice and State Constitutional Law," in *Learning from School Choice*, edited by Paul Peterson and Bryan Hassel (Washington, D.C.: Brookings Institution Press, 1998), 416–17.

14. Quoted in Joseph Viteritti, *Choosing Equality*, 175.

15. Joseph Viteritti, *Choosing Equality*, 175. See also Paul Peterson and Bryan Hassel, eds., *Learning from School Choice* (Washington, D.C.: Brookings Institution Press), 416–17.

16. For an analysis of the legal issues before the court, see *Amici Curia Brief for the Center for Education Reform, et al. in Support of Petitioners*, Nos. 00-1751, 00-1777, 00-1779, especially 14–30.

17. This is, of course, the dominant view of many Americans, rooted, in part, in the thought of Jefferson and adopted by Madison. Jefferson wrote in the Virginia Bill for Religious Liberty in 1786 "that no man shall be compelled to frequent or support any religious worship, place, or ministry whatsoever, nor shall

be enforced, restrained, molested, or burdened in his body or goods, nor shall otherwise suffer on account of his religious opinions or belief." Quoted in "State of the First Amendment: Freedom of Religion," *Update on Law-Related Education* 22, no. 1 (Winter 1998): 14.

18. Stephen Lazarus, "The Real Religious Establishment," *Capital Commentary* (October 5, 2001).

19. Stephen Lazarus, "What's Unconstitutional about School Choice," *Capital Commentary* (July 29, 2002).

20. Lazarus, "What's Unconstitutional about School Choice."

21. President Bush quoted in Peter Woll, *American Government: Readings and Cases* (15th ed.) (New York: Longman, 2003), 142.

22. Nathan Lewis, "Are Vouchers Constitutional?" *Policy Review* 93 (January/February 1999): 5–8.

23. For more on this, see Lewis, "Are Vouchers Constitutional?" 5–8.

24. Lewis, "Are Vouchers Constitutional?"

25. Great debates took place among legal scholars over such issues. For example, Alan Brownstein notes, "Indeed, challenges to the legitimacy of any doctrinal line distinguishing between vouchers and direct grants are raised from both sides of the voucher debate." See, e.g., Robert J. Bruno, *Constitutional Analysis of Educational Vouchers in Minnesota*, 53 Ed. Law Rep. 9, 13 (1989) (arguing that "where the school involved is a religious or religion-connected school, the voucher grant provision is a direct financial subsidy from the state to a religious organization" in violation of the Establishment Clause); *Mitchell*, 120 S.Ct. at 2546 (casting doubt on whether constitutionally permissible aid to religious schools must be in the form of vouchers or some other "indirect" mechanism since such a "formalistic line breaks down in the application to real-world programs"). Quoted in Brownstein, "Constitutional Questions about Vouchers," 125.

26. *Everson v. Board of Education* 330 U.S. 1 (1947) quoted in "State of the First Amendment: Freedom of Religion," *Update on Law-Related Education* 22 (Winter 1998): 10–16.

27. See Hubert Morken and Jo Renee Formicola, *The Politics of School Choice* (Lanham, Md.: Rowman & Littlefield, 1999), 16–17.

28. *Committee for Public Education and Religious Liberty v. Nyquist*, 413 U.S. at 797 (1973), quoted in Elizabeth Lugg and Andrew Lugg, "Vouchers as School Choice: An Analysis of *Jackson v. Benson*—the Milwaukee Parental Choice Program," *Journal of Law and Education* 29, no. 2 (April 2000): 175–92.

29. 413 U.S. at 786, quoted in Frank Kemerer, "Reconsidering the Constitutionality of Vouchers," *Journal of Law and Education* 30, no. 3 (July 2001): 435–44.

30. Lewis, "Are Vouchers Constitutional?" 5–8.

31. 413 at 783 n. 38, quoted in Kemerer, "Reconsidering the Constitutionality of Vouchers," 435–44.

32. Kemerer, "Reconsidering the Constitutionality of Vouchers," 435–44. For an excellent assessment of the impact of recent decisions on *Nyquist*, see William Howell and Paul Peterson, *The Education Gap: Vouchers and Urban Schools* (Washington, D.C.: Brookings Institution Press, 2002), 188–92.

33. *Mueller v. Allen*, 463 U.S. 388 (1983).

34. *Mueller v. Allen*, 463 U.S. at 401 (1983).

35. See Kirkpatrick, *Choice in Schooling*, 58.

36. For more on this, see Lugg and Lugg, "Vouchers as School Choice," 175–92.

37. Viteritti, "School Choice and State Constitutional Law," 423.

38. Viteritti, "School Choice and State Constitutional Law."

39. *Mueller v. Allen*, 463 U.S. 400 (1983), quoted in Kemerer, "Reconsidering the Constitutionality of Vouchers," 435–44.

40. *Mueller v. Allen*, 463 U.S. 387, 399 (1983), quoted in Viteritti, "School Choice and State Constitutional Law," 423.

41. *Lemon v. Kurtzman*, 403 U.S. 602, 612–13.

42. Quoted in Lisa Larson, "The Constitutionality of Education Vouchers under State and Federal Law," *Information Brief for the Minnesota House of Representatives* (July 1998): 7.

43. *Witters v. Washington Department of Services for the Blind*, 474 U.S. 481, (1985).

44. 474 U.S. 490-91 (Powell, J. concurring) (citations omitted). See also Viteritti, "School Choice and State Constitutional Law," 423.

45. As I argued in chapter 2, no school is neutral or value-free in the section on school choice's impact on public schools. If that is true, then any worldview that is funded by the government at the expense of other worldviews, constitutes an "establishment" of religion.

46. For a helpful overview of this and other cases, see Morken and Formicola, "*The Politics of School Choice,*" 26–28.

47. *Zobrest v. Catalina Foothills School District*, 113 S.Ct. 2462 (1993).

48. The vote in this case was 5–4 with Blackmun and Souter dissenting. Yet, the Supreme Court still lacks clarity into its religious freedom and establishment decisions. This case points to the Court's confusion over the exact meaning and application of the Establishment Clause when it comes to church–state issues. Chief Justice William H. Rehnquist said during oral argument on February 24, 1993, that the Court ought to "straighten out" its First Amendment jurisprudence. See Joan Biskupic, "Quips, Hypotheses Punctuate Court Arguments in Two Religion Cases," *Washington Post* (February 25, 1993): A-6.

49. Quoted in Lisa Larson, "The Constitutionality of Education Vouchers under State and Federal Law," *Information Brief for the Minnesota House of Representatives* (July 1998), 7.

50. *Zobrest v. Catalina Foothills School District*, 509 U.S. 22–23 (1993). Quoted in Kemerer, "Reconsidering the Constitutionality of Vouchers," 435–44.

51. For more on these cases, see Rayton Sianjina, "Parental Choice, School Vouchers, and Separation of Church and State: Legal Implications," *Educational Forum* 63, no. 2 (Winter 1999): 108–12. The Supreme Court upheld these principles, this time applying them to private schools only, on November 9, 1993, in *Florence County School District Four v. Carter*. The Supreme Court ruled that Shannon Carter's parents would receive the $35,000 that they had spent for their daughter's three years at the Trident Academy, a private school for children with learning disabilities. Trident was not a state-certified school. The Court awarded the parents the money because the public school system of Florence County, South Carolina, failed to meet her learning disability needs under the Individuals with Disabilities Education Act. In a unanimous decision, the Court upheld a lower court's order: 1) parents have the right to make a private school placement without school district approval, 2) parents who make this placement can seek reimbursement, and 3) parents can be reimbursed for a placement in a nonapproved private school. See *Florence County School District Four v. Carter*, 114 S.Ct. 361 (1993).

52. For more on these cases, see Lewis, "Are Vouchers Constitutional?" 5–8.

53. *Rosenberger v. Rector and Visitors of the University of Virginia*, 515 U.S. 830 (1995), quoted in Kemerer, "Reconsidering the Constitutionality of Vouchers," 435–55.

54. *Rosenberger v. Rector and Visitors of the University of Virginia*, 115 S.Ct. 2510, 2522 (1995) quoted in Viteritti, "School Choice and State Constitutional Law," 424.

55. Viteritti, "School Choice and State Constitutional Law," 424.

56. *Agostini v. Felton*, 521 U.S. 203 (1997). Joseph Viteritti suggests that while this case does not completely undo the three-pronged *Lemon* test, it does signal an important philosophical shift in the high court's approach to religion cases: "What changed was the willingness of the Court to accept certain assumptions that shaped previous decisions, specifically: that a public employee who works on the premises of a religious school is presumed to inculcate religion; that the presence of that employee creates a symbolic union between church and state; and, most significantly, that public aid that directly aids the educational function of a religious school impermissibly supports religious indoctrination. The Court affirmed the neutrality of the Title I services that are granted in a manner that

'neither favors nor disfavors religion,' because they are available to all eligible students 'no matter what their religious beliefs or where they go to school.'" Viteritti, *Choosing Equality*, 142.

57. Paul Peterson and Jay Greene, "Race Relations and Central City Schools: It's Time for an Experiment with Vouchers," *Brookings Review* 16, no. 2 (Spring 1998): 33–37.

58. Larson, "The Constitutionality of Education Vouchers under State and Federal Law," 7. See also "State of the First Amendment: Freedom of Religion," 10–16. Explaining the significance of *Agostini*, Charles Glenn writes: "The *Agostini* decision suggests that some amount of 'entanglement' necessarily associated with any system of accountability for the use of public funds need not be a barrier to supporting nonreligious educational activities in religious schools, provided that the services themselves are 'secular, neutral, and nonideological.'" *The Ambiguous Embrace: Government and Faith-Based Schools and Social Agencies* (Princeton, N.J.: Princeton University Press, 2000), 99.

59. *Mitchell v. Helms*, 120 S.Ct. 2530 (2000), at 2541 and 2544, quoted in Kemerer, "Reconsidering the Constitutionality of Vouchers," 435–55.

60. Kemerer, "Reconsidering the Constitutionality of Vouchers," 435–55.

61. See Viteritti, "School Choice and State Constitutional Law," 424–25.

62. Stephen H. Freid, "The Constitutionality of Choice under the Establishment Clause," *Clearing House* (November/December 1992): 92–95.

63. Lawrence Tribe, "Constitutional Scrutiny," *New York Times* (June 17, 1991).

64. Part of the challenge at the state level comes from states' adaptations of the Blaine Amendment. In 1875, Maine congressman James Blaine proposed an amendment prohibiting states from providing financial assistance to parochial schools. While the amendment failed to pass the two-thirds majority it needed by two votes, many states incorporated the amendment's intentions either through legislation or amendment. In fact, by 1890 over half the states had passed laws prohibiting public schools funds to be used in parochial schools. See Viteritti, "School Choice and State Constitutional Law," 419–21; Morken and Formicola, *The Politics of School Choice*, 15–16.

65. Viteritti, "School Choice and State Constitutional Law," 412.

66. See "State of the First Amendment: Freedom of Religion," 10–16 and see also Viteritti, "School Choice and State Constitutional Law," 417–19.

67. Viteritti, *Choosing Equality*, 176.

68. Viteritti, *Choosing Equality*, 178.

69. Viteritti, *Choosing Equality*, 178.

70. John Benson was the state superintendent of instruction.

71. Morken and Formicola, *The Politics of School Choice*, 33.

72. Viteritti, "School Choice and State Constitutional Law," 413.

73. Quoted in Viteritti, *Choosing Equality*, 173.

74. Larson, "The Constitutionality of Education Vouchers," 5.
75. Morken and Formicola, *The Politics of School Choice*, 34.
76. Viteritti, *Choosing Equality*, 172.
77. Viteritti, *Choosing Equality*, 172.
78. Viteritti, *Choosing Equality*, 172.
79. Lugg and Lugg, "Vouchers as School Choice," 175–92. Significantly, the Wisconsin Supreme Court also upheld the MPCP based upon state constitutional law. Viteritti explains, "The Wisconsin Supreme Court also rejected challenges made on the basis of state constitutional law. With regard to the state's public purpose doctrine, it explained, 'Education ranks at the apex of a state's function.' The decision continued, 'This court has long recognized that equal educational opportunities are a fundamental right . . . and that the state had broad discretion to determine how best to ensure such opportunities.' Citing *Pierce* and *Meyer*, as well as state precedents, the court affirmed, 'Wisconsin has traditionally accorded parents with the primary role in decisions regarding the education and upbringing of their children.' It then quoted at length from an 1899 decision of its own that went to the heart of the choice question, recognizing that: Parents as the natural guardians of their children [are] the persons under natural conditions having the most effective motives and inclinations and being in the best position and under the strongest obligations to give to such children proper nurture, education and training." *Choosing Equality*, 172–73.
80. Morken and Formicola, *The Politics of School Choice*, 34.
81. Viteritti, *Choosing Equality*, 172.
82. Cited in Lewis, "Are Vouchers Constitutional?" 8. See also Perry Zirkel, "What Will Be the Supreme Court's Choice on Choice," *Journal of Law and Education* 30, no. 3 (July 2001): 431–33.
83. James Dwyer has suggested that it is only a matter of time before someone files suit to extend the *Norwood* holding, which denies aid to racist schools, to include sexist schools. See James Dwyer, *Vouchers within Reason: A Child-Centered Approach to Education Reform* (Ithaca, N.Y.: Cornell University Press, 2002), 209.
84. See Viteritti, *Choosing Equality* 179.
85. Alan Brownstein echoes this writing: "I take it as a given that the public funding of religious schools is of substantial value to religious families and faith communities. It facilitates the free exercise of religion, helps children learn the substance of their family's religion, and strengthens and reinforces the beliefs and commitments of those faith communities that sponsor religious schools. There is no doubt that vouchers increase access to all of these religious benefits for some people. Whether the increased access and resulting religious advantages would be equally available to all religious families and communities under a voucher or subsidy program is less clear." I have argued it is. See Brownstein, "Constitutional Questions about Vouchers," 126.

Chapter Four

Elements of a
Good School-Choice Plan

Now that the Supreme Court has cleared the path for a just educational system including school choice, the focus falls to legislators to develop a comprehensive school-choice plan. What would a good school-choice system look like? In this chapter I describe the elements of a school-choice system, and then I examine the issues related to cost and regulation. Throughout I show that a well-designed plan will save states money and can provide sound education without over regulation.

ELEMENTS OF A SCHOOL-CHOICE SYSTEM

The purpose of a school-choice system is to improve education for children by empowering parents to choose a school for their child. This choice should be available regardless of religious commitment or financial status, and should enable teachers to teach with few restrictions. This goal, in turn, will create new schools.[1] A just statewide school-choice system should contain the following ten provisions:

1. All Parents Will Receive a Tuition Voucher

Progressive financial tactics, like a progressive income tax, are common in the United States. If a state does the tax collecting for education and progressively taxes the rich (whether through property taxes or otherwise), then all parents will receive a voucher worth 100 percent of the statewide average spent per student. However, if there is little progressivity in taxation, then a sliding scale voucher, like the following example, should be implemented. Between the highest and lowest incomes, a sliding scale will be in effect. The average tuition voucher should be 90 percent of the statewide average (which was approximately $6,500 per student in the 1998–99 school year and $7,300 in the 2000–2001 school year).[2]

Parents with incomes below the poverty line should receive a voucher worth 125 percent of the statewide average to help with education-related expenses. Parents at the poverty line up to 175 percent of the poverty line should receive 100 percent of the statewide average. From there, the voucher amount should progressively decrease to 50 percent of the statewide average for the richest 1 percent. No parent will be able to add on to the amount of the voucher beyond the 1–50 percent to get up to but not greater than 100 percent. Schools that agree to accept tuition vouchers must not charge more than 100 percent of the voucher amount. This will ensure equal protection for all children. If a parent wishes to opt out of this system by choosing a more expensive school that is not participating in the voucher program, all of the cost will come out of the parent's pocket. If this were not a provision of the program, state subsidies could go toward further segregation of society by allowing rich families to add on dollars to send their children to better schools that poor parents would be unable to afford.

If a state's system of taxation is not progressive, then a sliding scale voucher is fair, because it provides all parents, regardless of financial status or religious preference, with access to good schools. Moreover, states will save money because private and parochial schools cost less than public schools, and many well-to-do parents will be contributing to the cost of their children's education.[3] Former Clinton Secretary of Labor Robert Reich made this case in the *Wall Street Journal* when he argued for vouchers for all families based on a sliding income scale, with the poorest families receiving the greatest voucher credit. Reich wrote, "The only way to begin to decouple poor kids from lousy schools is to give poor kids additional resources, along with vouchers enabling them and their parents to choose how to use them."[4]

2. Schools Will Not Be Funded by the District

Public school systems have perpetuated the cycle of poverty and injustice. All tax dollars will go into a state "hopper," as has been done in Michigan, and distributed evenly to parents. This will prevent the uneven competition that could occur if education were funded by districts instead of by the state.[5]

3. Tuition Vouchers, Not Tax Credits

States should adopt tuition vouchers instead of tax credits. Tuition tax credits hinder poor parents, since they must first pay for education and only later receive the tax credit. Few poor parents can afford to do this.

4. Minimum Voucher Amounts

A voucher should cover no less than 50 percent of the average state school cost, since anything below that might be insufficient for a small group of parents to start a new school. A system of school choice must create new schools. Without new schools, choice is meaningless. If parents are empowered to choose, they must have real options from which to choose.

5. Transportation Supplements

A tuition voucher should provide a reasonable extra voucher amount for children needing additional transportation to reach the school of their choice, paid for through the savings provided by school choice. This supplement would only be necessary if there is no sliding scale voucher.

6. Gradual Implementation

A school-choice program should be implemented gradually. The enactment period would serve as a transition for the poor, who should be allowed to participate first before others join in (as in Milwaukee and Cleveland). Public schools should be given up to ten years to adjust to the changes.[6]

7. Private and Parochial Schools

Private and parochial schools must be included in the program since 85 percent of all nonstate schools are parochial. Twelve percent of all American students—nearly five million nationwide—attend private or parochial schools.[7]

8. Government and State Regulation

Schools should be free from extensive governmental regulation that might infringe on their autonomy and identity. But the state should have regulations for schools that receive public funds. Schools should be held accountable for how the money is spent. All funds going to schools must be used for educational goods, services, and facilities and may not be used for any church-related activities. The state should have certification requirements for the hiring and firing of teachers, ensure that certain subjects are taught in every curriculum, ensure that schools follow national civil rights laws, guarantee that school facilities do not present a safety risk to the students, fill out compliance reports, conduct financial audits, and enforce health regulations.[8] Private and parochial schools will have the ultimate safeguard: they can refuse to participate in choice programs if they believe the restrictions are too onerous. Private and parochial schools receiving public funds will also be required to take their share of difficult-to-educate children; this will impose limited new duties on private and parochial schools.[9]

9. Student Retention

Schools will set their own policies for retaining students. School choice ought to promote fair access. It ought not force schools to keep children they would otherwise expel.

10. Parent Information Centers

Each school district will establish a parent information center (PIC) to assist parents with information and counseling in choosing the best school for their child. Each school should be required provide the center with information in the following eight areas:

1. A mission statement and the supporting philosophy of education
2. Governing structure

3. Criteria for hiring and firing teachers, including the qualifications of all teachers and administrators
4. Matriculation and retention policies
5. The independent accrediting agency or state standards used in reviewing the school to ensure basic educational competencies and testing
6. Tuition charges and an independent financial audit showing how all money was raised, budgeted, and spent
7. Type of curriculum adopted and the type of teaching methods used
8. The aggregate scores of students on standardized tests, and the attendance, graduation, expulsion, and suspension rates[10]

The PIC should make this information readily available to the public. Providing this information will help to ensure the accountability of all schools receiving public funds. There should be consequences to a school if it fails to comply with these requirements.

DEALING WITH ISSUES OF CONCERN: COST AND REGULATION

Cost

Opponents argue that a system of school choice would cost a state more than it is presently spending on education. State legislatures will have to find extra money to fund private and parochial school tuitions, to pay transportation costs to the new schools of choice, and to finance information gathering, outreach, and training. Albert Menendez and Edd Doerr say:

> Including nonpublic schools in tax-funded school-choice plans will entail extremely high costs for taxpayers. Adding the costs of operating existing nonpublic schools to those of public schools will obviously increase elementary and secondary school costs across the nation by at least ten percent, as the number of students in tax-supported schools rise by at least ten percent.[11]

Critics claimed that California's Proposition 174 would have increased the state's education budget by $1.3 billion.[12] According to the Carnegie Foundation's widely acclaimed *School Choice, A Special Report*: "School choice, to be successful, requires significant administrative and financial support. It is not a cheap path to educational reform. . . . The point is clear . . . choice costs. . . . If choice is to work, added expenditures are required."[13] And the NEA writes, "Vouchers undermine reform efforts by shifting scarce resources away from public schools."[14]

To put the issue of expenditures into perspective, consider the current system, which is very expensive. The amount spent per pupil has increased from $974 per pupil in 1945 (in 1992 dollars) to $5,216 in 1992.[15] In the 1994–95 school year, Jersey City spent an average of $9,200 per pupil.[16] Federal, state, and local governments spent $253 *billion* on public education in the 1992–93 school year. In inflation-adjusted dollars, this was up 56 percent from 1980–81 dollars. The average amount spent per child was 50 percent higher than in West Germany and 85 percent higher than in Japan.[17] By the 1998–99 school year, the expenditures had risen to $311.6 billion. The average amount spent per child had risen to $6,696. When adjusted for current dollars, the overall dollars and the average per pupil are the following: 1986, $137.2 billion and $3,479; 1993, $220.9 billion and $5,160; and in 1999, $302.9 and $6,508. The National Center for Education Statistics projects that total expenditures by 2011 will range from $402.4 billion to $435.9 billion and the average per pupil will range from $8,538 to $9,250.[18]

Conversely, a well-designed school-choice proposal will save money for states. Many states will spend less in their state education budgets, because the average cost of private school education is about half that of public school education.[19] Consequently, even if a voucher paid for 80 percent of a private school tuition for the richest parents, the state would still save 20 percent on what it would have spent for a public school education. In other words, if the state can purchase an education with a voucher at a cost lower than average the state spends, then a state should support that proposal. Milwaukee, for example, saves over $2,000 per student when it provides a tuition voucher for a student instead of having to pay the full cost of a public school on tuition charge.[20] California's Proposition 174 received scrutiny from three Nobel Prize–winning economists, 140 leading economists, and every major antitax group in the state. Their verdict was that Proposition 174 would save the state money.[21]

The school-choice programs in Cleveland, Milwaukee, and Pensacola have not drained money from the public schools. According to the Ohio Department of Education, since school choice began in Cleveland, the general operating expenditures for the public schools have risen from

$559.6 million to $662.6 million. Per pupil spending increased from $7,970 to $8,814.[22] Part of this increase is because the public school still gets credit for the students who leave through the voucher. According to Dorman Cordell: "The president of the Ohio Federation of Teachers said the $5.25 million spent last school year on voucher students (about $3,300 per student when other costs are considered) was money being denied to public schools. But state officials pointed out that the public schools, which spent $6,506 per student in 1996–97, came out ahead because the state funding formula still counted the voucher students in Cleveland's enrollment."[23] As a result, Cleveland Public Schools had a net revenue gain of $118,473 in 1997.[24]

The Milwaukee school-choice program has also not drained vast resources from Milwaukee's public schools. Since the choice program began in Milwaukee, spending in the Milwaukee Public Schools (MPS) increased from $604.5 million to $968 million along with a per-pupil increase of $6,064 to $9,417.[25] According to the Institute for the Transformation of Learning at Marquette University, real state aid to the MPS increased 55 percent during the years of the MPCP.[26] In fact, the MPS spending rate grew three times faster than enrollment during the 1990s.[27] In 2001, the MPS itself tactically admitted that vouchers save money when it reported that if choice were eliminated and the 10,000 choice students returned to the MPS, the MPS would add $70 million of added operating expenses and would have to borrow up to $70 million for new facilities.[28] Summing up the impact of the MPCP on the MPS, Fuller and Mitchell write:

> During the first nine years of the Milwaukee Parental Choice Program, Milwaukee Public School's financial situation improved substantially after the program was expanded to include religious schools. Specifically, MPS enrollment rose eight percent while spending rose 29 percent, state aid increased 55 percent and the local tax levy decreased 33 percent.[29]

Similarly, the voucher plan in Florida has helped save the public schools money. According to FAQs about Florida's system of Opportunity Scholarships:

> Opportunity Scholarships themselves have no effect on the revenues for public schools. This is because the per-student spending in the public school will remain the same regardless of the number of students who use Opportunity

Scholarships. In fact, many private schools have tuition below what is currently spent to educate a child in public school. In these circumstances, the funding difference remains in the state treasury and can be allocated to enhance spending on public education. . . . In the two schools that are currently eligible for Opportunity Scholarships, funding has increased to help these schools improve. The Department of Education is providing more money, including a grant of over $87,000 for basic skills programs to help improve learning in the areas where it is needed most: reading, writing, and mathematics.[30]

In fact, under the Florida plan in which failing schools receive money to help them become succeeding schools, choice has meant more money for public schools. According to Tom Gallagher, Commissioner of the Florida Department of Education:

> For D and F schools in Florida the federal government authorized supplemental funds. The 78 F schools in 15 school districts will have $45,018,127 available in supplemental funding. The 613·D schools in 57 school districts will have $280,734,600 available in supplemental funding. Florida has also set aside $2,138,191 and $3,576,150 in supplemental funds for D and F schools, respectively.[31]

So, under Florida's plan, students may choose to leave failing schools and the failing schools receive extra financial assistance. *Education Week* explains:

> Under Florida's A+ Opportunity Scholarship Program, parents of some students at Spencer Bibbs and A.A. Dixon schools in Pensacola (Escambia County) chose to enroll them in other private or public schools. Bibbs and Dixon had been designated as "failing" by the state. As a result of the designation, Bibbs and Dixon received additional state financial aid. With these funds they hired full-time reading and writing specialists. Former Escambia County Schools Superintendent Jim May said, "To be fair, the [Florida] Department of Education has come through with significant contributions . . . to help us through a hard time."[32]

Consequently, when the *New York Times* visited those two schools, it found that the schools had "hired more teachers, reduced class size, stretched the school year by 30 days and added afternoon tutoring."[33]

States could also choose to reinvest the savings into education instead of saving the money. If they choose not to lower their state education budgets, they could instead increase the average amount the state spends on students who choose public education. James Foster explains:

Oregon, for example, spends over $4,700 on each public-school pupil (making the state thirteenth in the nation). An elementary school enrolling 500 students would receive over $2.3 million. If 10 percent of the students at the school took advantage of a $2,500 tax credit to attend a private school, the school would lose $125,000. But each departing student would leave behind $2,200. That money could then be used to improve the education of the students remaining in the public schools.[34]

And this savings is exactly what's happened in Milwaukee. Dorman Cordell explains:

About $7.1 million went to the Milwaukee private school program in the 1996–97 school year, when 1,650 students participated and payments were $4,400 per student. The Union said the money should have been used in the public schools to reduce class size and implement a new learning program. This argument ignored the fact that the district received about $7,500 for each of the students and sent the private schools only $4,400—giving the district an extra $3,100 for each of the children it no longer had to educate. Thus the public schools had more money per remaining student.[35]

In other words, states will save money in choice programs because instead of getting $7,500 and having to pay the $7,500 to educate the child with a net gain of $0, the states get $3,100 for free and get to spend that money on students already in the system. States make money when school choice is implemented. This is clearly described by Joe Williams:

In the worst-case scenario, state Department of Administration estimates showed that if 15,000 students left the district to attend choice schools, MPS would be left with $900 more per pupil to spend on education. . . . Expanded school choice could result in substantial overall savings for Milwaukee Public Schools and allow the district to ease classroom overcrowding, three reports presented Wednesday night to the School Board show. A June 28 report by the Legislative Fiscal Bureau, distributed to school officials Wednesday night by Gardner, said MPS would find savings in its educational programs "because these students would no longer be educated by

MPS and thus, costs in the district should be reduced. . . ." In addition, board members said the district would not be required to build new classroom space at its current pace, resulting in substantial long-term savings.[36]

States that adopt a system of school choice will either save money or will gain additional funds to spend on each pupil.

School choice could also decrease state expenditures through lower transportation and administrative costs. If a school-choice proposal created more schools, then transportation costs might decrease if multiple schools shared a building close to a child's home. Administrative costs would likely decrease, since there would be fewer layers of bureaucracy.[37] John Chubb has explained why there are fewer bureaucratic costs in a school-choice system: "There is every reason to believe that the administrative structure of a choice system would be less bureaucratized than today's public school systems, and look more like private educational systems, where competition compels decentralization and administrative savings."[38] Such savings have already been achieved. For example, the Vaughn Next Century Learning Center, a charter school near Los Angeles, saved $1.2 million in its first year because it accepted competitive bids for services and thus had lower bureaucratic costs.

Demographic trends also indicate that school choice will likely help states save money. Student enrollment figures are expected to increase over the next decade, which will require many school districts to build new buildings. In Detroit, school districts have floated bonds in order to pay for new buildings. Yet inner-city Detroit Catholic schools have available space that could be used without further expenditure. Had Pennsylvania passed education reform legislation in 1995, Philadelphia alone could have saved school districts millions of dollars in building costs.

In addition to saving states money, a well-constructed school-choice proposal will produce long-term socioeconomic benefits. Because schools of choice achieve higher graduation and attendance rates and better student performance, while also meeting the needs of "hard-to-educate" students (see chapter 6), they will be associated with fewer dropouts and better-educated graduates, who might contribute positively to society. Offering enhanced educational choices to individual students will produce long-range benefits for society as a whole. School choice makes moral and financial sense.

Regulation: Fringe Schools

Will school choice be so lax that fringe schools will be supported with public dollars?

Critics of school choice argue that a school-choice proposal will either overly restrict private and parochial schools' freedom with new regulations, or a school-choice proposal will be so lax that it will provide funding for "fly-by-night" schools backed by such extremist sects as the Moonies or America First. Estelle James has argued that increasing state regulation of private and parochial schools is "inevitable, given the political logic and supporting empirical evidence."[39] Former California Assembly Speaker Willie Brown says, "Can you imagine a KKK group, skinheads, witches, or other cult groups setting up schools to teach their philosophy and using taxpayers' dollars to do so? This country has a history of blocking religious and dangerous cult groups from using public funds which must be continued."[40] Similarly, Charles Glenn reports:

> Reporters found that at schools that have labored for accreditation from the respected Western Association of Schools and Colleges, for example, there is the sense that a host of new "diploma mills" might open with little regulation and low standards. "There's no doubt that a lot of them would form," said one administrator at an expensive private school in San Francisco. "There would be no financial oversight."[41]

David Berliner, former president of the American Educational Research Association, warned that "voucher programs would allow for splintering along ethnic and racial lines. Our primary concern is that voucher programs could end up resembling the ethnic cleansing now occurring in Kosovo." The Harrisburg, Pennsylvania, school superintendent told a television audience that school choice would help create "Hitlerian regimes."[42] And Professor Henry Levin has written that "educational choice leads to greater socioeconomic and racial segregation . . . [and] that inequalities in educational outcomes are likely to be exacerbated by vouchers."[43]

I would now like to consider the two arguments against vouchers more closely. Consider first the latter argument: funding private and parochial schools means funding unaccountable fly-by-night schools. Long considered the Achilles' heel of school choice, this argument no longer represents a death knell to school-choice proposals.

The strongest argument why fly-by-night schools won't be funded under a system of choice is also the most obvious one: fringe schools will not be able to comply with federal and state accountability laws. For example, federal legislation requires charter schools to be open to all students who apply or admit students based on a lottery system if too many apply. Other state laws help ensure that charters will be open to all, including the following stipulations: offering transportation for lower-income students, forbidding exclusion of children based on intellectual or academic ability, ensuring that enrollment reflects the district's student population demographics, and targeting a certain percentage of students who do not achieve their potential in the traditional public school.

Charter schools must also observe Title VI of the Civil Rights Act of 1964, which bans discrimination in any educational program receiving federal funding, and Title VII, which prohibits discrimination in employment. Adhering to civil rights legislation and other laws related to issues such as safety issues like the quality of school buildings, observance of fire codes, disaster preparedness, an emergency action plan, a transportation system, conducting employee background checks, reporting child abuse; respecting those with special needs; respecting family privacy rights; allowing one's records to be open to the public; establishing health policies related to immunizations, first aid, physical exams, disease prevention, drug/alcohol- and tobacco-free schools, and a school lunch program, and so forth does not place an unreasonable burden on charter schools nor infringe upon their academic freedom.[44] They do guarantee that radical schools will not receive funding.

Similarly, the Milwaukee choice plan concretely demonstrates that a middle course can be found between overregulation and no regulation. The Milwaukee plan requires that private schools in the choice program subject themselves to eight federal and state laws and to one of four programs of accountability to parents. Beyond that, schools are free to develop their own curriculum, hire and fire teachers according to institutional philosophy, and teach as they see fit. Further, the eight federal and state laws must be obeyed by *all* private and parochial schools, whether or not they are a part of the choice program. Yet schools remain responsible to parents, or else they lose their source of funding.[45]

Now let me examine how accountable public and private schools are today in the United States. To gain some initial perspective on this question, one should ask how accountable public schools are currently. At present, many public schools are not accountable to parents for their teachers, curricula, student achievement scores, or day-to-day operations. Parents and teachers are frustrated that school boards, heads of teachers unions, and bureaucrats are pulling the control levers. Jeanne Allen describes another consequence stemming from the lack of public accountability in public schools—the abuse of public funds:

> Consider the abuses of public funds in New York City schools occurring hand-in-hand with a decline in educational quality, or the Kansas City, Missouri fiasco in which a multi-million dollar funding increase, amounting to more than $36,000 per student, was actually followed by a drop in achievement scores. Likewise, the schools of Jersey City have been put into receivership (state control) and have received an additional $100 million infusion of funds—with no positive results to show for it.[46]

Contrast the lack of accountability of public schools with the accountability of private and parochial schools. The latter are subject to many federal guidelines that will not change in a school-choice system. Federal statutes promoting civil and religious rights while preventing discrimination on the basis of gender, age, handicap, and national origin also impose restraints on private and parochial schools.[47] Typically, state courts have ruled in favor of the state and against the school in cases dealing with state regulation of private and parochial schools.[48] Private and parochial schools have been, and will remain, highly accountable educational institutions.

For example, all private schools participating in the Cleveland Scholarship and Tutoring Program must register with the Ohio State superintendent of public instruction, observe discrimination law, not charge low-income voucher families more than 10 percent of the voucher amount, work with parents to allow them to provide in-kind contributions or services in lieu of the 10 percent figure, and they must meet all other standards for the state's nonpublic schools—things like educational goals, curriculum and instruction, teacher qualifications, instructional materials and equipment, and the quantity and quality of facilities—and their programs must be evaluated once every five years.[49]

The Milwaukee schools have also been evaluated and have been shown to be accountable. According to the Wisconsin Legislative Audit Bureau, most of the schools participating in the Milwaukee Parental Choice Program were providing high-quality academic programs and tests.[50]

Private and parochial schools are also accountable to parents, since parents will stop sending their children to these schools if the schools do not perform adequately. Furthermore, most private and parochial schools are accredited, as Charles O'Malley explains: "Approximately 96 percent of private school children attend schools which are accredited or evaluated by national, regional, or state private school organizations. These organizations maintain standards which have been accepted or recognized by federal, state, and local education agencies, as well as by foundations and corporations."[51]

The accountability of private and parochial schools has paid enormous dividends for society. Private and parochial schools contribute to the common good by producing good citizens: their graduates tend to vote regularly, repay student loans on time, and obey the laws.[52] Private and parochial school student achievements have been reflected in various studies. One 1986 study, for example, found that Catholic school students scored an average of 14.7 points higher (out of 500 points) in math and 15.7 points higher in science than the average public school seventh grader.[53] Student performance in choice schools was confirmed by a RAND study, which attributed student achievement in choice schools in part to students' sense of ownership in the school. Compared with students in non-choice public schools, students in choice public schools had 20 percent higher graduation rate and their mean SAT scores were 73 points higher. Students in choice parochial schools did even better: they had a 50 percent higher graduation rate and their mean SAT scores were 161 points higher.[54]

A well-designed school choice plan will not fund fly-by-night schools. Since all schools must comply with the aforementioned state and federal laws, fly-by-night schools would not be able to comply with those standards. The argument that school choice will lead to public funding of skinhead, KKK, and witch schools is based on the faulty premise that private and parochial schools are unaccountable. However, private and parochial schools are highly accountable, and broadening educational funding to include them will fund quality schools that contribute to the common good.[55] Moreover, choice systems must not impose too many restrictions upon private and parochial schools. I now turn to an examination of that issue.

Regulation: Restrictions

Will school choice be so restrictive that private and parochial schools will be suffocated? The issue then becomes not whether the government will regulate private schools; but rather, the issue is how much regulation is appropriate. Obviously, if the religious and private schools are to receive public funding, there will be some regulation. The type of regulation mentioned in the previous section is appropriate. The type mentioned in the upcoming paragraph is not. The standard that should guide regulation should be whether the government's regulation interferes with the identity of the school. Observing things like building codes and civil rights legislation should be a part of governmental regulation. Infringing upon the character and identity of the school should be opposed. Charles Glenn clearly explains that the danger with too much regulation could be that "at some point the combination of funding and regulation could have the effect of making it in the eyes of the law a 'state actor,' subject to all the constitutional and other obligations imposed upon government itself."[56] Schools must be free to retain their own distinctive identity without being morphed into a creature of the state. Again, Glenn explains, "Protecting the ability of faith-based agencies and schools to be unlike those operated by government is essential both to their own integrity and also to the contribution that they can make to a diverse society."[57] The standard should be this: retain the school's identity while observing nondiscrimination and compliance with health and safety standards. Period.[58]

The single most dangerous threat to a private or parochial school's freedom is the legislation relating to admissions. Many parochial schools attempt to match children from their parish with their school or recruit students whose parents' values are similar to those in the school. If freedom is restricted in the admissions process or if schools are forced to use a lottery, then churches may not have tithing members' children in their schools or the schools may get students who do not agree with the school's philosophy.

John Holmes, director of government affairs for the Association of Christian Schools International, says his organization's number one concern is the regulation of admissions. Though most of this group's 3,500 member schools admit children of all faith backgrounds, they never do so without the eager involvement of parents. "The admissions process is what makes it possible

to evaluate whether a child and his family would be comfortable with who
we are as a religious institution," he says. "Your whole philosophical frame-
work can be ruined by families who are opposed to what you are doing."[59]

The other potential problem would be a school choice plan that allows
for "opt-outs." "Opt-outs" means the following: a student would be able
to opt out of any religious activity in the school that offends a student's religious beliefs. The problem is that this clause can easily become a slip-
pery slope related to what constitutes a religious activity: a certain class
teaching ethics or moral character, a fund-raising activity, the reasons un-
derlying a teacher's discipline of a student, and so on.

The difference between the two issues I have highlighted here and the
previous list of state and federal guidelines is significant: the laws do not af-
fect directly upon the mission and integrity of the school, the later (admissions and opt-out) do. The first should be supported, the latter opposed.[60]

The Center on Education Policy noted such potential over-regulation by
the government in their analysis of twenty-two European countries with
choice. They concluded:

> We found that when private schools accept significant levels of public fund-
> ing, they usually must comply with a rather high degree of government reg-
> ulation. Countries that heavily subsidize private schools also regulate and
> inspect them in areas that many American private schools might find objec-
> tionable, such as course content, testing policies, student admissions, tuition
> levels, teacher hiring and salaries, and composition of governing boards.[61]

Such concerns are not merely theoretical. According to Glenn, the Milwaukee educational establishment "sought to choke it [the MPCP] to death
with regulation."[62] Fortunately, the judge hearing this case disagreed, writing: "I am not persuaded that this program turns private into public schools;
and if they are not public schools, they are not subject to the Uniformity
Clause. . . . Here it seems more accurate to characterize participating
schools as private schools that accept public school students."[63]

State supreme court rulings have buttressed the status of private schools
in school-choice plans. In *Jackson v. Benson* 213 Wis.2d 1, 570 N.W.2d 407
(1998), the Wisconsin Supreme Court ruled that private schools do not become de facto public schools under the Milwaukee voucher program. Consequently, private schools are not subject to the same regulations. The court

concluded, "The mere appropriation of public monies to a private school does not transform that school into a district school." The core reason is because no money flows directly to the private, religious school. Money first goes to the parents who are then free to determine the school to which they will give the money. Joe Loconte explains the significance:

> In principle, the ruling means that any attempt to convert private sectarian schools into public schools would violate the religion clauses of the First Amendment. According to the court, government may not interfere "in any ways with the schools' governance, curriculum, or day-to-day affairs." Moreover, state enforcement of minimal standards and oversight of private schools, the court said, "already exists."[64]

Therefore, the question may be posed this way: Will public aid to private and parochial schools open the door to government regulations of private and religious institutions, thereby jeopardizing schools' autonomy? Jeffrey Tucker, for example, cautions: "Like successful businesses, private schools do well because they are funded with private money and are managed independently of politics. Instead of making public schools more like private schools, which should be the goal, vouchers may well do the reverse."[65] Do real-world examples confirm these dire prophecies? Let us examine what has happened in other nations with publicly funded systems of public, private, and parochial school choice. Most of these countries share a tradition of church–state separation. Has school choice torn down the wall of separation and stripped away the unique identity of private and parochial schools?[66]

Every Western European nation has some form of public support for private or parochial schools.[67] In the aftermath of the Cold War, several Eastern European nations, including Poland and Czechoslovakia, have also adopted systems of school choice. In the words of Charles Glenn: "As the nations of Eastern Europe have overthrown or voted out their Communist governments, among the concrete expressions of a new-found freedom has been the enactment of laws guaranteeing the right to establish and operate nongovernment schools."[68] Other first-world nations, including Australia, New Zealand, Canada, and Japan, also have some form of school choice. School choice is popular throughout Europe, as the socialist governments in Spain and France found out when they tried to limit school choice in 1984. School choice has been considered even in the former Soviet Union, and in 1992 the Russian Federation authorized funding for private schools.[69] Have school-choice systems hindered the private and parochial schools in these countries?[70]

Although many of the nongovernment schools in Great Britain have a religious character, private schools are fully funded by the government. The Education Act of 1944 established three levels of schools: maintained schools, which are funded by the state and local governments; private schools, which are funded by private sources; and direct grant schools, which receive partial support from the government. Religious schools are found in all three categories, including the Anglican and Catholic schools which are not private but part of the public system. The Education Reform Act of 1988 strengthened this system by providing for school-based management, parental choice, and local accountability. Although the Act did not increase the supply of schools from which to choose, many schools have "opted-out" to become grant-maintained schools, which provides the schools with greater autonomy.[71] School choice has not destroyed nongovernment schools in Great Britain; in fact, 20 percent of all students study in nongovernment schools.

Canadians have been much more willing than Americans to accept the idea that "value-free" education is a mirage. Consequently, when a school meets minimal criteria, even one operated by a small religious or ethnic minority group, it receives public funds for schooling.[72] Despite a trend toward individualism and away from group rights, six out ten of Canada's provinces provide funding for independent schools. Significant differences emerge from province to province. Ontario provides two public systems, one secular and one Catholic, and offers limited funding to private schools. Alberta and British Columbia provide greater funding to private schools. These schools have not been burdened with heavy regulations (when compared with the fears of some), and the public school system remains intact.[73] Clifford Cobb has suggested that the key to improving the Canadian system is by redirecting the government's funds from going directly to the school to directly to the parent. This will reduce the possibility of state interference with the educational mission and activities of the school.[74]

In the Netherlands, nongovernment schools enjoy great freedom in a highly decentralized school system (despite extensive regulation). The Primary Education Act of 1920 states that parents have "a natural right and duty" to choose their child's school. Parents establish their own schools, provided they have a minimal number of students and meet minimal state requirements, such as teacher certification, a high-quality curriculum, and safe buildings (after a battle, Muslims and Hindus now have similar rights since 1988).[75] In terms of both funding and legal status, Dutch law recognizes no distinction between state and independent schools.[76] The private school system is strong in the Netherlands; 71 percent of students study in private schools and two-thirds of all schools have a religious identity.[77] The number of schools mushroomed in the 1920s, but it has fallen rapidly recently due to consolidation. According to Glenn, for Catholics and Protestants, there are "thousands of schools."[78] In fact, support for religious schools remains strong despite growing secularization throughout the country.[79]

In Belgium, parents have been able to choose their children's education since 1831, when educational freedom was made a principle in the Constitution. Catholic and other nonstate schools have been funded since the 1880s. The Belgian system is divided into three networks of schools: free, community, and municipal. Free schools (both Catholic and non-Catholic) are eligible for public funding. School choice has not hindered private education in Belgium, where about half of all students attend private schools.[80]

Germany has a long history of supporting "confessional schools" that were either Protestant or Catholic. A 1987 decision by the Federal Constitutional Court required states to support nongovernment schools on a neutral, nondiscretionary basis. Confessional schools were shut down during the Nazi era, and the U.S. common-school system was rejected after the war since "the American model of a common school, dependent exclusively on state and local government and ignoring confessional differences, seemed to some Germans uncomfortably close to the Nazi's German Community School." As Cobb writes, "Preserving freedom of thought depends on protecting the institutions in which unorthodoxy can flourish."[81] Even though many Protestant and Catholic schools in Germany have lost their religious character in recent decades, many Germans still support funding for religious schools, even those who do not regularly attend religious services.[82]

Denmark allows any group of parents representing more than twenty-eight students to form a school at the state's expense. The state typically covers 78 percent of the entire operating cost per pupil. Private schools are thriving. Schools have been founded by Montessori and Waldorf educators, humanists, Jews, Muslims, socialists, and more. The Danes have offered freedom of choice through education.[83]

The conclusion is clear: Private and parochial schools have not lost their freedom in countries with choice. In fact, private and parochial schools are thriving.[84] The United States is an exception in the Western world in that it does not provide public funding for independent schools. Inconsistencies exist in the United States system, as it already has school choice and a voucher program at the college and university level. It should be extended into the elementary and secondary schools, where currently only the government schools receive public funding.[85]

Things are starting to change.[86] Congress has approved a D.C. voucher bill and there is growing support for school choice.[87] In fact, the momentum for school choice continues to grow.[88] In poll after poll Americans favor choice. State coalitions supporting choice are now up and running in most states, legislation continues to be introduced, and every day students benefit from the programs in both Milwaukee and Cleveland. Quentin Quade used to say that as more and more parents see other parents benefiting from choice, they will begin to develop "parent envy."

WHY HAS SCHOOL CHOICE BEEN
SO SLOW IN COMING TO THE UNITED STATES?

If private and parochial schools are accountable, contribute to the common good, and are widely funded throughout the First World, then why has school choice been so slow in coming to the United States? There are three principal reasons. First, some of the proposals have not been drafted as well as they should have been: they have included a tuition tax credit instead of a voucher; their experimentation period has been too short; they have included only "nonsectarian" schools; or they provided insufficient funds to create new schools. Second, Americans maintain a strong love for public education. Many hold a deep, almost religious, reverence for the public school system and cannot imagine how any "tampering" with it could lead to improvement.

A third reason is that school choice has been opposed by the powerful teachers' unions—the National Education Association (NEA) and the American Federation of Teachers (AFT). The NEA's opposition to school choice has been overt. In California it raised teachers' dues by $63 in order to oppose Proposition 174. Political opponents to the various school-choice proposals have often used scare tactics. For example, the California Teachers Association fiercely opposed the proposition by showing television commercials about the type of radical schools that may open if school choice were passed, though the likelihood of the scenarios they described was slim.[89] Charles Glenn explains:

> Funded by the teachers' unions and other elements of the educational establishment, the antivoucher advertising campaign claimed "that the dearth of government regulations will lead to the proliferation of secretive, fraudulently operated voucher schools." Television was saturated with antivoucher ads, including one showing the holocaust in Waco, with a voiceover suggesting that David Koresh could have used vouchers to run a school.[90]

Another way that the teachers unions have opposed vouchers politically is to support the party that opposes vouchers. In 1992, the NEA PAC endorsed thirty-nine candidates for the U.S. Senate and only one, Arlen Specter of Pennsylvania, was a Republican. He received $2,000.[91] Other voucher opponents have run unfair ads against vouchers.

Why are the teachers' unions so opposed to vouchers? The NEA states its opposition with these words:

> Ensuring every student a quality public education should be a top national priority. The National Education Association (NEA) opposes taxpayer-funded private and religious school vouchers because they drain critical resources from public schools, while offering little or no benefit to a small minority of students. Instead of diverting public tax dollars to private school vouchers, Congress should invest in public education by promoting the highest teacher quality and academic standards, universal access to classroom technology, lower class size, and safe, modern public buildings.[92]

The NEA and the AFT now meet together calling themselves the NEAFT. At the second joint council of the two organizations on January 30–31, 2002, the council set out its agenda including a commitment to "counter private school vouchers and tuition tax credits."[93] Summing up its position, the AFT writes, "The AFT supports parents' right to send their children to private or religious schools but opposes the use of public funds to do so."[94]

Why is union opposition to vouchers so vehement? The answer is simple: Teachers will lose the guarantee of their jobs and the union will lose its power with many fewer teachers as part of the union. According to research on the state of Michigan conducted by the Mackinac Center for Public Policy, teachers' unions oppose school choice because very few charter and private school teachers are unionized. Their research reveals that while 100 percent of traditional government school teachers are unionized, only 3.6 percent of charter school teachers are members of unions, and only 0.2 percent of private school teacher are. The study concludes, "This study reveals that unions have powerful financial incentives to maintain the current barriers to school choice, including the Michigan constitutional ban on K–12 tuition vouchers and tuition tax credits." The study goes on to say:

> To union officials, expanded school choice may mean a reduction in their organizations' income and political power as greater numbers of low- and middle-income families choose to send their children to charter and private schools with non-unionized workforces. . . . This study shows that union officials have strong financial and political incentives to spend millions of dollars to prevent parents from simply being able to choose the safest and best schools for their children. . . . Unions have not been successful at organizing the employees of charter and private schools. Preservation of school employee union power and influence therefore requires union officials to defend the system they now dominate, and resist the growth of schools in which they have been unable to gain a foothold.[95]

Consequently, the unions work hard at opposing school choice at any cost. Myron Lieberman has examined their tactics and describes them as "all out opposition to any legislation, no matter how small the scale, which could provide vouchers or tuition tax credits to parents who wish to enroll their children in private schools."[96]

Such power comes from a union that has many advantages when compared with other unions. Myron Lieberman details these teacher union advantages:

> Most union revenues, including PAC funds, are deducted from payroll and transmitted promptly to the union *at no cost to the union*. . . . The typical teacher union contracts not only require school boards to collect and transmit funds for the union PAC *at no cost to the union*; they accord the union a veto power over any other deduction, such as for a Republican PAC. . . . The teacher unions are organized to influence legislative and public opinion; the unions raise teacher compensation this way, not by providing better service at a lower cost. . . . In school districts in which NEA/AFT affiliates

are the bargaining agent, teachers who do not wish to support union bargaining or political agendas must act to avoid contributing to these agendas. . . . The teacher unions assert that most of their revenues are devoted to collective bargaining, not political action. As I and others have argued elsewhere, collective bargaining *is* political action in the public sector.[97]

Lieberman then goes on to explain the main objective is to reduce the power of the teachers' unions financially if one wishes to promote genuine educational reform in the United States: "Although not exhaustive, the foregoing considerations virtually dictate educational reform strategy in the immediate future. That strategy must be to weaken the teacher unions financially."[98] He then provides three ways to achieve this objective: "1. Reduce union revenues, 2. Eliminate various taxpayer subsidies to the unions which never should have been allowed in the first place, and 3. Impose the requirements that apply to private sector unions under the National Labor Relations Act to the teacher unions under state bargaining statutes."[99]

CONCLUSION

School choice scares some education bureaucrats, chills some teachers, and downright frightens the unions—but it will be good for American children. Why should substandard teachers or schools continue to be subsidized? America's children deserve the best education they can get, and a system of school choice will improve their educational options.

   Despite strong objections from powerful, entrenched critics, school choice should become the new educational system in America. School choice should be implemented under a very carefully designed plan. The evidence shows that school choice saves states money when compared with the current system. The lesson of school choice from Europe and other First-World nations is that in systems of choice, private and parochial xschools experience vibrant growth while fly-by-night schools weaken and fail. The United States is on its way toward learning this lesson.

NOTES

   1. In developing these points, I am indebted to two of the nation's leading school-choice advocates, John Coons and Stephen Sugarman. In *Scholarships for*

Children, they construct a detailed bill that could serve as the basis for a school-choice bill in a state legislature. *Scholarships for Children* (Berkeley: University of California, 1992). Two other significant school-choice proposals deserve mention. Stephen Arons argues for a school-choice plan based upon the First Amendment's guarantee of religious liberty in *Compelling Belief: The Culture of American Schooling* (New York: McGraw-Hill, 1983), and "Out of the Fire and into the Frying Pan," *First Things*, January 1991. John Chubb and Terry Moe argue for a school-choice plan based upon the free market system in *Politics, Markets and America's Schools* (Washington, D.C.: Brookings Institution Press, 1990), and "Politics, Markets, and the Organization of Schools," *American Political Science Review,* December 1988. For a thorough critique of Chubb's and Moe's argument, see *Teachers College Record* 93 (Fall 1991): 137–73; and D. L. Evans, "The Marketplace Mythology in School Choice," *Education Digest* 56 (March 1991): 28–30.

2. See the U.S. Census Bureau, "Public Education Finances: 2001" quoted in "The Notebook," *The Christian Science Monitor* (March 18, 2003): 12. The total expenditures were $302.9 billion. See "Projections of Education Statistics to 2011," *National Center for Education Statistics*, http://nces.ed.gov/pubs2001/proj01/tables/table33.asp. The state spending the highest per pupil was New Jersey at $10,594, followed by the District of Columbia $10,069, New York $9,757, Connecticut $9,720, and Rhode Island $9,073. The districts spending the most were Boston $10,293, Buffalo $8,994, Minneapolis $8,488, the District of Columbia $8,474, and Montgomery County (Md.) $8,287. See "The Top 10 Lists," *American School & University* 74, no. 5 (January 2002): 45–49. By the 2002–03 school year, the top five spending states were the following: District of Columbia $13,525, New York $11,089, Alaska $11,066, New Jersey $10,892, and Connecticut $10,258. The bottom five were North Dakota $4,459, Utah $4,755, Arizona $5,218, Alabama $5,512, and Mississippi $5,624. See "Where Mississippi Ranks among Nation's Schools," *The Christian Science Monitor* (June 3, 2003): ·14. Similarly, the 9th Bracey Reports puts the average public school expenditure at $6,500 per public school student and $2,915 for the average sectarian school student. See Gerald W. Bracey, "Public and Private Schools Compared," *Phi Delta Kappan* 81, no. 8 (April 2000): 633-34. The expenditure per pupil was about $6,000 in 1992–93 according to Coons and Sugarman, *Scholarships for Children*, 9, 10. See also footnotes 19 and 31 from chapter one.

It should be emphasized that private schools are already handling a number of the public schools' difficult-to-educate children. In fact, private schools currently educate about 100,000 of the 5.6 million special education students in the United States. They are paid for with public dollars totaling about $2 billion annually. For an excellent overview of this trend and of how a choice program will impact special needs students, see Jonathan Fox, "Sending Public School Students to Private Schools: The Untold Story of Special Education," *Policy Review*, no. 93 (January/February, 1999): 25–29.

3. Other popular voucher plans include the Sizer-Whitten plan, in which the government would provide a tuition voucher only to parents whose income is below the national average. This policy aims to make the least well-off more attractive to schools. Christopher Jencks's regulated-compensatory model was tried in the Alum Rock experiment: each student would receive a voucher equivalent to the price of education in their school district, with the poor receiving an extra amount. A local Education Voucher Agency would distribute the funds and information regarding vouchers. Christopher Jencks, *Education Vouchers: A Report on Financing Elementary Education by Grants to Parents* (Washington, D.C.: Center for the Study of Public Policy, 1970). Another plan promotes vouchers only within the public school system. Advocates believe that since the problem with the public school system is its bureaucratic inflexibility, an increase in flexibility within the system will improve education.

4. Quoted in Dale McDonald, "Reclaim the 'V' Word!" *Momentum* (Washington, D.C.) 31, no. 4 (November/December 2000): 72–73.

5. On the disparities in district spending within states, see James J. Hilton, "States' School-Spending Disparities," *Education Week* (17 June 1992): 28. Hilton argues that choice will exacerbate the problems in inner cities because schools will be unable to compete with schools from rich school districts. Consequently, poor children will leave these schools and the buildings will rot and decay in the inner city. But Hilton presupposes the status quo in terms of district-funded education. Statewide-funded education, similar to Governor John Engler's program in Michigan, will empower schools in poor districts by granting them the same funding per pupil as rich school districts. Choice will aid, not hinder, inner-city schools. See Hilton's "Local Autonomy, Educational Equity, and School Choice: Constitutional Criticism of School Reform," *New England Journal Public Policy* (Summer/Fall 1994): 293–305. Even if Hilton is correct that some districts would lose students, those districts would then become more responsive to parental pressure and would be forced to improve, or face the spectacle of closure altogether. Massachusetts Governor William Weld explains: "Some local officials and school administrators have complained that [school choice] puts pressure on districts that lose students. And my response is, 'That's right! That's what it's supposed to do.' I have heard from parents in districts that are losing students that they delighted with the newfound responsiveness of the officials in their schools. These are parents who are not choosing to send their kids to other places, but who are benefiting because competitive pressures are improving their kids' schools." Adam Meyerson, "Bay State Boomer: Bill Weld Talks Tough on Taxes, Tough on Crime," *Policy Review* (Spring 1993): 14.

6. For a summary of the difficulties of implementing school-choice plans, see Charles Glenn, "Will Boston Be the Proof of the Choice Pudding?" *Educational Leadership* 48 (December/January 1990/1991): 41–43; Charles Glenn, "Putting School Choice in Place," *Phi Delta Kappan* 71 (December 1989): 295–300; Charles Glenn, "Just Schools for Minority Children," *Phi Delta Kappan* 70 (June 1989): 777–79.

7. Stephen L. Carter, *The Culture of Disbelief: How American Law and Politics Trivialize Religious Devotion* (New York: Basic Books, 1993), 195.

8. See P. Lines, *Compulsory Education Laws: Their Impact on Public and Private Education* (Denver: Education Commission of the States, 1984); Dennis Encarnation, "Public Finance and Regulation of Nonpublic Education: Retrospect and Prospect," in *Public Dollars for Private Schools: The Case for Tuition Tax Credits*, edited by T. James and H. M. Levin (Philadelphia: Temple University Press, 1985).

9. One noted state example is *Council of Children with Special Needs, Inc. v. Cooperman* 501 A.2d 575 (N.J. Super. Ct. App. Div. 1985).

10. James W. Skillen, "Biblical Principles Applied to National Education Policy," *Biblical Principles and Public Policy: The Practice* (Colorado Springs: Navigator's Press, 1989): 229. This ten-point proposal meets the minimum criteria established by the 1992 Carnegie Foundation Report on School Choice for a just system of school choice: "By any standard of fairness, then, statewide programs demand a level playing field. At minimum, this means adequate transportation for all students; accessible, reliable information for parents and students about the plan itself and about the quality of schools and their programs; and serious attention to reducing the huge disparities between rich poor districts" (*A Special Report: School Choice*, 62). On how parents of different socio-economic status go about obtaining information on schools, see Mark Schneider, Paul Teske, and Melissa Marschall, *Choosing Schools: Consumer Choice and the Quality of American Schools*, (Princeton, N.J.: Princeton University Press, 2000), 108–45. They sum up their findings this way: "These patterns suggest that policies informing parents about schooling options must take into account the social context in which parents live. Policies in low-income urban areas must acknowledge the greater importance of informing well-educated community leaders, as well as the importance of assuring parents easy access to individuals (and information) directly associated with the schools. As school choice diffuses, especially in central cities, outreach activities to inform parents are essential" (Schneider, Teske, and Marschall, *Choosing Schools*, 145). My list has also been influenced by the Public Policy Forum Report entitled "Choice School Accountability: A Consensus of Views in Ohio and Wisconsin," *Public Policy Forum Report*, at www.publicpolicyforum.org/pdfs/choice_accountability.pdf.

11. Edd Doerr and Albert Menendez, *Church Schools and Public Money: The Politics of Parochiaid* (New York: Prometheus Books, 1991), 130.

12. See Larry Armstrong, "California May Choose School Choice," *Business Week* (18 October 1993): 35.

13. "School Choice: Possibilities and Problems," in *School Choice, A Special Report* (Princeton, N.J.: The Carnegie Foundation for the Advancement of Teaching, 1992), 22–24.

14. "Private School Vouchers," *National Education Association Topic Legislative Action Center* (June 2001): 1, at www.nea.org/lac/papers/vouchers.html.

15. Peter Brimelow and Leslie Spencer, "The National Extortion Association?" *Forbes* (7 June 1993): 72, 73.

16. David Boaz, "Learning Opportunities," *National Review* (12 September 1994): 52. Chester E. Finn Jr. describes the federal government's overexpenditures: "Hundreds of separate federal K–12 education programs spend upward of $18 billion a year. They are highly prescriptive and heavily regulated, substituting Washington's judgments for those of states, communities and families. They are hostile to such innovations as choice, charter schools and private management. Almost all of them strengthen the monopoly and the 'education governance' system—superintendents and school boards—rather than empowering governors, legislators or mayors. Parents, of course, have little or no say." "A Primer for Education Reform," *The Wall Street Journal* (January 13, 1995).

17. "Significant Gains for School Choice," *USA Today Magazine* (August 1994): 14.

18. "Projections of Education Statistics to 2011," *National Center for Education Statistics*, http://nces.ed.gov/pubs2001/proj01/tables/table33.asp. Of this amount, approximately $45 billion comes from the federal budget, representing just over 2 percent of the total federal government's budget. See Lawrence Hardy, "The President's Plan," *American School Board Journal* (April 2001): 22–23.

19. John Coons, "Is Choice Still a Choice?" *First Thing* (November 1994): 2. In Oakland, Catholic schools spend one-third the amount that public schools do per pupil; see Stuart Steers, "The Catholic Schools' Black Students," *This World* (23 December 1990): 9.

20. For an excellent discussion on how school choice would lower costs, see Quentin Quade, "School Reform: Toward Parental Choice," *Current* (February 1993): 21–25.

21. William Bennett, "Golden State Opportunity," *National Review* (1 November 1993): 13.

22. Ohio Department of Education, Expenditure Flow Model Reports. Cited in "School Choice Does Not Drain Money from Public Schools," *Center for Education Reform* at www.edreform.com/school_choice/facts/money.htm.

23. Dorman E. Cordell, "The Voucher Wars," *Brief Analysis No. 264, National Center for Policy Analysis* (April 29, 1998), quoted in "School Choice Does Not Drain Money from Public Schools," *Center for Education Reform*.

24. "Cleveland Schools Profit from Scholarship Program," *Policy Note*; Buckeye Institute for Public Policy Solutions (June 1997), quoted in "School Choice Does Not Drain Money from Public Schools," *Center for Education Reform*.

25. Milwaukee Public Schools Comprehensive Annual Financial Reports, quoted in "School Choice Does Not Drain Money from Public Schools," *Center for Education Reform*.

26. Howard L. Fuller and George Mitchell, "The Fiscal Impact of School Choice on the Milwaukee Public Schools," *Institute for the Transformation of Learning, Marquette University* (March 1999): 2, quoted in "School Choice Does Not Drain Money from Public Schools," *Center for Education Reform*.

27. "Vouchers Enter Second Decade," *USA Today* (October 24, 2000); "The Fiscal Impact of School Choice on the Milwaukee Public Schools," *Marquette University Institute for the Transformation of Learning* (March 1999), quoted in "School Choice Does Not Drain Money from Public Schools," *Center for Education Reform*.

28. "Analysis of FY02 Fiscal Impact on MPS if MPCP Is Eliminated," *Milwaukee Public Schools* (June 25, 2001), quoted in "School Choice Does Not Drain Money from Public Schools," *Center for Education Reform*. Similarly, Fuller and Mitchell write, "If choice did not exist, Milwaukee Public Schools also would incur added expenses to educate thousands of students who would likely transfer to MPS schools." Howard L. Fuller and George Mitchell, "The Fiscal Impact of School Choice on the Milwaukee Public Schools," *Institute for the Transformation of Learning, Marquette University* (March 1999): 3, quoted from the Center for Education Reform.

29. Fuller and Mitchell, "The Fiscal Impact of School Choice," 1.

30. "FAQs about Florida's A+ Plan," website of Governor Jeb Bush (January 14, 2000), quoted in "School Choice Does Not Drain Money from Public Schools," *Center for Education Reform*.

31. Florida Department of Education, Tom Gallagher, Commissioner, "Assistance and Activities in Schools with Performance Grade D or F," testimony before the Committee on Education/K–12 (February 8, 2000), quoted in "School Choice Does Not Drain Money from Public Schools," *Center for Education Reform*.

32. "Schools Hit by Vouchers Fight Back," *Education Week* (September 15, 1999), quoted in "School Choice Does Not Drain Money from Public Schools," *Center for Education Reform*.

33. "Florida's Vouchers a Spur to 2 Schools Left Behind," *New York Times* (March 14, 2000), quoted in "School Choice Does Not Drain Money from Public Schools," *Center for Education Reform.*

34. James D. Foster, "Say Yes to School Choice," *Christianity Today* (August 19, 1991): 29. See also Michael Barone, "School Choice: Its Time Has Come," *US News and World Report* (October 18, 1993): 57.

35. Dorman E. Cordell, "The Voucher Wars," *Brief Analysis No. 264, National Center for Policy Analysis* (April 29, 2998), quoted in "School Choice Does Not Drain Money from Public Schools," *Center for Education Reform.*

36. Joe Williams, *Milwaukee Journal Sentinel* (September 21, 1995): 1, quoted in "School Choice Does Not Drain Money from Public Schools," *Center for Education Reform.*

37. See Quade, "School Reform," 21–25.

38. John Chubb, cited in Jeanne Allen, *Nine Lies about School Choice* (Washington, D.C.: Center for Education Reform, 1999), 21, 22.

39. Estelle James, "Private School Finance and Public Policy in Cross-Cultural Perspective," paper delivered at the U.S. Department of Education Conference on the Economics of Private Schools, Washington, D.C. (May 1991).

40. Willie L. Brown Jr., "Voucher Business Is Bad Business," *Sacramento Observer* (15 September 1993), quoted in Allen, *Nine Lies about School Choice,* 16.

41. Asimov, "Many Private Schools War," A-19, quoted in Charles Glenn, *The Ambiguous Embrace: Government and Faith-Based Schools and Social Agencies* (Princeton, N.J.: Princeton University Press, 2000), 117–18.

42. The first quote is from "Experts Differ on Vouchers," *Albuquerque Journal* (May 8, 1999): A-1. The second is from "Pa. Voucher Plan Dies Amid 'Mean-spirited' Attacks," *School Reform News* 3, no. 8 (August 1999): 4. Both of these quotes are found in Jay Greene, "Choice and Community: The Racial, Economic, and Religious Context of Parental Choice in Cleveland," *The Buckeye Institute* (November 1999): 1.

43. Henry M. Levin, "Educational Vouchers: Effectiveness, Choice, and Costs," *Journal of Policy Analysis and Management* (Stanford University, September 1997): abstract, 12, quoted in Dan Murphy, "When You Weigh the Evidence: Voucher Programs in Milwaukee and Cleveland," *American Educator* (Fall 1998): 20.

44. The other related laws are the following: Title IX of the Education Amendments of 1972, the Elementary and Secondary Education Act of 1965, the Improving America's School Act of 1994, Goals 2000: Educate America Act, the Age Discrimination Act of 1975, the Americans with Disability Act of 1990, and Section 504 of the Rehabilitative Act of 1973, the Family Education Rights and Privacy Act of

1974, the Equal Access Act of 1984, the Fair Labor Standards Act, the Family and Medical Leave Act of 1993, the Occupational Safety and Health Act of 1990, the Drug-Free Workplace Act of 1988, and the Public Records Act. For an overview of these, see Joyce Ley, "Charter Starters Leadership Training Workbook 2: Regulatory Issues" (July 1999): 1–12, from the Northwest Regional Educational Laboratory.

45. The seven federal or state laws are the following: The Wisconsin Pupil Nondiscrimination Act; Title IX of the Education Amendments (1972); the Age Discrimination Act (1975); Section 504 of the Rehabilitation Act (1973); the Family Education Rights and Privacy Act (1973); the Family Education Rights and Privacy Act; the Drug-Free School and Communities Act (1986). Each of these federal and state laws guarantees and protects the rights and liberties of individuals, including freedom of religion, expression, association, unreasonable search and seizure, equal protection, and due process.

The four outcomes, at least one of which must be met, are the following: 1) at least 70 percent of the pupils in the program advance one grade level each year; 2) the private school's average attendance rate for the pupils in the program is at least 90 percent; 3) at least 80 percent of the pupils in the program demonstrate significant academic progress; and 4) at least 70 percent of the families of pupils in the program meet parent involvement criteria established by the private school. See Frank Kemerer, Joe Hairston, and Keith Lauerman, "Vouchers and Private School Autonomy," *Journal of Law and Education* 21 (Fall 1992): 614, 615.

46. Allen, *Nine Lies about School Choice*, 19.

47. See the Family Educational Rights and Privacy Act, 20 U.S.C. 1232g (1988), Title IX of the 1972 Civil Rights Act, 20 U.S.C. 1681 (1988), the Individuals with Disabilities Act, 20 U.S.C.A. 1400-1482a (West. Supp. 1992), *Runyon v. McCrary* 427 U.S. 160 (1976).

48. Two leading cases are the Nebraska State Supreme Court's decision in 1981, *State v. Faith Baptist Church*, 301 N.W.2d 571 (Neb. 1981) and *New Life Baptist Church Academy v. East Longmeadow*, 885 F.2d 940, 950-51 (1st Cir. 1989). One notable exception is the 1976 Ohio Supreme Court Decision. *State v. Whisner*, 351 N.E.2d 750 (Ohio 1976).

49. "School Vouchers: Publicly Funded Programs in Cleveland and Milwaukee," *U.S. Government Accounting Office*, GAO-01-914 (August 2001): 10, 11.

50. Wisconsin Legislative Audit Bureau, at www.legis/state.wi.us/lab/windex.htm, quoted in Jennifer Garrett, "Progress on School Choice in the States," *Heritage Foundation Backgrounder* (May 16, 2001): 9.

51. Charles O'Malley, "Who Says Private Schools Are Not Accountable?" Paper prepared for Temple University and Manhattan Institute, presented at the Western Regional Science Association conference, 21 February 1993. Cited in Allen, *Nine Lies about School Choice*, 16.

52. Private and parochial schools are even more racially and culturally tolerant than public schools, since private and parochial schools are, on the whole, less
segregated than public schools. This is in part because they are able to teach that
God disapproves of the mistreatment of blacks, whites, or any of the "least of
these."

On the desegregation of private schools, see James S. Coleman et al., *High
School Achievement: Public, Catholic, and Private Schools Compared* (New
York: Basic Books, 1982), 194; James Coleman and Thomas Hoffer, *Public and
Private High Schools: The Impact of Communities* (New York: Basic Books,
1987); "School Choice and a Nation's Character: An Interview with Cardinal An-
thony J. Bevilacqua," *Christian Perspectives: A Journal of Free Enterprise* 5
(Spring 1993): 1, 17–19; Stephen Sugarman, *Chicago Legal Forum* #18; Rockne
McCarthy, "Independent Schools: What Works," Office of Educational Research
and Improvement, 1989; Ken Sidey, *The Blackboard Fumble: Finding a Place for
Values in Public Education* (Wheaton, Ill.: Victor Books, 1989).

53. Carter, *The Culture of Disbelief*, 196.

54. P. T. Hill, G. E. Foster, and T. Gendler, *High Schools with Character*
(Santa Monica, Calif.: RAND, 1990). These findings confirmed similar studies:
Coleman and Hoffer, *Public and Private High Schools*; and Chubb and Moe, *Pol-
itics, Markets, and America's Schools*.

55. Yet the NEA still states, "Vouchers encourage 'fly-by-night' schools and
provide less accountability for public resources than public schools." "Private
School Vouchers," *National Education Association Topic Legislative Action Center* (June 2001), at www.nea.org/lac/papers/vouchers.html.

56. Charles Glenn, *The Ambiguous Embrace*, 102. Glenn goes on to explain,
"The issue at stake is not *whether* but *how intrusive* that regulation may be before
the nongovernmental school or agency loses its distinctive character and becomes
in effect part of the state apparatus, subject to all of the constraints that have made
the human service bureaucracy and the public education system so unwieldy and
so ineffective." Glenn, *The Ambiguous Embrace*, 103.

57. Glenn, *The Ambiguous Embrace*, 104.

58. The MPCP is an outstanding example of these criteria. It required the Milwaukee superintendent to submit an annual report to the legislature which compared public and nonpublic school's performance in terms of academic achievement, daily attendance record, percentage of dropouts, percentage of pupils
suspended and expelled, and parental involvement activities of pupils attending
private schools. See Glenn, *The Ambiguous Embrace*, 116. Glenn goes on to cite
Coons and Sugarman who elaborate on these criteria writing: "In order to assure
scholarship schools that they will be able to operate in distinctive ways, the legislature (and other organs of government) are specifically disabled from enlarging

controls upon curriculum, facilities, and school employment politics beyond the modest regulations that have traditionally applied to private schools (although we acknowledge that those controls vary from state to state). It is a practical motto of choice supporters that, whatever state laws have proved benign for the children of the rich should be adequate for us all." Glenn, *The Ambiguous Embrace*, 118, from Coons and Sugarman, *Scholarships for Children*, 32.

59. Joe Loconte, "Paying the Piper: Will Vouchers Undermine the Mission of Religious Schools?" *Policy Review* no. 93 (January/February 1999): 30–36.

60. Joe Loconte raises the specter of future state and federal regulations being developed to place further restrictions on schools participating in voucher programs. To date, no such serious new regulation has been developed in Wisconsin, Ohio, or Florida. See Loconte, "Paying the Piper," 30–36.

61. Nancy Kober, "Lessons from Other Countries: Higher Public Funding for Private Schools Usually Means More Government Regulation," *Center on Education Policy*, introduction.

62. Glenn, *The Ambiguous Embrace*, 115.

63. Kemerer, Hairston, and Lauerman, "Vouchers and Private School Autonomy," 616, quoted in Glenn, *The Ambiguous Embrace*, 116.

64. Loconte, "Paying the Piper," 30–36.

65. Jeffrey Tucker, "Evils of Choice," *National Review* (1 March 1993): 46.

66. On this, see Charles Glenn, *Choice of Schools in Six Nations: France, Netherlands, Belgium, Britain, Canada, West Germany* (Washington, D.C.: Office of Educational Research and Improvement, 1989). See also Charles Glenn, "Who Should Own the Schools?" *Equity and Choice* 9: 59–63; John Ambler, "Who Benefits from Educational Choice? Some Evidence from Europe," *Journal of Policy Analysis and Management* 13 (1994): 454–76; Charles Glenn, "Controlled Choice in Massachusetts Public Schools," *Public Interest* (Spring 1991): 88–105. For a summary on the status of school choice in other regions, such as the newly independent countries of Eastern Europe and Germany, see Charles Glenn, "What's Really at Stake in the School Choice Debate?" *Clearing House* 66 (November/December 1992): 75–78; and Charles Glenn, *Educational Freedom* (Washington, D.C.: CATO Institute, 1995).

67. Glenn, *Choice of Schools in Six Nations*.

68. Glenn, "What's Really at Stake?" 76.

69. See Rockne McCarthy, James Skillen, and William Harper, *Disestablishment a Second Time: Genuine Pluralism for American Schools* (Grand Rapids, Mich.: Christian University Press, 1982), 107–23.

70. Chile has had a system of school choice for the past two decades. Students in fee-paying schools did perform significantly better than students at traditional schools. However, there may be many factors explaining this difference, including the extra funding available to these schools. For a detailed account and analy-

sis, see Alejandra Mizala and Pilar Romaguera, "School Performance and Choice: The Chilean Experience," *Journal of Human Resources* 35, no. 2 (Spring 2000): 392–417.

71. John Chubb and Terry Moe, *A Lesson in School Reform from Great Britain* (Washington, D.C.: Brookings Institution Press, 1992). See also Jack Tweedie, "The Dilemma of Clients' Rights in Social Programs: Effects of Parental Rights of School Choice in England, Scotland and Wales," *Law and Society Review* 23 (1989): 175–208.

72. Mark Noll, *A History of Christianity in the United States and Canada* (Grand Rapids, Mich.: Eerdmans, 1992), 259–60, 453.

73. Rockne McCarthy et al., *Society, State, and Schools: A Case for Structural and Confessional Pluralism* (Grand Rapids, Mich.: Eerdmans, 1981), 189–91.

74. Clifford W. Cobb, *Responsive Schools, Renewed Communities* (San Francisco: ICS Press, 1992), 160.

75. Cobb, *Responsive Schools*, 158.

76. Cobb, *Responsive Schools*, 141–44; also see Charles Glenn, *The Myth of the Common School* (Amherst: University of Massachusetts Press, 1988), 244–49.

77. Glenn, *The Ambiguous Embrace*, 143.

78. Glenn, *The Ambiguous Embrace*, 136.

79. Glenn, *The Ambiguous Embrace*, 138.

80. McCarthy et al., *Society, State, and Schools*, 141; Grover G. Norquist, "Engler's Moment," *American Spectator* (October 1993). The percentage of students studying in private schools in other nations should also be noted: 28 percent of Japanese high school students, 15 percent of all French students, 22 percent of all Australian students, 20 percent of Irish primary students, and 50 percent of Irish high school students. In all of these countries, private schools receive public funding.

81. Cobb, *Responsive Schools*, 155, 156.

82. Glenn, *The Ambiguous Embrace*, 153. Many children (more than 70 percent) attend Catholic or Protestant kindergarten because of the kindergarten exception—kindergarten is not part of the school system but is typically provided by other denominational institutions.

83. Cobb, *Responsive Schools*, 157, 158.

84. International experience allays another concern for school choice in the United States, as fly-by-night schools have not sprouted up all over the world.

85. Glenn, "What's Really at Stake?" 76. In addition to attempting to expand voucher programs, choice advocates in the United States are also working to curtail state legislatures' role in regulating private and parochial schools by limiting their ability to introduce new and burdensome legislation on schools after implementation of a school-choice program. See *Kentucky State Board for Elementary*

and Secondary Education v. Rudasill, 589 S.W.2d 877 (Ky. 1979); the Oregon Educational Choice Initiative (1990); and the California Scholarship Initiative (1993).

86. The international enthusiasm for school choice has encouraged grassroots movements throughout the states. A widely publicized May 1994 report by the Heritage Foundation gave the following facts: school-choice legislation was introduced or pending in thirty-four states in 1993, governors in thirty-three states had indicated support for school choice, at least thirty-five states had significant parental and grassroots coalitions working for school choice, and a total of nine states had implemented charter school legislation. Allyson Tucker and William Lauber, *School Choice Programs: What's Happening in the States* (Washington, D.C.: Heritage Foundation, 1995), 4. For a succinct summary of the results from statewide ballot initiatives in 1992, see Carroll Doherty's "How Initiatives Fared," *Congressional Quarterly Weekly Report* (7 November 1992): 3595. Specifically, on Pennsylvania's House Bill 1133, and Senate Bill 992, see William Cooley, "School Choice or School Reform?" *Pennsylvania Educational Policy Studies Series* No. 12 (November 4, 1991): 1–14; and John Golle, "Advocates of School Choice Undaunted by Setbacks," *Congressional Quarterly Researcher* (March 25, 1994): 277. For more on the Colorado vote, see Anne Lewis, "Private-School Vouchers," *Education Digest* (January 1993): 59, and her "Choice: Vouchers and Privatization," *Phi Delta Kappan* (September 1992): 6, 7; and Scott Pattison, "More School Choice," *Consumer's Research Magazine* (October 1992): 40. For a practical guide to grassroots educational reform, see Jeanne Allen, *The School Reform Handbook: How to Improve Your Schools* (Washington, D.C.: Center for Education Reform, 1995).

87. Another example occurred in 1994, when forty-two senators voted for local test programs providing low-income families with federal vouchers redeemable at either public or private schools.   ·

88. *School Reform in the United States: State by State Summary* (Winter 1995), Center for Education Reform, 3. According to the Center for Education Reform, in January 1995, eleven states allowed statewide public school choice; nine states allowed public school choice within some or all districts; eleven states had charter schools, either offering real autonomy or in need of improvement; twelve states had private sector scholarship programs; and three states had publicly sponsored full school choice. The eleven states that allow public school choice throughout the state are Arkansas, California, Colorado, Idaho, Iowa, Massachusetts, Minnesota, Nebraska, Ohio, Utah, and Washington; states that allow public school choice in some or all districts are Connecticut, Michigan, New Jersey, New York, North Carolina, Oregon, and South Carolina; the six states that have charter schools offering real autonomy are Arizona, California, Colorado, Massachusetts, Michigan, and Minnesota; five states that offer charter schools

needing improvement are Georgia, Hawaii, Kansas, New Mexico, and Wisconsin; the twelve states that offer private sector scholarship programs are Arizona, Arkansas, California, Colorado, District of Columbia, Florida, Georgia, Indiana, Michigan, New Jersey, New York, and Texas; and offering publicly sponsored full school choice are Milwaukee, Wisconsin, Vermont, and Puerto Rico. (Puerto Rico's program continued only through the end of the 1994–95 school year.)

89. "A Fierce Fight South of the Border," *Alberta Report* (November 1993): 11; Peter Brimelow and Leslie Spencer, "The National Extortion Association?" *Forbes* (June 7, 1993): 72.

90. Glenn, *The Ambiguous Embrace*, 117.

91. Glenn, *The Ambiguous Embrace*, 3.

92. "Private School Vouchers," *National Education Association Topic Legislative Action Center* (June 2001) at www.nea.org/lac/papers/vouchers.html.

93. "NEAFT Partnership Council Charts Ambitious Agenda," at www.aft.org/neaft/index.html.

94. "The Many Names of School Vouchers," *AFT on the Issues*, at www.aft .org/Edissues/schoolchoice/Index.htm.

95. Matthew Brouillette and Jeffrey Williams, "The Impact of School Choice on School Employee Labor Unions: Unionization Rates among Private, Charter, and Traditional Government Schools Suggest Reason for Union Opposition to School Choice," *The Mackinac Center for Public Policy, Midland, Michigan* (June 1999):1–16.

96. Myron Lieberman, "Teacher Unions: Is the End Near? How to End the Teacher Union Veto over State Education Policy," Claremont Institute, Golden State Center for Policy Studies (December 15, 1994) at www.education policy.org/files/tchrunio.htm.

97. Lieberman, "Teacher Unions," 4, 5.

98. Lieberman, "Teacher Unions," 5.

99. Lieberman, "Teacher Unions," 6.

Chapter Five

What Is Happening in the United States with School Choice?

AN ENCOURAGING START

There have been many positive developments in school choice in the United States over the past few years. The momentum for choice has translated into concrete schools, both in terms of charter schools and schools of choice. This is an encouraging start.

Given the critical importance of parental choice in education, compare the present system with the options available to children with school choice. Choice frees students from significant hurdles by enabling them to study in schools that are specifically designed to meet their needs: magnet schools; charter schools; or high-quality public, private, or parochial schools.[1]

For over two decades, students have attended over 1,000 magnet schools in over 100 cities nationwide offering specialized education. The most popular themes in elementary schools are individualized basic skills, foreign languages, science/math/computers, programs for the gifted and talented, and programs in the arts. The most popular themes in high schools are science/engineering, vocational/career preparation, business/marketing, and creative/performing arts.[2]

Student performance has risen dramatically in magnet schools. For example, the Montclair, New Jersey, school district turned all its schools into magnet schools in the early 1980s, and student test scores improved significantly. In Buffalo, New York, student test scores rose dramatically in the lower grades while the declining test scores of high school students were reversed after the city created a number of magnet schools. Student test scores have also risen in magnet schools in Montgomery County, Maryland; Austin and Dallas, Texas; and San Diego, California.[3]

This exiting trend is just the tip of the iceberg. The most significant school choice reforms have been in charter schools and the school-choice programs in Milwaukee and Cleveland.

CHARTER SCHOOLS

Choice for more parents is becoming a reality through the growing charter school movement, which offers options to all children including the poor. A charter school is an autonomous educational entity that operates under a contract (i.e., a charter) among the educators, the teachers or parents, and the sponsors (frequently a local school board, a state education board, or a state university). The state pays the average per-student cost and waives most regulations and union rules. In turn, the charter school teachers must deliver specific academic results. If the school fails to produce, the limited term charter (usually about three years) is revoked. Many teachers want this challenge. For example, most of the California charter schools indicated that they started their school to free themselves from rules and regulations and to gain control over decisions related to curriculum and instruction. The number of charter schools nationwide increased quickly from 41 as of May 1994, to about 140 in March 1995.[4] Today there are well over 2,000.

Charter schools assist students because the schools offer stimulating and innovative academic environments. In particular, poor, at-risk, and disadvantaged students benefit in two ways: 1) they can attend a regular charter school; 2) a required number of all charter schools must service them. This system is in place in California, Massachusetts, Colorado, and Minnesota. The nation's first charter school, City Academy in St. Paul (opened in 1992), was created specifically for high-school dropouts and can only accept those students.

Charter schools attract teachers and parents because the schools are innovative, responsive to their communities, and less constricted by bureaucracy and regulation. Teachers are freed from the educational bureaucracy and empowered to teach. Since teachers and parents best know teaching and the students, charter schools are thriving. Poor parents favor charter schools because charter schools are accountable, empower teachers and parents, offer equal opportunity, prove cost-effective, promote innovation, and reduce conflict and dissent.

When the Minnesota legislature passed the nation's first charter law in 1991, it cited four benefits of charter schools:

1) Charter schools fit with current thinking on outcome-based education and parent choice. Children with different needs and aspirations need different educational settings; parents can select a charter school that best meets the needs of child and family.
2) Charter schools contribute to teacher empowerment since teachers can manage the schools, if they choose.
3) Charter schools have student learning at heart. The entire system—its birth and continued existence—depends on student outcome as the measure of its success or failure.
4) Regular schools face restrictions that charter schools do not. A regular school might have to accept all students; a charter school could sharpen its focus to address needs of at-risk students only.[5]

The Vaughn Next Century Learning Center typifies the progress made when parents and teachers are freed to be innovative. Located near Los Angeles in an impoverished barrio, 95 percent of the students are poor enough to qualify for the breakfast and lunch. The center, which works closely with parents in eight committees, has operated with a $1 million surplus because it cut layers of bureaucracy and took competitive contract bids for supplies. The school reinvested the surplus in a new building and in school supplies, such as computers. Consequently, the center has seen the academic achievement of its 1,107 students rise significantly.[6]

Since the City Academy opened in St. Paul in 1992, over 2,700 charter schools have opened their doors in thirty-seven states and Washington, D.C., serving more than 575,000 students. All this in only ten years! The states with the most charter schools in the 2002–03 school year were the following: Arizona 468, California 452, Florida 232, Texas 228, and Michigan 186.[7] The Heritage Foundation rates twenty-two states as having medium to strong charter school laws and sixteen as having weak charter school laws.[8] The most significant recent developments in terms of charters are the following: on May 2, 2001, Indiana's governor signed that state's first charter law; and an effort to overturn Oregon's charter school law failed in 2000 when opponents obtained fewer than half of the signatures needed to place it on the ballot. No state has overturned a charter school law.[9]

Charters tend to be smaller than traditional public schools and serve a disproportionately high number of minorities. Charters typically enroll an average of 137 students compared with public school average enrollments of 475. In 1998, white students made up 48 percent of charter school enrollment but 59 percent of the public school enrollment.[10]

There are obviously struggles with all new programs, including charters. For example, a September 2002 report by the Brookings Institution of 376 charter schools in ten states found that charters in four states were performing worse than the traditional schools while charters in six states were performing indistinguishably from the traditional public schools.[11] However, while the success in suburban areas has not been amazing, Marjorie Coeyman describes the success in urban areas: "Since then (1992), the movement has spawned some exciting success stories. Particularly in urban areas—where such stories were badly needed—high-profile charters moved into low-income neighborhoods and proved that they could take the same kids and, with less public money, produce better results."[12]

Coeyman cites five specific examples of successful charter schools. The Academy of the Pacific Rim in Boston, Massachusetts, offers a challenging curriculum focused on Eastern education and tradition combined with Western learning and culture. Students study Mandarin Chinese, tai chi, and Shakespeare. The school's test scores are among the highest in the Boston public schools. The New School for the Arts in Tempe, Arizona, started off in a storefront in a strip mall. Today its college-preparatory curriculum has helped its graduates get into some of the most prestigious arts schools and Ivy League colleges. The Minnesota New Country School in Henderson, Minnesota, provides self-directed learning without any specific courses. The Bill and Melinda Gates Foundation was so impressed with the school that it offered $4.5 million to start fifteen similar schools. The Bronx Preparatory Charter in New York holds classes from 7:15 A.M. to 5:15 P.M. 200 days a year and provides its students with 50 percent more instruction time than students at regular New York public schools. The North Star Academy in Newark, New Jersey, offers a challenging curriculum in which students attend classes eleven months of the year. On state tests, students scored twice the district average in language arts and almost triple in math. All of which makes the point that the problem is not the inner-city child, it's the school system. "We've proven schools can do it," says Ms. Jordan of Bronx Prep. Every time a charter school accepts students who lag behind the average academically, and then turns their performances around, that school "makes the case that the problem is not the kids," she says.[13]

Disadvantaged children have been disproportionately assisted by charters. One shining example is the Maya Angelou Public Charter School in Washington, D.C. The school has eighty-five high school students who have either been in jail or have dropped out of the public school. As founder David Domenici says, "We want to give options to kids that no one wants to give options to." Students are in school eleven hours a day and work at one of the school's two businesses, either in catering or in technology. Sixty percent of the students who make it through one year end up graduating.[14]

Similar gains are found in the Advantage Charter Schools. Covering fifteen inner-city schools in seven states and the District of Columbia, these inner-city students showed a 9.1 point gain on two national standardized tests: the Woodcock Reading Mastery Tests Revised and the ninth edition of the Sanford Achievement Test.[15] And charters have benefited children in their districts who remain in the traditional public school. For example, one Minnesota school district opened a public Montessori grade school after a group proposed opening a charter one. One Michigan district created smaller classes and started offering Spanish, art, and computer science after charter schools started attracting students. One Connecticut district began to ask parents for feedback on how to better meet parents needs after a group discussed starting a new charter school.[16] As a result of charter schools opening up in Arizona, "districts made greater attempts to inform parents about school programs and options; districts placed greater emphasis on professional development for teachers; and school principals increased consultations with their teaching staffs."[17]

Despite the success of charter schools, the teachers' unions raise objections. In the American Federation of Teachers' "Issues on Charter Schools," the union wrote, "Currently, no state meets all of the AFT criteria for charter school legislation." This is, in part, because some of the AFT criteria would limit the very freedom that charters represent. For example, two of the AFT criteria are that charter schools should hire certified teachers and charter school employees should be covered by the collective bargaining agreement.[18]

We find similar wording in the NEA statement regarding charters: "The NEA believes that charter schools can be a positive vehicle for public school reform, depending on their development, funding, structure, and governance. Charter schools must be held to high levels of educational and public accountability and must be prepared to welcome and educate all students."[19] In fact, in its official recommendations, the NEA recommends 1) private and parochial schools should not be involved, 2) there should be no sectarian focus in programs, admissions, employments, materials, or any other operations, limiting the number of charter schools, strict controls over admission, a prohibition on charging tuition, and requiring charter teachers to be under the same due process and collective bargaining rights.[20] Gone in this statement are freedom over admissions policies, freedom from many public school restrictions, and freedom from bureaucratic oversights. While saying they are for charters, the NEA limits the very power of the charters' freedom. But the very success of charters has come from freeing schools from the restrictions that the public school system places upon teachers.[21]

OTHER TYPES OF SCHOOL CHOICE

Charter schools are but one piece of the school-choice pie. They represent a positive start in school-choice reform, but they are just that—a first step. We must keep focused on the main goal: full parental choice of any legally certified school—public, private, or parochial. School choice must not, it cannot, end with charters.

Under a full-fledged voucher program, like the one described in chapter 4, a poor child could also choose from high-quality public, private, or parochial schools. A child could attend a school within its own district (intradistrict choice) or in another district in the state (interdistrict choice). Some of the most often cited intradistrict programs are those in East Harlem, New York; Montclair, New Jersey; and Cambridge, Massachusetts. Ann Bastian, a senior program officer at the New World Foundation, has found that intradistrict programs have helped poor students because they contain six key elements: 1) choice is part of a districtwide school improvement effort; 2) every school becomes a school of choice; 3) choice grants teachers more latitude in teaching; 4) choice provides all parents and students with real opportunities; 5) sufficient information is available to parents; and 6) choice districts have acquired higher funding.[22] Moreover, interdistrict choice programs have brought racial integration to the suburbs in Milwaukee and St. Louis.[23]

In addition to magnet schools, charter schools, intradistrict choice, and interdistrict choice, school choice is becoming an increasing reality for many students through privately sponsored choice programs. The growth in the privately funded scholarships programs has been impressive. Seventeen such programs have been established to assist children in making tuition payments to private or parochial schools through the 1994–95 school year. Typically, the programs pay up to half of the tuition bill. The Choice Charitable Trust sponsored the first children in 1991 and provided between $650 and $800 for ten students in the 1994–95 school year. The Partners Advancing Values in Education (PAVE) in Milwaukee is presently the nation's largest program providing tuition assistance ranging from $516 to $1,000 for 1,799 elementary school students, and from $1,225 to $1,500 for 469 high school students. The Scholarship Fund for Inner-City Children in Newark, New Jersey, is presently the nation's second largest program, providing $300 for 1,800 children. In the 1994–95 school year, there were 8,761 students in 583 schools nationwide participating in private scholarship programs.[24] By 1996, 13 percent of the country's public school students were involved in some form of public school choice.[25] Roughly a quarter of all children in America are in some form of a choice school, either public or private.[26]

By 2000, there were nearly 100 privately funded scholarship programs and five publicly funded scholarship programs that together empower almost 70,000 disadvantaged students to attend a better school. Children First America sponsors private voucher programs in seventy cities nationwide. The Children's Scholarship Fund sponsors thirty-six private voucher programs throughout the country. They have provided scholarships to nearly 40,000 children to attend over 7,000 private schools.[27]

In fact, there has been strong growth in many different areas of choice in recent years. By 2000, at least twenty-one states considered legislation to create charter schools or voucher programs for low-income students. At least eighteen states considered tax deductions or tax credits to assist parents with their educational expenses.[28] Jennifer Garrett of the Heritage Foundation sums up the status of choice in 2001:

Amendments to strengthen charter school laws are pending in Minnesota, Missouri, Connecticut, Florida, Nevada, Illinois, and Alaska. Charter school legislation is moving through the Iowa legislature for the first time. Voucher legislation has been proposed in eight states, including Connecticut, Florida, Maryland, New York, and Texas. A corporate income tax credit for private school tuition, already approved by the Florida House, was recently passed by the state Senate. A similar tax credit bill was recently passed in Pennsylvania. Tuition tax credit bills have been introduced in 10 states.[29]

THE SCHOOL CHOICE PROGRAMS IN
MILWAUKEE AND CLEVELAND

The most promising of all areas of choice has been the two major choice programs in Wisconsin and Ohio and the one smaller program in Florida. As of 2004, there are three full state-financed school-choice programs up and running: in Milwaukee, Cleveland, and Pensacola.[30]

In 1990, Wisconsin passed legislation creating the Milwaukee Parental Choice Program. The MPCP allowed Milwaukee to become the country's first district to use vouchers. The program began in 1990 on the initiative of Polly Williams, an African American Wisconsin legislator. The $2,500 vouchers were awarded based on a lottery to low-income families. Originally, the voucher could only be used at secular private schools and parents could not add on to the voucher amount. Schools had to accept the voucher without add-on charges. The legislature funded up to 1,500 vouchers. Three hundred forty-one vouchers were used in the 1990–91 school year and the number was raised to 830 in 1994–95. The number of schools increased from seven in 1990–91 to twelve in 1995–96. By the 1999–2000 school year, there were 7,621 students enrolled in ninety-one private schools. All students must come from families at 175 percent of the federal poverty line or less.

In the mid-1990s, the Wisconsin legislature expanded the voucher program to include 15,000 low-income students and changed the program to include religious schools. On June 10, 1998, the Wisconsin State Supreme Court upheld the use of vouchers for private and parochial schools. The U.S. Supreme Court decided not to hear an appeal of that decision, in effect, upholding the state's decision. Voucher students started attending religious schools in the 1998–99 school year. About 8,000 students took advantage of the vouchers that were worth the amount of the Milwaukee's public school expenditure per pupil.

By 2001–02 school year, about 10,000 children used vouchers at over 100 mostly religious schools in Milwaukee. Presently, up to 15,000 students may participate in the program and may use their vouchers to attend any private school, religious or nonreligious. The amount of the voucher is as large or larger than the cost per student in Milwaukee's public school. Hence, it is significantly larger than Cleveland's. Wisconsin spent about $38.9 million on the Milwaukee voucher program in the 1999–2000 school year.[31] Wisconsin spent $5,106 per student in the voucher program—less than the $6,011 it spent per pupil in the Milwaukee Public School (MPS) District.[32]

The schools participating in the program are held to strict accountability standards. Each school must admit students randomly if there are more applications than available slots, submit an independent financial audit each year, and allow students to opt out of religious instruction and activities. Each school must also meet at least one of the following criteria: 1) at least 70 percent of students advance to the next grade, 2) attendance must average at least 90 percent, 3) at least 80 percent of the students must demonstrate "significant academic progress," or 4) at least 70 percent of the families must meet parental involvement criteria established by the private school.

The results of the Milwaukee program have been impressive. First, students have performed well in the Milwaukee choice program. According to research conducted by John Witte, while urban students scores usually decline over time, "there is no substantial difference . . . between the Choice and MPS students. . . . On a positive note, estimates for the overall samples, while always below national norms, do not substantially decline as the student enters higher grades. This is not the normal pattern in that usually urban student average scores decline relative to national norms in higher grades."[33] Greene, Peterson, and Du, in their research, found that students who had been in the choice program for three and four years had average gains in math 6.8 percentile points and in reading 4.9 percentile points.[34] The Harvard team also found improvements in voucher students' language and math scores.[35] And Cecilia Rouse found that "being selected to participate in the choice program appears to have increased the math achievement of low-income minority students by 1.5 to 2.3 percentile points per year."[36]

Similarly, Martin Carnoy writes: "When all the results are compared, it appears that voucher-using (choice) students in Milwaukee probably made greater gains by their third and fourth years in private schools—at least in math—than did students in public schools. But the achievement effect was not large, and only a fraction of voucher students stayed in private schools for this long even though the voucher fully covered tuition."[37]

Second, parents are satisfied with the Milwaukee Program. John Witte writes, "Satisfaction of Choice parents with private schools was just as dramatic as dissatisfaction was with prior public schools. . . . There was also, in each year, overwhelming support among participants that the Choice program should continue."[38]

Third, the Milwaukee program has been successful at targeting the poor. Witte found that choice students

> were from very low-income families, considerably below the average Milwaukee Public Schools family and about $500 below the low-income (free-lunch-eligible) MPS family. . . . Blacks and Hispanics were . . . overrepresented. . . . Choice students were considerably less likely to come from a household in which parents were married. . . . Prior test scores of Choice students showed they were achieving considerably less than MPS students and somewhat less than low-income MPS students.[39]

Similarly, David Ruenzel wrote that the Milwaukee program

> has . . . deeply involved long-alienated parents in their children's schooling. This is of crucial importance, standing as a powerful retort to educators who have long suggested that parents burdened by social and economic problems could devote but minimal attention to educational issues. . . . If choice parents were largely invisible in their old public schools, they are visible everywhere in their new schools—in the corridors, in the office, and even in the classroom, where they sometimes work as aides.[40]

Finally, recent studies have shown that the Milwaukee program also benefits students remaining in Milwaukee's public schools. According to Harvard economist Caroline Hoxby, Milwaukee's public elementary schools have improved as a result of the private school-choice program. Significantly, Jay Greene found similar results in Florida.[41]

In April 1992, Ohio Governor George Voinovich established a Commission of Educational Choice to create an alternative model for educating the low-income families who had no choice other than the public schools. In March 1995, the Ohio General Assembly created the Cleveland Scholarship and Tutoring Programs (CSTP) appropriating funds for 3,700 (1,500 students used them) scholarships worth up to $2,250 each for low-income families. The scholarship covered up to 90 percent of tuition (up to $2,500, hence the $2,250 figure) and was set at roughly one-third of the cost of a Cleveland public school pupil of $6,507 (so the voucher amount is much smaller than Milwaukee's). Students whose family income was at or below 200 percent of the poverty line received 75 percent of the school's tuition, up to $2,500, and those below the poverty line received 90 percent, up to $2,500. Since the voucher paid between 75 and 90 percent of the tuition, parents could add on the rest of the tuition amount. The legislation said that one-half of the scholarships could be redeemed at private schools but the Ohio Department of Education reduced that number to one-fourth.[42] The 25 percent guideline was ultimately eliminated, but the proportion attending private schools must still remain within the limits established by the law.

In August 1996, Cleveland began the country's second state-financed school-choice program. The Cleveland school-choice program eventually offered scholarships to all low-income applicants that it was able to contact.[43] Any low-income parent with a child in kindergarten through third grade was eligible to apply and the program added one grade per year so that by 2001–2002, parents with children up to eighth grade are eligible to apply. Each year the program adds about 1,000 new students who enter at the kindergarten level.

By 1997, 79 percent of the scholarships were granted to children who had been in public schools or were just starting kindergarten. Twenty-one percent went to children who had already been attending private schools.[44] The Cleveland program gave the poor preferential treatment. If a family's income was 200 percent of the poverty line or lower, the family received 90 percent of the school's tuition, up to $2,250. In the first lottery held, only those families whose income was below the poverty line were eligible. For voucher students who do not come from low-income families, the voucher is limited to 75 percent of tuition, to a maximum of $1,875.[45]

In August 1999 the Federal District Court of Ohio ruled the program unconstitutional, but the outcry was so great that Judge Solomon allowed the students to remain in the program, pending an appeal to the Ohio's Sixth Circuit Court of Appeals. On June 20, 2000, the Sixth Circuit Court of Appeals heard the case and on December 11, 2000, ruled that program was unconstitutional, giving unconstitutional aid to religious schools. The court ruled that the program had the effect of advancing religion and that it constituted an endorsement of religion and sectarian education in violation of the First Amendment. However, a stay was put into effect until the case could be heard by the U.S. Supreme Court. In 2002, the Supreme Court ruled that publicly funded school vouchers do not violate the separation of church and state as long as parents have a range of secular choices as well.

During the 1999–2000 school year, 3,400 voucher students enrolled in fifty-two private schools. During the 2000–2001 school year, about 3,968 students participated in the program. Catholic schools enrolled 3,138 children, roughly 79 percent. Of the fifty-one schools participating, thirty-one are Catholic and nearly 80 percent are religiously affiliated. Because the demand for the scholarships is so high, a lottery is used. Vouchers are issued in the name of the parent, sent to the school, signed by the parent, and then deposited by the school. Ohio spent about $7.7 million on the program in the 2000–2001 school year.[46] In the 1999–2000 school year, it spent $1,832 per pupil in the choice program, compared with $4,910 per pupil in the Cleveland School District.[47]

The Cleveland program has had many successes. First, it has helped integrate students of different races. According to research conducted by Jay Greene of The Buckeye Institute, school choice in Cleveland contributes to racial integration by providing families with access to private schools that are, on average, better racially integrated than public schools. Nearly 20 percent of voucher recipients attend a private school whose racial make-up resembles that of Cleveland, compared with only 5 percent of Cleveland public schools students who attend comparably integrated schools. More than three-fifths (60.7 percent) of Cleveland public school students attend schools that are almost entirely white or almost entirely minority, but only 50 percent of voucher students attend comparably segregated schools. Significantly, religious schools contribute to this integration. Greene writes, "Yet the evidence on racial integration suggests that access to a choice program that includes religious schools makes a significant contribution to promoting racial integration in Cleveland schools."[48]

That choice helps racial integration should not surprise us. Public schools are frequently limited in their ability to offer racial integration because they assign students based on where they live. As Jay Greene has found, "Public schools in Cleveland are remarkably segregated."[49] The U.S. Department of Education has reported that students attending a private school are more likely to be in racially mixed classes than students in public schools.[50] Greene concludes, "The evidence is clear that contrary to the expectations of critics, school choice helps promote integration."[51]

Furthermore, vouchers are provided to the poorest in Cleveland, helping them find more integrated schools for their children. Greene writes, "We know that choice students, on average, have significantly lower family incomes than do Cleveland city public school students."[52] Many of these parents choose nonreligious schools. Greene reports that only 16.5 percent of the parents enrolled their children in religious schools.[53]

Similarly, the Ohio Department of Education found that the CSPS program "effectively serves" the low-income families it was established to assist, and does so while maintaining the same racial mix as Cleveland's public schools.[54]

A second Cleveland success is that preliminary test scores in mathematics and reading at two schools formed in response to the adoption of school choice for students attending choice schools showed gains while language scores declined. Greene, Howell, and Peterson described the students' performance:

> The scores of Hope School students show moderate gains in reading and large gains in math. After one year, students in kindergarten through third grade scored, on average, 5.4 percentile points higher on the reading test and 15.0 percentile points higher on the math concepts test. Reading scores of students in first through third grade increased by 5.4 percentile points, math concepts scores by 12.8 percentile points, and total math scores by 11.5 points. Students in all grades experienced improvements.[55]

To put these improvements into perspective, compare these gains with students in the Cleveland public school during the time. Jay Greene and others report the following: "Cleveland public school reading scores declined, on average, by 1 to 2 percentile points between both the first and second grades and the second and third grades in the years 1994–95 to 1995–96."[56] And these two schools chose students who were the "poorest and most educationally disadvantaged."[57] If choice has worked for them, it can likely work for anyone. Broader studies of the choice students were conducted by the Ohio Department of Education. It found that voucher students show "small but statistically significant gains" in two of five academic areas, specifically, language and science.[58]

Third, parents selected their school based upon academic reasons. According to the research by Greene and others, 85 percent of parents new to choice schools said they chose their school to "improve the academic quality" of their child's education. Second in importance was their desire to find "greater safety" for their child, a reason given by 79 percent of the parents. "Location" ranked third.[59]

Fourth, parent satisfaction was very high with their child's choice school. Two-thirds of new choice parents were "very satisfied" with the "academic quality" of their school, compared to less than 30 percent of public school parents. Nearly 60 percent were very satisfied with school safety, compared with 25 percent of nonrecipients in public schools, and 55 percent were satisfied with discipline compared to only 23 percent of nonrecipients in public schools. Seventy-one percent of parents were "very satisfied" with the "teaching moral values," compared with only 25 percent of nonrecipients in public schools. Similar parental satisfaction was found in "private attention to the child," "parent involvement," "class size," and the school "facility."[60] Similarly, the Ohio Department of Education found that voucher parents were "much more satisfied" with their schools, indicating that school safety and improved quality of education were the most important factors to them.[61]

Finally, choice schools do well at retaining students both during the school year and from one school year to the next. Ninety-three percent of all families kept their child in the same school throughout the year. According to the Greene survey, 88 percent of private school parents intended to send their child to the same school the following year and 81 percent of the public school-choice parents.[62]

These gains are quite impressive when one realizes that it typically *costs* parochial and private schools to accept low-income students as part of the choice program. Mary Lou Toler explains:

By enrolling scholarship students, parish communities support them financially because the scholarship covers only 90 percent of the tuition, not 90 percent of the total cost to educate a child. On an average, tuition and fees last year were $1,737, yet the average cost per pupil was $2,373, with the difference provided through the generosity of the parish community. Other private schools in Cleveland that participate in the program have tuition fees exceeding $4,000 per student and they have accepted children without a parish to support them. Although the arguments on the national stage often state that Catholic schools experience large financial gains by accepting scholarship students, enough to "build chapels and buy crucifixes," the reality is quite different.[63]

The Public Policy Forum conducted a study of taxpayers in both Wisconsin and Ohio. They found broad, enthusiastic support for both Milwaukee's and Cleveland's programs. They reported four principal findings:

1) An "overwhelming majority" of taxpayers support the choice programs and "most" favor expanding choice in three ways: making the programs statewide, allowing religious schools to participate, and allowing all children to participate.
2) Each choice school should be required to make certain school-related information available for accountability purposes.
3) Representatives from private and public schools should gather each school's information.
4) For schools that don't comply, schools should be subjected to a probationary period.[64]

The Government Accounting Office (GAO) conducted a study of both the Cleveland and Milwaukee programs. The four consequential findings: 1) the two programs successfully targeted the poor since "voucher students were more likely than public school students to come from families that had less income and were headed by a parent who was single or not married to the person he or she [was] living with," and that these parents were more likely to have completed high school[65]; 2) the programs were attracting students at need since "researchers found that voucher schools in Milwaukee were attracting lower-performing public school students"; 3) the Cleveland program offered at least a similar educational package when compared with the public schools since, "Cleveland voucher schools, compared to public schools, had less-experienced teachers and smaller class sizes"[66]; and 4) the programs are successfully attracting

students of minority status since "well over two-thirds of the students enrolled in Cleveland's and Milwaukee's voucher programs and public
schools were minority group members."[67]

The GAO went on to note that "both Ohio and Wisconsin spend less on
each voucher student than on each public school student." Then, it went
on to observe that "contract researchers found little or no significant improvement in voucher students' achievement, but other investigators
found some positive effects."[68] In other words, the GAO found that *for
less money*, voucher schools *at worst* did as well as public schools and *at
best* did better.[69] Case closed.

CHOICE AND REFORM IN OTHER STATES

In 1999, Pensacola, Florida, began the country's third state-financed
school-choice program.[70] Earlier that year, Florida adopted the A-Plus Accountability and School Choice Program. This system offered vouchers to
students in schools that received repeated failing grades. Based on average student scores achieved on the Florida Comprehensive Assessment
Test, a school receives a grade of A, B, C, D, or F. If a school receives an
F in two out of four years, its students may receive a voucher to attend another school, either public or private. In the 1999–2000 school year, two
Pensacola schools met the failing criteria. As a result, fifty-three students
left to attend five private (four religious and one nonreligious) schools and
eighty-five children left to attend other public schools, out of a total student population of approximately 900 (the voucher maximum was $3,353
per student in kindergarten to third grade and $3,178 per student in fourth
through eighth grades). In the 2000–2001 school year, no schools qualified for vouchers.[71]

How did schools improve so that none qualified for vouchers one year
later? Jay Greene has analyzed test scores in Florida. He found that the
threat of vouchers in Florida caused math and writing scores to improve
in Florida's lowest-performing schools. Greene has demonstrated that
vouchers are indeed an effective way to improve students' academic performance. By comparing scores in 1998–99 and the 1999–2000 school
years, he found that all seventy-eight schools that received an F in 1999
received a higher grade in 2000. He concludes, "Performance of students

on academic tests improves when public schools are faced with the prospect that their students will receive vouchers."[72] Similarly, according to the "Competing to Win: How Florida's A+ Plan Has Triggered Public School Reform," school choice not only sparked widespread reform, it also helped to bring about success at other local public schools.[73]

Michigan is facing problems with overcrowding of public school students and the possibility of raising taxes to construct additional schools. The Mackinac Center for Public Policy conducted a survey of private schools in which they found that "conservative projections based on the survey data indicate that Michigan privately funded schools could have accommodated a total of more than 55,000 additional students over their 1998–99 enrollments. The results of the survey suggest that proposals to expand parental choice in education or to use privately funded schools to ease overcrowding in government schools could be both practical and efficient."[74]

Students in Maine have had limited school choice since 1873. If a child's town does not have a public school, the parents may choose another approved school, private or public, but not religious. In the fall of 1999, 5,614 students from fifty-five different communities attended private schools while 30,412 attended nearby public schools. The state's Department of Education reports that the average voucher amount for children to attend an alternate school is roughly $6,000 per student, approximately 20 percent less than the state's average per pupil expenditure for public education.[75]

Students in Vermont may choose from a large pool of public schools and eighty-three independent schools, but no religious schools. With the approval of the local school board, parents may elect to send their child to any one of these approved schools. During the 1998–99 school year, the state paid tuition for 6,505 students to attend a school of their choice. The state supreme court ruled that payments may not go to sectarian schools. The Vermont voucher program has been running since 1869.[76]

Students in Washington, D.C., may apply for a randomly assigned Washington Scholarship Fund to attend a school of their choice. After two years of scholarships, Wolf, Peterson, and West conducted a study of 1,000 students who participated in the private scholarship program. They found that scholarship students provided more tolerant responses to civil liberties questions, were assigned more homework, and had fewer problems with fighting. Moreover, their parents reported much higher grades for their school of choice than did parents with children in the traditional public schools. Significantly, African American students who switched to a private school scored 9 national percentile rank points higher than their public school peers in combined math and reading achievement.[77]

CONCLUSION

These encouraging developments in school choice go hand in hand with increased public support for choice. Public recognition of the potential benefits of school choice is growing. A 1992 Gallup Poll found that 64 percent of the American public favored public funding for public and private school choice (including religious schools). Approximately half of the respondents in a 2000 survey by the Center on Policy Attitudes favored the use of vouchers for tuition at private and religious schools. A clear majority of Americans surveyed by the National Education Association and released in March 2001 supported President Bush's proposal to give parents of children in chronically failing schools a voucher to send their child to a school of their choice. Sixty-three percent favored giving the students a voucher worth $1,500, and 82 percent of parents said they wanted to be in charge of their children's education, according to a survey conducted by Parents in Charge and released in April 2001.[78] From the early 1970s to the early 2000s, a majority has moved from opposing to supporting school choice.

The popularity for choice continues to grow, especially in the African American community. Significantly, some of the nation's most prominent African Americans support school choice, including former Atlanta Mayor Andrew Young, Martin Luther King III, the president of the Southern Christian Leadership Conference, and the former Colorado NAACP President Willie Breazell.[79] Their support is not surprising since a November 2000 survey by the Joint Center for Political and Economic studies found that 57 percent of African Americans support vouchers.[80]

Politicians are getting this message. In his 2004 budget, President Bush set aside $756 million for school-choice programs, including money to be used for seven or eight pilot programs across the country.[81] This is not surprising since President Bush has long supported school choice. A provision to fund a large-scale school-choice demonstration project was in the original version of the No Child Left Behind Act of 2001 but was removed during committee mark-up. John Boehner (Rep., Ohio) said: "Americans support giving parents the power to do what they think is best for their children's education. The president's plan gives this power as a last resort to the parents of children trapped in chronically failing schools after those schools have been given every opportunity to change. A solid majority of Americans support this approach."[82]

With the growing popularity of choice, comes a warning: choice must not end with charters. Charters are a significant step toward the end of a fully comprehensive school-choice system, like the one described in the previous chapter. They help build momentum toward a system where all four types of schools are considered public. However, some consider charters the culmination of school choice. This should not occur because that type of system falls far short of the comprehensive type of system described in the previous chapter. Charters are a helpful step toward full school choice, not the final destination.

At the Seventy-First Classical Middle Charter School in North Carolina, children study a classical education. They can take French, Latin, Socratic seminars, read books like *A Tale of Two Cities*, and observe a strict dress code policy. More than 90 percent of the school's students earned "proficient" or better on state tests. The school was named a North Carolina School of Excellence.[83] These are the opportunities that come with a choice system.

The North Star of school choice is what is best for the children. Diane Thorne described the difference in her daughter, Jordan, who is in the first year at Long Hill (a Blue Ribbon choice school in North Carolina): "She's just a different child this year. Last year, she was begging not to go to school."[84] Choice is about improved opportunities for disadvantaged children like Jordan Thorne and six-year-old Andrew Carney, whose mom said, "We wanted Andrew to be exposed to a second language. And Glendale offered Spanish. . . . [Being able to choose] just gives me more peace of mind."[85]

Choice can help to ensure that justice is brought to all children so that all children are provided with an opportunity to succeed. As has been shown in Milwaukee and Cleveland, school choice enhances the performance of at-risk children, provides more opportunities for parental involvement, and increases school's accountability. The time has come to provide all Americans with equal educational opportunity and enhanced parental empowerment. Now is the time for a nationwide system of school choice. It is time to ensure that all children, regardless of their parent's wealth, have the opportunity to succeed.

NOTES

1. For an excellent discussion of how school choice will assist the poor, see John Coons and Stephen Sugarman, *Education by Choice: The Case for Family Control* (Berkeley: University California, 1978), 109–30.

2. Rolf Blank and Douglas Archbald, "Magnet Schools and Issues of Education Quality," *Clearing House* 66 (November/December 1992): 82.

3. Blank and Archbald, "Magnet Schools," 34, 35.

4. Sarah Lubman, "Breaking Away: Parents and Teachers Battle Public Schools by Starting Their Own," *Wall Street Journal*, May 19, 1994; Jeanne Allen, "Monthly Letter to Friends of the Center for Education Reform, No. 14," 3. Lubman also found that the forty-one schools established by 1994 taught approximately 12,700 students. For an overview of the development of charter schools through October 1994, see the following: Stephen Tracy, "Charter Schools: Choices for Parents, Chances for Children," *Clearing House* 66 (November/December 1992): 90–91; Ruth E. Randall, "What's after School Choice? Private-Practice Teachers and Charter Schools," *The Education Digest* (April 1993): 38–41; Louann Bierlein and Lori Mulholland, "The Promise of Charter Schools," *Educational Leadership* (September 1994): 34–40; Linda Diamond, "A Progress Report on California's Charter Schools," *Educational Leadership* (September 1994): 41–45; Mary Ellen Sweeney, "How to Plan a Charter School," *Educational Leadership* (September 1994): 46, 47; Claudia Wallis, "A Class of Their Own: Bucking Bureaucracy, Brashly Independent Public Schools Have Much to Teach about Saving Education," *Time* (31 October 1994): 52–61.

5. Randall, "What's after School Choice?" 40.

6. "Charter Status Pays Off, in Cash," *Los Angeles Times* (5 April 1994); Wallis, "A Class of Their Own," 54, 55. Philadelphia, where half the public school students now attend charter schools, provides another example of charter schools' record of improved student achievement results. A disproportionately large number of the students tending charter schools are African American and Latino. Student attendance is 5.8 percent higher in charter schools than in regular public

schools. Charter school students in grades 9 through 12 outperform regular public school students in course passage rates in English by 8.5 percent, in social studies by 3.9 percent, in mathematics by 4.9 percent, and in science by 7.8 percent, according to Robert Schwartz, "Restructuring Philadelphia's Neighborhood High Schools: A Conversation with Constance Clayton and Michelle Fine," *Journal of Negro Education* 63 (1994): 117.

7. Marjorie Coeyman, "Charter Schools Dig In: Ten Years Later, What Have We Learned?" *Christian Science Monitor* (January 7, 2003): 15–19.

8. Jennifer Garrett, "Progress on School Choice in the States," *The Heritage Foundation Backgrounder* (May 16, 2001): 6. For an excellent overview of the Arizona charter schools, see April Gresham, Frederick Hess, and Robert Maranto, "Desert Bloom: Arizona's Free Market in Education," *Phi Delta Kappan* 81, no. 10 (June 2000): 751–57.

9. Garrett, "Progress on School Choice in the States," 1.

10. Garrett, "Progress on School Choice in the States," 4.

11. Coeyman, "Charter Schools Dig In."

12. Coeyman, "Charter Schools Dig In."

13. Coeyman, "Charter Schools Dig In."

14. Melanie Kaplan, "Education Innovators Make Their Mark," *The Christian Science Monitor* (January 7, 2003): 20.

15. Henry, "Scores Up for Charter Schools," quoted in Garrett, "Progress on School Choice in the States," 10. For entire report, see Advantage Schools Annual Report on School Performance, March 2001, located at www.advantage-schools.com/news/AnnualReport99-00.pdf.

16. Garrett, "Progress on School Choice in the States," 19. Moreover, charter school laws were upheld by the state supreme courts in New Jersey and Utah. On April 21, 2000, a circuit court judge in Illinois dismissed a lawsuit filed by the Illinois Education Association and others that would have struck down Illinois' tax credit for education-related expenses. See Garrett, "Progress on School Choice in the States," 2. (Illinois' tax credits offer a credit of up to 25 percent of educational-related expenses that exceed $250 per child or $500 per family.)

17. Nina Shokraii Rees, *School Choice 2000: What's Happening in the States,* (Washington, D.C.: Heritage Foundation, 2000), quoted in Garrett, "Progress on School Choice in the States," 4.

18. "AFT on the Issues: Charter Schools" at www.aft.org/issues/charter schools.html.

19. "Charter Schools," *National Education Association Legislative Topic Action Center* (June 2001) at www.nea.org/lac/papers/charter.html.

20. "Charter Schools," *National Education Association,* 4. See also "Charter Schools Overview," *National Education Association* at www.nea.org/issues/charter.

21. Charles Glenn writes: "Ideally, *every* public school should become a charter school, with a clear sense of purpose linked to specific outcomes, with scope to be distinctive, and with the opportunity to gather teachers and parents who share a vision for education." Lawrence Hardy, "Public School Choice," *American School Board Journal* (February 2000): 24.

22. Ann Bastian, "Which Choice? Whose Choice?" *Clearing House* 66 (November/December 1992), 96. Similarly, Stephanie Counts and Beverly Lavergneau found that school-choice programs are most effective when they: 1) have collected data and done community outreach, 2) supply distinct and diverse schools, 3) have a clearly articulated student selection process, 4) provide adequate transportation, and 5) make a financial commitment to the children and to cost effectiveness. See "Choice as a Vehicle for Urban Educational Change in the 1990s," *Clearing House* 66 (November/December 1992): 79, 80.

23. "Bringing Racial Integration to the Suburbs," *School Administrator* (May 1993): 12–17; see also Robert S. Peterkin and Janice E. Jackson, "Public School Choice: Implications for African American Students, *The Journal of Negro Education* 63 (1994): 126–38.

24. "Choice Opportunities: Private Scholarship Programs," Center for Education Reform, 5.

25. Hardy, "Public School Choice," 23.

26. Hardy, "Public School Choice," 23.

27. Garrett, "Progress on School Choice in the States," 5.

28. Garrett, "Progress on School Choice in the States," 2.

29. Garrett, "Progress on School Choice in the States," 2.

30. For a complete analysis of the effect of vouchers, see *Revolution at the Margins* by Frederick Hess (Washington, D.C.: Brookings Institution Press, 2002).

31. U.S. General Accounting Office, *School Vouchers: Publicly Funded Programs in Cleveland and Milwaukee* (August 2001): 4, GAO-01-914.

32. U.S. General Accounting Office, *School Vouchers*, 4. The GAO goes on to note that the Milwaukee school district in 1999–2000 had about 105,000 students enrolled in 165 schools supported by $917 million in total revenues.

33. John Witte, "The Milwaukee Voucher Experiment," *Educational Research and Policy Analysis* (Winter 1998), quoted in Howard Fuller, "Evidence Supports the Expansion of the Milwaukee Parental Choice Program," *Phi Delta Kappan* 81, no. 5 (January 2000): 390–91.

34. Witte, "The Milwaukee Voucher Experiment," 390.

35. U.S. General Accounting Office, *School Vouchers*, 30.

36. Cecilia Rouse, "Private School Vouchers and Student Achievement: An Evaluation of the Milwaukee Parental Choice Program," *Quarterly Journal of*

Economics (May 1998), quoted in U.S. General Accounting Office, *School Vouchers*, 391.

37. Martin Carnoy, "School Vouchers: Examining the Evidence," *Economic Policy Institute* (2001): 32.

38. Witte, "The Milwaukee Voucher Experiment," quoted in Fuller, "Evidence Supports the Expansion," 390–91.

39. Witte, "The Milwaukee Voucher Experiment," quoted in Fuller, "Evidence Supports the Expansion," 390–91. Despite all the evidence, voucher opponents still argue that choice does not aid the least well-off. Dan Murphy writes, "So far, we know that both the Milwaukee and Cleveland programs have favored relatively advantaged students, leaving the most disadvantaged students in public schools with even fewer resources." See his "When You Weigh the Evidence . . . Voucher Programs in Milwaukee and Cleveland," *American Educator* (Fall 1998): 43.

40. David Ruenzel, "A Choice in the Matter," *Education Week* (September 27, 1995), quoted in Fuller, "Evidence Supports the Expansion," 390–91.

41. Caroline Hoxby, "School Choice and School Productivity," *Harvard University* (February 2001). See http://post.economics.harvard.edu/faculty/hoxby/papers/school_choice.pdf.

42. The decision to reduce the number from one-half to one-fourth was made by John M. Goff, then the state superintendent of public instruction.

43. Jay Greene, William Howell, and Paul Peterson, "Lessons from the Cleveland Scholarship Program." Paper prepared for presentation before the Association of Public Policy and Management, Washington, D.C. (November 1997): 5.

44. See also Zach Schiller, "Cleveland School Vouchers: Where the Students Come From," *Policy Matters Ohio*. Schiller finds similar numbers. Published in 2001, he finds that 33 percent of students had previously been in private schools whereas two-thirds had not (21 percent had gone to public schools in Cleveland and 46 percent were kindergarteners or came from elsewhere).

45. U.S. General Accounting Office, *School Vouchers*, 6.

46. U.S. General Accounting Office, *School Vouchers*, 3.

47. U.S. General Accounting Office, *School Vouchers*, 4.

48. Jay P. Greene, "Choice and Community: The Racial, Economic, and Religious Context of Parental Choice in Cleveland," *The Buckeye Institute* (November 1999). According to the U.S. GAO, the Cleveland school district in 1999–2000 had about 76,000 students enrolled in its 121 schools and had $712 million in revenue (of which $371.9 million was from the state of Ohio). The Cleveland programs also sets aside funding for tutoring students who remain in the Cleveland public schools. U.S. General Accounting Office, *School Vouchers*, 5.

49. U.S. General Accounting Office, *School Vouchers*, 7.

50. U.S. General Accounting Office, *School Vouchers*, 3.

51. U.S. General Accounting Office, *School Vouchers*, 16, 17.

52. U.S. General Accounting Office, *School Vouchers*, 13.

53. U.S. General Accounting Office, *School Vouchers*, 14.

54. Mary Lou Toler, "School Choice Works in Cleveland," M*omentum* 32, no. 3 (September/October 2001): 60–61.

55. Greene, Howell, and Peterson, "Lessons from the Cleveland Scholarship Program," 23.

56. Greene, Howell, and Peterson, "Lessons from the Cleveland Scholarship Program," 24.

57. Greene, Howell, and Peterson, "Lessons from the Cleveland Scholarship Program," 22.

58. Toler, "School Choice Works in Cleveland," 60–61. In a study largely suspect of pro-voucher research, where Martin Carnoy points out that gains were not found in many areas and that student performance lacked in commercial schools, he still writes, "In Cleveland, the most reliable results suggest that, after two years, choice students who used their vouchers to attend existing (religious) private schools made greater gains in science than did non-choice students." Carnoy, "School Vouchers," 32.

59. Greene, Howell, and Peterson, "Lessons from the Cleveland Scholarship Program," 10.

60. Greene, Howell, and Peterson, "Lessons from the Cleveland Scholarship Program," 14.

61. Toler, "School Choice Works in Cleveland," 60–61.

62. Greene, Howell, and Peterson, "Lessons from the Cleveland Scholarship Program," 19. Martin Carnoy of the Economic Policy Institute has analyzed some of the findings by Peterson, Greene, and other school-choice proponents. He has pointed out some of the challenges in their research. However, even Carnoy concludes that there are still benefits to students from vouchers even though they are "significantly smaller" than voucher proponents argue. See his "School Vouchers: Examining the Evidence," 1–58.

63. Toler, "School Choice Works in Cleveland," 60–61. For another view, see Martin Carnoy, "School Choice? Or Is It Privatization?" *Educational Researcher* 29, no. 7 (October 2000): 15–20.

64. "Choice School Accountability: A Consensus of Views in Ohio and Wisconsin," *Public Policy Forum Report* at http://publicpolicyforum.org/pdfs/choice_accountability.pdf.

65. According to the GAO for the 1998–1999 school year in Cleveland, 70 percent of the voucher students' families were head by a single mom compared

with 62 to 65 percent of public school families and the mean family income was $18,750 compared with $19,814 by public school families. Also, 91.6 percent of mothers and 89.2 percent of fathers had completed high school compared with 78.1 percent and 77.7 percent of moms and dads of public school students. Finally, 14.2 percent of voucher moms and 12.1 percent of voucher dads had a four-year college degree, compared with 7.8 percent of public school moms and 8.1 percent of the dads. For the 1998–99 school year in Milwaukee, the gap was even more significant. For voucher parents: 76.5 percent were headed by a unmarried parent, the mean family income was $11,430, 84.9 percent of the moms had a high school degree or GED, 73.1 percent of the dads had similar education, and 8.9 percent of the moms and 9.4 percent of the dads had a four-year college degree. For the public school families at large, 49 percent of the families were headed by an unmarried parent, the mean family income was $22,000, 75 percent of the moms and 76 percent of the dads had a high school degree or GED, and 11 percent of the moms and 15 percent of the dads had a four-year college degree. U.S. General Accounting Office, *School Vouchers*, 14, 15.

66. For the 1998–99 school year, in Cleveland, voucher schools averaged 201 to 300 students, had a range of enrollment of 51 to over 500, had an average of 6 to 10 full-time teachers, averaged 20.6 students per class, and the average teacher had 8.6 years of experience. Public schools averaged 401 to 500 students, had an average of 150 to over 500 in enrollment, averaged 21 to 25 full-time teachers, averaged 23.6 students per class, and had 14.2 years of average teacher experience. Kim Metcalf, *Evaluation of the Cleveland Scholarship and Tutoring Grant Program 1996–1999* (Bloomington: Indiana University, 1999), quoted in U.S. General Accounting Office, *School Vouchers*, 16.

67. U.S. General Accounting Office, *School Vouchers*, 3, 4, 17. The GAO reported that 79 percent of the students in the Cleveland public schools were of minority status compared with 73.4 percent in the choice program. The GAO's statistics are from Kim Metcalf, *Evaluation of the Cleveland Scholarship and Tutoring Grant Program 1996–1999*. The Milwaukee figures are comparable. The report finds that 61.4 percent of Milwaukee's public school children are African American and 62.4 percent of the voucher students are African American. Also, 13.3 percent of the public school children are Hispanic and 13.2 percent of the voucher students are Hispanic. Overall, 79.8 percent of students in Milwaukee's public schools are of minority status compared with 79 percent in voucher schools. U.S. General Accounting Office, *School Vouchers*, 20.

68. U.S. General Accounting Office, *School Vouchers*, 25, 27. Similar findings were observed by the Wisconsin Legislative Audit Bureau. See www.legis.state .wi.us/lab/windex.htm.

69. Harvard economist Caroline Hoxby found that school choice improves academic achievement while lowering educational costs. See her report, "Does Competition among Public Schools Benefit Students and Taxpayers?" *American Economic Review* (December 2000); see also "The Difference That Choice Makes," Economics Focus, *Economist* (January 27, 2001), quoted in Garrett, "Progress on School Choice in the States," 10.

70. Technically, Milwaukee and Cleveland are city choice programs only. Vermont and Maine offer publicly sponsored choice only at nonreligious private schools and only if there isn't adequate space in the public schools.

71. In October 2000 the First District Court of Appeal for the State of Florida ruled that the Opportunity Scholarship Program was consistent with Article IX, Section 1, of the Florida Constitution. In April 2001, the Florida Supreme Court declined to review the appellate court's ruling.

72. Jay Greene, *An Evaluation of the Florida A-Plus Accountability and School Choice Program* (New York: Manhattan Institute for Policy Research, Center for Civic Innovation, 2001), 2. See also www.edreform.com/press/2001/apluseval.htm. In addition to Florida's program, Maine and Vermont have offered limited school choice for more than a century. These two states offer private, secular education for students whose public school districts do not have sufficient school capacity.

73. Garrett, "Progress on School Choice in the States," 9. See also Center for Education Reform, "Groundbreaking Report Shows Competition from School Choice Sparks Widespread Public School Reform" (October 2000).

74. Matthew J. Brouillette, "Unused Capacity in Privately Funded Michigan Schools: Survey of Excess School Capacity to Help Ease Overcrowded Classrooms and Accommodate School Choice," *The Mackinac Center for Public Policy* (March 1999): 1.

75. Frank Heller, "Lessons from Maine: Education Vouchers for Students since 1873," *CATO Institute Briefing Papers* (September 10, 2001): 1.

76. Libby Sternberg, "Lessons from Vermont: 132-Year-Old Voucher Program Rebuts Critics," *CATO Institute Briefing Papers* (September 10, 2001): 1. See also Clifford Cobb, *Responsive Schools, Renewed Communities* (San Francisco: ICS Press, 1992), 163–64.

77. Patrick Wolf, Paul Peterson, and Martin West, "Results of a School Voucher Experiment: The Case of Washington, D.C., after Two Years." Paper prepared for the annual meeting of the American Political Science Association (August 30–September 2, 2001), San Francisco, California.

78. Garrett, "Progress on School Choice in the States," 1.

79. Garrett, "Progress on School Choice in the States," 1.

80. Garrett, "Progress on School Choice in the States," 11, quoted from "Black v. Teachers," *Economist* (March 10, 2001). See "The Black Vote in 2000," at www.jointcenter.org/whatsnew/index.html.

81. Justin Blum and Michael Fletcher, "Bush Aide Says Voucher Offer Would Require D.C.'s Agreement," at www.washingtonpost.com/wp-dyn/articles/A20952-2003Feb3.html.

82. Press release, "New Poll for NEA Shows Majority of Americans Back President Bush's Approach to School Choice," Committee on Education and the Workforce, U.S. House of Representatives, 107th Congress, 1st Session (March 8, 2001), quoted in Garrett, "Progress on School Choice in the States," 10.

83. Hardy, "Public School Choice," 26.

84. Hardy, "Public School Choice," 26.

85. Hardy, "Public School Choice," 26.

Chapter Six

The Poor Benefit from School Choice

As demonstrated in chapter 1, poor children suffer in today's American schools.[1] School-choice expert Joseph Viteritti powerfully described how choice will aid the poor: "Should we expect that providing the poor with the same choices that most middle-class people enjoy would have a detrimental effect on the political order?"[2] In this chapter, I describe how choice is already helping poor children.

Education is the key for poor children. Many different voices have proclaimed choice as the vehicle for empowering poor children. Let's listen to some of them. Newark Councilman Cory Booker said, "If we are ever going to break the cycle of poverty within inner cities, we have to focus on education. . . . Wealthy people seem to have that choice. We say to the poorest, most vulnerable Americans that they cannot choose. We as a government force them into failing institutions."[3] Former governor and presidential candidate and now Senator Lamar Alexander agrees that vouchers are the way out. "What we're simply trying to do is give people without money more of the same choices of schools that people with money already have."[4]

In the summer of 2000, the Black Alliance for Educational Options (BAEO; an intergenerational coalition of black leaders from many different political persuasions) was formed to transform the American educational system so it could offer choices to students of color. The BAEO wrote:

It is un-American to accept conditions that deny the possibility of equity for all of our children. We intentionally use the metaphor of struggle, because the history of our people is grounded in a consistent battle for equity and injustice.[5]

Urban League president Hugh Price said, "If urban schools . . . continue to fail in the face of all we know about how to improve them, then parents will be obliged to shop elsewhere for quality education. We Urban Leaguers believe passionately in public education. But make no mistake. We love our children even more."[6]

The relationship between schooling, children living in poverty, and the hope for a better future for these children was powerfully summarized by Peterson and Greene who wrote:

> Some say U.S. race relations are improving; other say not. Some say that affirmative action has fostered racial progress; others say not. But almost all Americans, liberal and conservative, agree that in the long run racial equality can be fully achieved only by eliminating disparities in the average educational performances of blacks and whites. Most Americans, we submit, would go so far as to say that if the next generation of blacks and whites acquire similar academic skills, the remaining barriers to racial equality could well slip away of their own accord.
>
> But despite the broad consensus for education's central importance, the United States tolerates the isolation of half of its African American children in public school within an unsafe and severely underperforming system. Any serious attempt to eliminate racial inequities must correct this glaring blot on the nation's racial report card.[7]

Along this line, former Democratic Congressman Floyd Flake said, "We cannot offer our children any hope for the future if we do not first furnish them with a quality education. The public schools in the city have not been able to provide that opportunity for the great majority of poor children."[8]

In *The Condition of Education 2000*, the authors wrote: "By choosing the school that their children attend, parents may perceive that they can influence the quality of education their children receive. In addition, with parents choosing their children's school, schools may be prompted to compete for enrollments by improving the programs they offer."[9]

Why have so many voices from so many perspectives come to support school choice for the poor? They believe school choice will assist the poor because school-choice programs offer poor students an open door to a better education. Now the evidence is in—school choice is empowering poor children.

THE CRITICS ARE WRONG: SCHOOL CHOICE IS BETTER FOR THE POOR

The Poor Want School Choice

Yet critics argue that school choice will hurt the poor. They cite four possible ways. First, they argue that the poor prefer the present system to a system of school choice. But polls taken of the poor demonstrate that not only do poor parents overwhelmingly favor school choice, they have usually been the strongest advocates of school choice.

Since a disproportionate number of the poor in the cited states are minorities, listening to the opinions of groups such as African Americans may give insight regarding the will of the poor. Throughout the 1980s, when the polls controlled for socioeconomic factors, whites participated in private schools with only 1 percent more frequency than other ethnic groups. In a 1983 Gallup Poll, 51 percent of all Americans favored school choice, but 64 percent of all African Americans favored choice. In a 1986 Gallup Poll, nonwhites favored school choice more than whites by a nearly 2–1 ratio.[10] In a 1989 poll, 60 percent of all Americans—but 65 percent of African Americans—approved of vouchers or school tax credits that would enable children to attend private as well as public schools.[11] In a 1992 poll, African Americans favored school choice more than whites.[12] The conclusion is clear: African Americans do not support the educational status quo. Their bitter experiences with the educational establishment have taught them that the system discriminates against them.

In recent years, support for school choice has grown among the poor. In poll after poll, people of minority status strongly favor school choice. A 1997 national survey conducted by the Joint Center for Political and Economic Studies found the greatest amount of support for vouchers was among African Americans—57 percent.[13] Similarly, in a 1997 Phi Delta

Kappa poll, 72 percent of African Americans favored vouchers.[14] A 1997 nationwide poll conducted by Terry Moe found that 79 percent of the inner-city poor favor a voucher plan (including 61 percent who said they strongly favor school choice. The survey also found that 82 percent of the inner-city poor and 76 percent of the advantaged whites agreed that school choice would be "especially helpful to low-income kids, because their public schools tend to have the most problems").[15]

A 1997 Ohio poll found that 77 percent of African Americans supported school choice.[16] Another 1997 poll found that 65 percent of Latinos, 70 percent of African Americans earning less than $15,000 per year, and 86 percent of African Americans aged twenty-six to thirty-five support vouchers.[17] A 1998 Florida poll found that only 26 percent of Floridians opposed school choice.[18] In one poll, 60 percent of African Americans supported school choice in 1999.[19] Another 1999 poll found that 71 percent of African Americans supported vouchers.[20] Additionally, a 1999 poll showed that 68 percent of all minorities' supported vouchers.[21] A 1999 *Washington Post* survey found that 65 percent of African Americans with incomes under $50,000 favored school choice.[22] And a 1999 Ohio poll found that 87 percent of African Americans ages twenty-six to thirty-five and 66.4 percent of Africans Americans ages eighteen to twenty-five support school choice.[23] Furthermore, 6,244 parents applied for the 1,700 available seats in the Cleveland choice program.[24] A Milwaukee poll, in 1999, found that 74 percent of African Americans, 77 percent of Hispanics, 81 percent of people making less than $11,000 per year, and 81 percent of people with less than a high school education favored school choice.[25] A 1999 Atlanta poll found that 63 percent of minority parents felt that students in failing schools should receive a voucher to select of a 'school of their own choosing.[26] Finally, a 2000 poll conducted in New York City found that 87 percent of Hispanics, 86 percent of Asians, and 83 percent of African Americans favored vouchers.[27]

And it's obvious why the poor would so greatly favor school choice. Under the current system, they lack options. Under a school-choice plan, they would have options. Consequently, it was not surprising that the Black Alliance for Educational Options stated their goal in the following way:

BAEO is allied together to actively and aggressively support parent choice to empower families and increase educational options for Black children.

We will work with any individuals or groups, irrespective of race and eth-
nicity, that share our goal of expanded educational options for low-income
families. BAEO has its eye on a single prize—the effective education of
ALL of our children. We can no longer tolerate a situation that leaves far too
many of our children stranded in an educational wasteland waiting for the
next "five-year plan" to unfold.[28]

And why shouldn't the poor prefer such a just system? They suffer disproportionately under the current system; as Margonis and Parker say,
"Under-funded public schools, operating within the conditions created by
housing segregation and economic discrimination, have failed their students in countless cases."[29] Similarly, Howell and Peterson explain:

African Americans, more than other groups, live in the poorest, least attractive, and most dangerous communities within metropolitan regions. Because students are assigned to schools on the basis of where they live, public schools inherit all of the racial inequalities that plague housing markets.
Precisely because African Americans suffer most under a system of public
education based on residency, they stand to benefit the most from the new
education opportunities that vouchers afford.[30]

Obviously, then, the poor do not prefer the current system or their current school. Joseph Viteritti has written:

The reach and effectiveness of these institutions (inner-city ministry-
related schools) is stifled by a system of school funding that refuses to
support the educational preferences of parents who choose to send their
children to private or parochial schools, but invests valuable public resources in government-run institutions that have failed generations of minority children. The strict separationist philosophy that has dominated educational policy in America for more than a century is so out of step with
the culture and needs of racial minorities that it must share a large part of
the blame for the years of educational neglect that has been visited on
poor communities.[31]

Similarly, Peterson and Greene point out: "A *New York Times* article reported last December, for example, that 93 percent of blacks in Denver
agreed that 'some children in the Denver public school system are receiving a substandard education.'"[32]

In contrast to the current system, we now have the evidence: the poor have seen the benefits from the experiments around the country because they are the ones who have been specifically targeted in the voucher programs. The poor are the beneficiaries. The poor are those who are benefiting from the well-designed voucher programs; the average family income of those receiving vouchers in Milwaukee was $11,600, in Cleveland $18,750, in New York's privately funded program $10,000.[33] In the choice experiments in the United States, at least two-thirds of all recipients have been people of color.[34]

For example, the Milwaukee program, as we saw in chapter 5, specifically targets the poor.[35] This program offers concrete assistance to poor children, concludes Daniel McGroarty, a fellow at the Institute for Contemporary Studies, since "the average parental choice student is more likely to have been a discipline problem than a stand-out scholar at his old school and was no better off educationally or financially than his old public-school peers."[36]

Some schools have been set up specifically to assist children in need. School choice would improve the educational situation for "difficult-to-educate" children. Minnesota, for example, has developed specific "second chance" choice programs to meet the needs of students who are at least one year behind their grade level, two years behind in performance level, pregnant or a custodial parent, chemically dependent, or absent from school for three weeks straight. The program empowers 30,000 students per year to choose from any one of the state's 130 public or private alternative programs. Student surveys demonstrate that alternative school students are less likely to get into trouble or to drop out. Students remain in the system where their atypical needs are met. The same is true in New York, where the Preparation through Responsibility, Empowerment, and Purpose (PREP) school teaches girls ages eleven to fifteen who are either pregnant or already have a child.[37] Furthermore, charter schools in three states have been created to meet the needs of poor or "difficult-to-educate" students: Massachusetts, Colorado (with thirteen of fifty slots reserved for such schools), and over half of California's fifty-plus charter schools.[38]

Not surprisingly, poor parents approve of their schools of choice. According to *The Condition of Education 2000*, only 48 percent of parents assigned to their school were satisfied with it, compared with 78 percent of parents who chose their private school. The numbers were similar in terms of satisfaction with teachers, 53 percent compared with 75 percent, satisfaction with academic standards, 53 percent compared with 81 percent, and satisfaction with discipline, 54 percent compared with 85 percent.[39] The poor are clearly dissatisfied with the current system.

And the poor are clearly satisfied with their school when they get to pick it. John Witte reports that in Milwaukee, "satisfaction of choice parents with private schools was just as dramatic as dissatisfaction was with prior public schools." Kim Metcalf found that in Cleveland, "across the range of school elements, parents of scholarship students tend to be much more satisfied with their child's school than other parents. Scholarship recipient parents are more satisfied with the child's teachers, more satisfied with the academic standards at the child's school, more satisfied with order and discipline, more satisfied with social activities at the school." Paul Peterson and others found in Cleveland that "choice parents were significantly more satisfied with almost all aspects of their children's education than was a random sample of parents from Cleveland public schools. Nearly 50 percent of choice parents reported being very satisfied with the academic program, safety, discipline, and teaching of moral values in their private school."[40] Margaret Hadderman sums up the studies, writing, "Analyzing several evaluations of the Cleveland, Milwaukee, and New York City programs, WestEd researchers found consistent, generally positive results regarding inclusion of low-income families, parent satisfaction, parent education levels, parent marital status and family size, race-ethnicity, and attrition and mobility."[41] Summing up their findings from all of the privately funded scholarship programs, Howell and Peterson write, "They were noticeably more satisfied than public school parents generally."[42] Peterson sums up the surveys of parents in choice schools:

In their answers to almost all questions, parents are more enthusiastic about choice schools, usually by large margins. For example, forty-four percent more of the San Antonio choice parents than public school parents said they were satisfied with school discipline. Forty-one percent more were satisfied with the amount their child learned. Of those who moved to choice schools from public schools in Cleveland, the percentage of parents "very satisfied" with the school's academic quality was thirty-four percent higher than that of those who applied but did not enter the program. Thirty-four percent more were satisfied with school safety, thirty-six percent with school discipline. Similar results were obtained in Milwaukee and Indianapolis. If the only thing that counts is consumer satisfaction, school choice is a clear winner.[43]

Newark Councilman Booker tells this story which makes the statistics come to life:

> Many of the poorest parents, mostly single mothers, especially during the summer months, approach me and beg me to help them find available scholarships that might liberate their children from failing pubic schools, public schools that have decade-long records of failures. I sit with parents and listen to their stories that the only hope for their children and their families' future is a good education for their child. They are convinced, because of great evidence, that their child cannot succeed in the public school system. This is a problem.[44]

The conclusion is clear: the poor want choice. They do not want the status quo.

The Poor Make Wise Choices

Second, critics argue that poor parents lack the essential resources, such as time, energy, know-how, and education, to make a wise choice of schools. Consequently, they will make decisions based on factors other than quality of education. Thomas Fowler-Finn, superintendent of Haverhill Public Schools (Massachusetts), makes this argument in his study of an intradistrict choice program in his district. He found that the three top reasons parents chose a school were: 1) school location, 2) school and classroom size, and 3) additional services, such as after-school activities and computer labs. School quality ranked fourth.[45] Similarly, Nicholas Lemann said that when a major impediment to poor student's academic success is "their parents' impoverishment, poor education, lax discipline, and scant interest in education," it's unlikely they will become "tough, savvy, demanding education consumers."[46] And, from the Carnegie Foundation for the Advancement of Teaching 1992 report on school choice: "When parents do select another school, academic concerns often are not central to the decision."[47] So too, Poetter and Knight-Abowitz suggest, "Studies show, however, that parents often use an array of indicators to choose a school, many of which are unrelated to academic achievement or curricular quality, including race and class makeup of the student body."[48]

Furthermore, research on the "psychology of poverty" suggests that the poor might perceive that they have fewer options than they actually do. This is Katie Cannon's point in *Black Womanist Ethics*, where she points out that black women's choices are affected by the perception of limited options, because they have been told since birth that "their range of freedom has been restricted."[49]

To the extent that poor parents lack certain resources, this fact is more of an argument for extending the resources available to the poor than it is an argument against school choice. Supporters have developed centers for information on school choice, daylong fairs, church meetings, and home-counseling visits to give parents resources. For example, in Lowell, Massachusetts, a small city with a diverse population, the school district has established parent information centers with bilingual staffing and multilingual materials; conducted site workshops; and placed multilingual resources in libraries, churches, temples, medical care facilities, neighborhood variety stores, restaurants, shopping centers, laundromats, housing developments, public agencies, schools, and homeless shelters. The district has also sent neighborhood recruiters door-to-door to answer questions to provide application assistance.[50]

The research contradicts the aforementioned statements. Poor parents in choice programs select their schools based upon significant academic criteria. Eighty-five percent of the parents in the Cleveland voucher program selected the voucher because they said that they wanted to enhance the academic quality of their child's school.[51] Therefore, it is not surprising that Booker challenges the idea that poor parents will make poor choices:

> I always respond to that, and I challenge it. I challenge anybody to come into my city and walk with me and simply talk to these mothers. You will see that they care more about the education of their children and are more informed than suburban soccer moms are in the towns where I grew up. They know what it is going to take to help their children achieve the American dream. They believe in it, and they still hold onto it.[52]

Moreover, parents' financial status is a precarious predictor of their motivation for their children's education. Poor parents have made excellent decisions when given a choice. In Minnesota, a national leader in school choice reform, 113,000 parents (14 percent overall) of Minnesota's K–12 students actively selected their schools in the 1992–93 school year. Of those, a survey found that the primary reason for choosing a school was academics.[53]

When parents in East Harlem School District Four were given intradistrict public school choice in 1974, their children ranked last in state testing in New York City. After twelve years of choice, students in District Four ranked sixteenth out thirty-two districts in math and reading. After eighteen years of choice, the percentage of students reading at or above the appropriate grade level had skyrocketed 23 percent, from 15.3 percent to 38.3 percent. Meanwhile, the citywide test scores improved less than 13 percent, from 33.8 percent to 46.4 percent. This statistic means that from 1974 to 1992, District Four did a better job at improving student reading levels than New York City as a whole.[54] Math scores, graduation rates, and admissions into selective high schools had also jumped significantly in District Four. Poor parents chose good schools in District Four, and their children benefited.[55]

While these were the early positive results of school choice, they were not an aberration. In the more recent privately funded choice programs in New York, Washington, and Dayton, choice students have demonstrated amazing academic improvement.[56] Wealthy individuals began private scholarship programs to offer poor children the opportunity of gaining a first-rate education. John Walton and others funded private school education, which, according to Adam Meyerson, focused "public attention on the merits of Catholic, Baptist, Lutheran, Muslim, Jewish, and other religious schools that, despite shoestring budgets, are giving superior education to poor children in the same neighborhoods as their local dead-end public schools."[57] Parents typically received half the tuition amount from a private voucher. Adam Meyerson explains the logic:

> This may sound harsh for families whose average income is $18,000. But this "hand up, not a handout" strategy, as Patrick Rooney has described it, makes a tremendous difference in opening educational opportunity. When parents have to scrimp and save to pay tuition, they think of education as an investment. They take charge. They pay attention to whether they are getting their money's worth, to what school will be best for their children. And children take school more seriously when they know their parents are sacrificing for the sake of their future.[58]

In each of these programs, poor students were randomly chosen.[59] Paul Peterson describes the results for the students in New York: "After one year, the national percentile ranking of students attending private schools was, on average, two points higher in reading and mathematics than the ranking of the comparison group that remained in public schools."[60] After two years, African American students in New York scored 4 percentile points higher on standardized tests, African American students in Dayton scored 7 percentile points higher, and those in Washington, D.C., 9 points higher.[61] Peterson reports that according to the National Assessment of Educational Progress, minority students attending private schools have made enormous gains over the past twenty years.[62] In the privately funded scholarship program in Charlotte, Jay Greene found that "students given by lottery a voucher to attend private school outperformed their counterparts who failed to win a voucher by 6 percentile points after one year's time."[63] He also found that students who received a scholarship from private donors in the Edgewood School District near San Antonio also benefited tremendously from school choice.[64] Similarly, Peterson reports, "The scores of students participating in the school-choice program in San Antonio increased between 1991–92 and 1993–94, while those of the public school comparison group fell."[65]

In addition to these privately funded scholarship programs, there are also the state-funded voucher programs in Cleveland and in Milwaukee. Students enrolled in the Cleveland choice program also had amazing academic improvement. After just the first year, Peterson found that "two newly established choice schools serving 25 percent of the students previously attending public schools gained 9 national percentile rank points in math and 6 percentile points in reading."[66] According to Metcalf, Peterson, Howell, and Greene, "The results after two years indicate that scholarship students in existing private schools had significantly higher test scores than public school students in language (45.0 versus 40.0) and science (40.0 versus 36.0).[67] As a result, Metcalf concluded:

The scholarship program effectively serves the population of families and children for which it was intended and developed. The program was designed to serve low-income students while maintaining the racial composition of the Cleveland Public Schools. . . . The majority of children who participated in the program are unlikely to have enrolled in a private school without a scholarship.[68]

Greene, Peterson, and Howell found similar gains in two of the most disadvantaged Cleveland schools. "We found that after two years, students at the two schools we examined had gains of 7.5 in reading and 15.6 national percentile points in math."[69] Greene also conducted a study in which he linked educational freedom with student performance. He found that student performance increased when there was greater choice offered to parents.[70]

Students enrolled in the Milwaukee Parental Choice Program scored similar impressive results. Students who won lotteries to go to the choice schools scored, according to a study conducted by Paul Peterson, Jiangtao Du, and Jay Greene, "6 percentile points higher on their reading scores and 11 percentile points higher on their math scores than students who did not receive a voucher."[71] And the most dramatic improvements came in the third and fourth years of participating in the Milwaukee School Choice program.[72] Peterson and Greene explain:

> Our examination of the Milwaukee data showed that a student's enrollment in the program had only modest effects during the first two years. But by years three and four, choice students began outstripping their peers in the control group. If such gains can be duplicated nationwide, they could reduce by between one-third and one-half the current difference between white and minority test score performance.[73]

As a result, in the Joint Legislative Audit Committee report on the Milwaukee Program, 71.1 percent of parents chose their private school because of the high educational standards, 70.4 percent chose their school because of good teachers, and 67.8 percent because of the safe and orderly classrooms.[74] Clearly, poor parents were choosing their schools for significant academic concerns.[75]

Summing up the findings of all the studies done on the academic achievement of students in choice programs, Paul Peterson writes, "All in all the evidence that school choice enhances the achievement of low-income students has not become quite substantial."[76] Similarly, Patrick McEwan writes, "The combined results suggest that attendance at private, mainly Catholic schools may improve the mathematics—and, to a lesser extent, reading achievement—of poor, black students in elementary schools. However, it bears emphasis that the effects are not consistently observed for all grades and the effects do not appear to exist for poor, non-black students."[77] In other words, poor students either achieve better or the same in schools of choice, often at a far lower cost. Jay Greene explains:

> The authors of all ten studies find at least some benefits from the programs and recommend their continuation, if not expansion. No study finds a significant harm to student achievement from the school choice programs. The probability that all ten studies would be wrong is astronomically low. It is also worth noting that the private schools participating in these various school choice programs tend to have per pupil operating costs that are nearly half the per pupil expenditure in the public schools. Even if we were to find no significant academic benefit from school choice, we might still endorse the policy because parents like it, and because it costs half as much money to produce the same level of academic achievement. To increase student achievement significantly, while spending less money per pupil and making parents more satisfied, as the evidence from these ten studies consistently shows, provides strong support for school choice.[78]

In half of the private scholarship programs, parents are chosen by lottery to participate. Paul Peterson explains some parents' reactions to finding out that they had been selected:

> When the winners of the New York lottery were announced last May, winners were ecstatic: "I was crying and crying and crying," smiled Maria Miranda, a permanently disabled single mother living in Brooklyn. "It was the best Mother's Day present I could have asked for." A year into the Cleveland choice program, Pamela Ballard, parent of a new choice-school student in Cleveland, exclaimed, "After being in the Cleveland public schools, my daughter was listed a behavior problem. She was a 'D and F' student. . . . [Now my daughter's] behavior and grades are wonderful. . . . I wish lots of other scholarships . . . were available (because) many cannot afford . . . private schools."[79]

Consequently, choice students are more likely to remain in their school throughout the entire year. In Milwaukee, 77 percent of all choice students remained in their schools throughout the entire year compared with only

35 percent of Milwaukee's low-income public school students. Only 5 percent of elementary school choice students left their schools.[80] Fewer students leave their schools and so there's far less turmoil for the students in their lives. There are fewer adjustments to new teaching, new environments, and new expectations. There are fewer disruptions in the child's life. She can learn with more consistency.

One parent summed up the transformation in her son's life now that he attended a choice school: "I must admit there was a period of transition, culture shock you might call it. He had to get used to the discipline and the homework. . . . But Alphonso began to learn about learning, to respect the kids around him and be respected, to learn about citizenship, discipline, and doing your lessons. . . . My son has blossomed into an honor-roll student."[81]

These test scores translate into an increased long-term likelihood of success for these students. Peterson writes, "Students who score higher on standardized tests are more likely to remain in school, more likely to achieve a college degree, more likely to remain married and avoid welfare dependency, and more likely to enjoy a higher family income."[82] A University of Chicago study supports this, saying that there is "a substantial private school advantage in terms of completing high school and enrolling in college, both very important events in predicting future income and well-being. Moreover . . . the effects were most pronounced for students with achievement test scores in the bottom half of the distribution."[83]

Clearly, poor parents want a choice. The evidence has shown that they make wise choices based on significant criteria. And their children improve academically in schools of choice. The debate should be over. Give the poor choice.[84]

Such results should not surprise us, for the research has convincingly demonstrated the benefits of private, parochial, and charter schools. According to a March 2001 report commissioned by New York University, City Catholic fourth and eighth graders score higher on standardized tests than do public city students. Co-chair Joseph Viteritti said, "The study demonstrates that Catholic schools are more effective in severing the connection between race or income and academic performance."[85] According to an August 2000 study of privately funded voucher programs in New York, Dayton, and Washington, D.C., African American choice students' test scores increased 6.3 percentile points in their second year in the program.[86] A study of Pennsylvania's charter schools, which serve a higher percentage of at-risk and minority students than do the state's public schools, found that their students outscored public school students on state assessment tests by eighty-six points.[87]

The evidence therefore is in. Parents make wise choices for their children. They choose a new school based upon significant criteria. Most importantly, the new schools that they select for their children assist their children in performing significantly better on standardized testing. By getting their children into better schools, poor parents demonstrate that they make very wise decisions.

School Choice Promotes Integration

The third argument against school choice is that vouchers will create a two-tier system, with upper-class students attending good schools and poorer students attending lesser quality schools. As Kevin Smith concludes after a lengthy quantitative analysis, "Competition between public and private schools appears to result in a creaming effect."[88] Critics believe that public schools and second-rate private schools will become the "dumping grounds" for the least well off. One scholar contends: "Under the pretense of compassion for the poor, they [choice advocates] are simply proposing a privatized caste system in which the rich will continue to go to elite prep schools, and the poor, at very best, would be able to go another category of private schools, either parochial schools or very poorly funded sort of second-rate private academies."[89] Similarly, American Federation of Teachers president Sandra Feldman said that vouchers would take "money away from inner city schools so a few selected children can get vouchers to attend private schools, while the majority of equally deserving kids, who remain in the public schools, are ignored."[90] So too, Thomas Poetter and others argued, "The choices also come with dangers of re-segregating students and communities based on race and class, further exacerbating rather than addressing the problem of equity."[91] In short, critics argue that school choice will be the road to educational apartheid.[92]

School choice cannot *create* a two-tier system of education. The present system is *already* two-tiered.[93] Arthur Bestor characterizes the current system as "educational wastelands," and Jonathan Kozol describes the

disparity between rich and poor as "savage inequalities."[94] William Julius
Wilson has documented the current situation:

> In major cities such as New York, Chicago, Atlanta, Washington, D.C.,
> Philadelphia, St. Louis, and Detroit not only have public schools become over-
> whelmingly populated with minority students, but the background of both mi-
> nority and white students is primarily working or lower class. And in certain
> underclass neighborhoods in the inner city, neither children from middle-class
> families nor those from working-class families are represented in the public
> schools. The more affluent white and minority families are increasingly opting
> to send their children to parochial or private schools if they remain in the cen-
> tral city or to suburban schools if they move to the metropolitan fringe.[95]

Wilson explains the situation in Chicago in detail. In the fall of 1980, a
total of 39,500 freshmen entered public high schools; in the spring of
1984, only 18,500 graduated. Only 6,000 of those graduates could read at
a twelfth-grade level. The situation was even worse for African Americans
and Hispanics in segregated inner-city schools. In the fall of 1980, 25,500
African American and Hispanic freshmen entered high schools; in the
spring of 1984, only 9,500 graduated. Only 2,000 of those graduates could
read at a twelfth-grade level, and only 4,000 could read at a junior high
level.[96]

And things have remained the same. In the fall of 1993, over 85 percent
of the students in Chicago, Dallas, Detroit, Houston, Los Angeles, and
Washington, D.C., were of minority status.[97] Explaining the current situation in detail, Poetter and Knight-Abowitz write, "Orfield and Eaton
(1996) found that current racial segregation in some U.S. schools is at levels equal to or surpassing the levels in existence when the *Brown v. Board
of Education* decision was handed down."[98]

In other words, the problem is the worst in the major cities throughout
the United States. According to Peterson and Greene, 85 percent of the
public school students in Chicago, Dallas, Detroit, Houston, Los Angeles,
and Washington are of minority background. Only 20 percent of all white
students attend public schools in major cities.[99]

And these schools are failing the children. Peterson and Greene point
out that only 46 percent of urban students read at a "basic" level compared
with 63 percent in nonurban areas; and only 23 percent of students at ur-

ban high-poverty areas read at a "basic" level compared with 46 percent in nonurban high-poverty areas. And children's scores fall further behind as they advance through the school system. Urban high-poverty children scored 3 percent behind the New York average in third grade, 6 percent in sixth grade, and as much as 15 percent behind in high school.[100]

The present system puts poor children at a disadvantage. A choice system could empower poor children to get into better schools. School choice offers poor children "dignified equality" instead of "savage inequalities." Moreover, choice programs help many schools achieve a better racial balance.[101]

Contrast the segregation of the current public school system with private schools that are more integrated. Peterson and Greene report:

Today's private schools are less racially isolated than their public school peers. According to 1992 Department of Education data, 37 percent of private school students are in classrooms whose share of minority students is close to the national average, compared with only 18 percent of public school students. Not only are private school students more likely to be in well-integrated classrooms, they are less likely to be in extremely segregated ones (either more than 90 percent white or more than 90 percent minority). Forty-one percent of private school students are in highly segregated classrooms, as compared with 55 percent of their public school peers.[102]

Peterson and Greene go on to point out that private school students are also more likely to have positive relationships with students from other racial and ethnic groups and have more community spirit. Moreover, the students from choice programs are anything but elite. Jay Greene explains:

In Milwaukee, 76 percent of choice students were from single, female-headed households. In Cleveland, the figure was 70 percent. In Washington it was 77 percent, and in Dayton it was 76 percent. The standardized test scores of choice students before they began private school averaged below the 31st percentile in Milwaukee, below the 27th percentile in New York, below the 33rd percentile in D.C., and below the 26th percentile in Dayton. In other words, choice students were generally performing in the bottom third academically. If this is cream, then none of us needs to go on a diet.[103]

School choice programs are designed to assist poor inner-city children. The children, trapped in failing schools without any choices, are precisely the students who have been participating in school-choice programs. Peterson points this out: "Among the applicants to New York City's choice program, only 26 percent were performing at grade level in reading and 18 percent in mathematics, far below the 55 percent reported for all New York City elementary students reported by the city school system."[104] Choice programs help reduce the gap between the rich and the poor by offering integration instead of segregation.

This assistance is precisely why poor inner-city parents want school choice. Terry Moe conducted a nationwide survey in which he found that 79 percent of inner-city poor parents favored a voucher plan and that 61 percent of the inner-city poor "strongly" favored vouchers.[105]

The benefits of choice expand beyond education. A system of school choice can help revitalize urban areas. Paul Peterson and Jay Greene explain:

> Speaking to a Pittsburgh conference on urban renewal last July, Milwaukee's visionary mayor, John Norquist, argued that if school choice becomes a reality, "public schools will respond to private-sector competition with an aggressive effort to maintain their clientele, just as United and American Airlines did." Empowered to choose among a variety of schools, young parents with children entering school will forgo the expensive move to the suburbs and pick instead a local school suited to their needs. Other families, offered better schools in the cities, will give up their suburban homes to live closer to their jobs. Businesses will open schools so their employees can bring their children with them on their daily commute. The central-city economy will pick up, property values will rise, racial integration will increase, and central-city test scores will rise.[106]

A school-choice program can even help those students who choose to remain in the public schools. Caroline Hoxby found an 8 percent improvement in the test scores of the students who remained in public schools in areas where some type of school choice had been implemented. And where just public schools competed for the same students, Hoxby still found a 3 percentile overall improvement in test scores.[107] School choice is good for the students who pick a school of choice and it's good for those who choose to remain in their local public school. School choice works.

School Choice Opens the Doors of Good Schools to the Poor

Fourth, critics argue that an insufficient voucher might deny a poor child access to a private or parochial school, since poor parents would be incapable of paying the difference between tuition costs and the voucher amount. Furthermore, critics argue that an insufficient voucher would empower only large groups of parents to start a new school.

This is more of an argument for getting a school-choice program right than it is an argument against choice. A poor parent should receive an amount of money equal to the average state cost per student, or else the poor will be incapable of sending their children to the best schools, and parents will be incapable of starting new schools. John Coons, one of the nation's foremost school-choice advocates, opposed California's Proposition 174, a school-choice ballot initiative in November 1993, because the scholarship was worth only $2,600: "The mass of low-income children would have no schools in which to spend their scholarships. As a similar experiment in Milwaukee demonstrates, $2,600 does not start many new schools in the city."[108]

The Milwaukee plan addresses the "creaming" criticism well, by stipulating that any school that chooses to receive voucher students cannot charge more than the amount of the voucher. This is a positive step, since a voucher plan should not allow parents to supplement the voucher with their own contribution, as this would contribute to further segregation and inhibit a poor child's ability to gain access to the best schools, as David Osborne explains:

Let's say a voucher was worth five thousand dollars a child. Some affluent people would add ten thousand dollars and send their kids to the fanciest private school. Some upper-middle class people would add five thousand dollars and send their kid to the ten-thousand-dollar school. The working class and the poor would go to five-thousand-dollar schools—you'd lose the mixing by social class.[109]

While school choice offers justice for all children, it markedly improves the situation for poor and minority children by granting them fair access to the best schools. Making this point clearly, one-time critic of school choice Diane Ravitch wrote:

> It is not just to compel poor children to attend bad schools. It is not just to prohibit poor families from sending their children to the school of their choice, even if that school has a religious affiliation. It is not just to deny free schooling to poor families with strong religious convictions, any more than it would be just to prohibit the use of federal scholarships in non-public universities like Notre Dame, Marymount, or Yeshiva.[110]

That the poor are empowered through greater educational opportunities may be the strongest argument in favor of school choice. Good schools may ameliorate social problems within poor districts by alleviating some of the causes of unrest. Edward Marciniak argues that a school choice plan will help the poor combat significant youth problems: poverty, unemployment, dropping out of school, juvenile crime, alcohol and drug abuse, and early parenthood. Charles Glenn summarizes the critical role of school choice for the poor in a speech entitled "Choice and the Purposes of Schooling":

> The people whom this will help the most are those who sometimes suffer the greatest estrangement from, and disadvantage in, the larger society. The children of minorities are, in general, most poorly served by the schools to which they are involuntarily assigned, and they are less able to purchase private education or to move to areas with better schools.[111]

CONCLUSION

Vast quantities of research now have clearly demonstrated that school choice aids children in low-income families. In August 2000, Jay Greene released results of a study he conducted of a private scholarship program in Charlotte, North Carolina, entitled "The Effect of School Choice: An Evaluation of the Charlotte Children's Scholarship Fund." Greene found that the scholarship program improved student's test scores, had high rates of parental satisfaction, provided schools with safe environments, reduced racial conflicts, cost less than traditional public schools, offered smaller class size, and helped low-income parents.[112] Similarly, John Witte, the official evaluator of Milwaukee's school choice program, concluded in his recent evaluation, *The Market Approach to Education: An Analysis of America's First Voucher Program*, that school choice is a "useful tool to aid low-income parents."[113] In addition, a report released by the private scholarship group Children First America shows that academic performance and parental involvement increase while neither money nor talented students are drained from the public schools.[114]

Advocates of school choice should thus advance proposals that aid poor children. Schools in districts that have choice, magnet schools, and charter schools have clearly demonstrated that multiple school choices' have helped poor students.[115] The poor want school choice because it will provide them with the options they find lacking in the present system. Poor children will have access to better schools, poor parents will experience a sense of empowerment, and poor parents will increasingly participate in a more just educational system. More poor students should get school choice.

Typifying student achievement in choice programs, Pamela Ballard described the transformation of her child: "Hope Academy was my last hope. I took my third-grade child, who had been in several Cleveland schools and was labeled a 'problem child.' I now have a successful child. Where there were Ds and Cs, there are now As and Bs."[116]

Newark Councilman Cory Booker tells the story of Ms. Cooper, whose daughter was shot but lived. Ms. Cooper was determined to stay in Newark and transform her city instead of leaving. With passion in her eyes, she asked Mr. Booker, "Cory, who will fight with me?"[117]

NOTES

1. Obviously, our entire educational system is broken, and the poor are hit the worst because they have no way to get out. Dary Ann Olsen and Matthew J. Brouillette explain the state of today's public educational system: "America's education system is failing. It is failing to provide parents with choices in education services and, consequently, failing to provide children with the educations they deserve. Since 1970 disturbing trends in American education have been well documented: per pupil expenditures have doubled, class sizes have shrunk, and teachers salaries have grown; yet, despite those infusions of spending and the adoption of countless

other reforms, student achievement has stagnated and even declined." "Reclaiming Our Schools: Increasing Parental Control of Education through the Universal Education Credit," *Policy Analysis* no. 388 (December 6, 2000): 12.

2. Joseph Viteritti, *Choosing Equality: School Choice, the Constitution, and Civil Society* (Washington, D.C.: Brookings Institution Press, 1999), 197.

3. Cory Booker, "School Choice and Government Reform: Pillars of an Urban Renaissance," *Manhattan Institute Civic Bulletin*, no. 25 (February 2001): 5, 8.

4. Quoted in Carnegie Foundation (1992), 3, quoted in Frank Margonis and Laurence Parker, "Choice: The Route to Community Control?" *Theory and Practice* 38, no. 4 (Autumn 1999): 203–208.

5. Black Alliance for Educational Options, *The Continuing Struggle against Unequal Educational Opportunity* (August 24, 2000).

6. Quoted in Paul Peterson and Jay Greene, "Race Relations and Central City Schools: It's Time for an Experiment with Vouchers," *Brookings Review* 16, no. 2 (Spring 1998): 33–37.

7. Peterson and Greene, "Race Relations," 33–37.

8. Viteritti, *Choosing Equality*, 202.

9. *The Condition of Education 2000*, Section 4, 61, quoted in Black Alliance for Educational Options, *The Continuing Struggle*.

10. David Kirkpatrick, *Choice in Schooling: A Case for Tuition Vouchers* (Chicago: Loyola University Press, 1991), 105; see also "Gallup/Phi Delta Kappa Poll of the Public's Attitudes toward the Public Schools," *Phi Delta Kappan* (September 1986). These Gallup Poll results compare with the 63 percent of all Californians who wanted school choice in the 1993 Proposition 174 pre-vote 011; see Larry Armstrong, "California May Choose School Choice," *Business Week* (October 18, 1993): 38.

11. A report by National Public Radio's "All Things Considered," November 7, 1990. See also William Julius Wilson, *The Truly Disadvantaged: The Inner City, the Underclass, and Public Policy* (Chicago: University of Chicago Press, 1987), 63.

12. Jonathan Sandy, "Evaluating the Public Support for Educational Vouchers: A Case Study," *Economics of Education Review* (1992): 249–56. This was supported by a 1989 Gallup poll in which school choice was favored by 60 percent of interviewees overall, but by 6 percent of minorities; see *Phi Delta Kappa* (September 1989).

13. Peterson and Greene, "Race Relations," 33–37.

14. Peterson and Greene, "Race Relations," 33–37.

15. Terry Moe, address before the "Rethinking School Governance" Conference, sponsored by the Program on Education Policy and Governance, Kennedy

School of Government, Harvard University (June 1997), quoted in Paul Peterson, "School Choice: A Report Card," *Virginia Journal of Social Policy and the Law* 6, no. 1 (Fall 1998): 47–80.

16. Sandy Theis, "Most Ohioans Back School Voucher Plan, Survey Finds," *Cincinnati Enquirer*, October 19, 1997: B-1.

17. A 1997 Joint Center for Political and Economic Studies Poll, quoted in Margonis and Parker, "Choice: The Route to Community Control?" 203–208.

18. Mark Silva, "Poll: Many Support Funding Private Schools," *Miami Herald* (August 20, 1998): B-5.

19. David Bositis, "1999 National Opinion Poll, Education," *Joint Center for Political and Economic Studies* (1999).

20. Brian Gill et al., *Rhetoric versus Reality* (New York: Rand Education, 2001), 143.

21. *Florida Times-Union* (Jacksonville, Fla.), May 25, 1999, B-3.

22. *Des Moines Register*, May 11, 1999.

23. Dave DeSchryver, "School Choice Today," *Center for Education Reform* (October 1999).

24. "Giving Choice a Chance: Cleveland and the Future of School Reform," *Buckeye Institute for Public Policy Solutions* (September 1998): 17.

25. Alan Borsuk and Joe Williams, "Choice, Voice, Basics and Values: That's What People Demand in Their Schools, According to Poll," *Milwaukee Journal Sentinel*, October 17, 1999: 1.

26. "Education Reform: Thinking Too Small," *Atlantic Journal-Constitution*, August 2, 1999: 8-A. Many of the citations in this paragraph come from *School Choice Facts* compiled by the Institute for Justice and printed by the Center for Education Reform.

27. McDonald, "Reclaim the 'V' Word!" 72–73.

28. Black Alliance for Educational Options, *The Continuing Struggle*. Similarly, the board members of the Milwaukee public school board signed a fundraising letter on September 10, 1998, supporting PAVE (Partners Advancing Values in Education), a private scholarship foundation for poor children in Milwaukee, writing: "Parents have the rights and responsibility to determine the course of their children's education. . . . As members of the Board of MPS, our task is to support them in carrying out that responsibility. . . . MPS can provide quality education for all our children . . . but until we make it happen, we ask that you contribute to PAVE's scholarship fund, both for the sake of the thousands of children immediately at risk and for the sake of public education reforms in Milwaukee," quoted in Nina Rees, "Public School Benefits of Private School Vouchers," *Policy Review* no. 93 (January/February 1999): 16–19.

29. Margonis and Parker, "Choice: The Route to Community Control?" 203–8.

30. William Howell and Paul Peterson, *The Education Gap: Vouchers and Urban Schools* (Washington, D.C.: Brookings Institution Press, 2002), 187.

31. Viteritti, *Choosing Equality*, 203.

32. Peterson and Greene, "Race Relations," 33–37.

33. Gill et al., *Rhetoric versus Reality*, 144.

34. Gill et al., *Rhetoric versus Reality*, 146.

35. The program was established in 1990; see Wisconsin Statute 119.23 (1990). The Wisconsin State Supreme Court upheld the constitutionality of the program in *Davis v. Grover*, 480 N.W2d 460 (Wis. 1992). In 1995, the Wisconsin legislature decided to extend the legislation to include religious schools. The Milwaukee Parental Choice Program provided tuition assistance, or a scholarship worth $3,200 in the 1994–95 school year, to children from low-income families to attend nonsectarian private schools. To qualify, a family may not earn more than five times the poverty line; 60 percent of the families in the program earn less than $10,000 per year. In 1994, 95,830 students participated. Over 90 percent of the students are African American or Hispanic. See also "School Reform in the United States: State by State Summary," *Center for Education Reform* (Winter 1995): 18; see also Allyson Tucker and William Lauber, *School Choice: What's Happening in the States* (Washington, D.C.: Heritage Foundation, 1994), 53–55.

36. Daniel McGroarty, "Private Choice, Public Dumping," *National Review* (November 1, 1993): 24.

37. Cheryl Lange and James E. Ysseldyke, "How School Choice Affects Students with Special Needs," *Educational Leadership* (November 1994): 84. See also Rachel Scheier, "Teen Mothers Get an Education: New York City Program Targets 'Babies Having Babies,' and Tries to Keep Them in School," *Christian Science Monitor* (January 23, 1995): 9–11.

38. *School Reform in the United States: State by State Summary, Winter, 1995* (Washington, D.C.: Center for Education Reform, 1995).

39. *The Condition of Education 2000*, Section 4, 72, quoted in the Black Alliance for Educational Options, *The Continuing Struggle*.

40. Jay Greene, "The Surprising Consensus on School Choice," *Public Interest*, no. 144 (Summer 2001): 9–35.

41. Margaret Hadderman, "Educational Vouchers," *ERIC Digest* 137 (May 2000): 2.

42. Howell and Peterson, *The Education Gap*, 186.

43. Peterson, "School Choice: A Report Card," 47–80.

44. Booker, "School Choice and Government Reform," 7.

45. Thomas Fowler-Finn, "Why Have They Chosen Another School System?" *Educational Leadership* (December 1993/January 1994): 61. For surveys that

find similar results, see Arizona Department of Education, "Results of the Non-Resident Student Enrollment Survey," *Research and Development* (December 13, 1989); *The Carnegie Foundation for the Advancement of Teaching: Survey of Chief State School Officers* (1992), appendix C; Minnesota House of Representatives, "Open Enrollment Study: Study and District Participation, 1989–90, Working Paper #1," (February 1990), 2; Michael Rubinstein et al., "Minnesota's Open Enrollment Option," (Washington, D.C.: Policy Studies Associates and the U.S. Department of Education, 1992): 13, 14; and David Bechtel, "Open Enrollment: Preliminary Report for the 1989–90 and 1990–91 School Years," Iowa State Department of Education, 15.

46. Abigail Thernstrom, *School Choice in Massachusetts* 40 (1991) (quoting Nicholas Lemann, "A False Panacea," *Atlantic* January 1991: 104), quoted in Peterson, "School Choice: A Report Card," 47–80.

47. Carnegie Foundation for the Advancement of Teaching, *School Choice: A Special Report* 13 (1992), quoted in Peterson, "School Choice: A Report Card," 47–80.

48. Thomas Poetter and Kathleen Knight-Abowitz, "Possibilities and Problems of School Choice," *Kappa Delta Pi Record* 37, no. 2 (Winter 2001): 58–62.

49. Katie Cannon, *Black Womanist Ethics* (Atlanta: Scholars Press, 1988).

50. Stephanie Counts and Beverly Lavergneau, "Choice as a Vehicle for Urban Educational Change in the 1990s," *Clearing House* 66 (November/December 1992): 80.

51. Peterson, "School Choice: A Report Card," 47–80.

52. Booker, "School Choice and Government Reform," 8.

53. Joe Nathen and James Ysseldyke, "What Minnesota Has Learned about School Choice," *Phi Delta Kappan* (May 1994): 685.

54. Seymour Fliegel and James Macguire, *Miracle in East Harlem: The Fight for Choice in Public Education* (New York: Times Books, 1993), 230. See also Rees, "Public School Benefits of Private School Vouchers," 16–19.

55. Fliegel and Macguire, *Miracle in East Harlem*. For more on the good choices that poor parents make, see John McKnight, "Why 'Servanthood' Is Bad," *The Other Side* (January/February 1989); Charles Glenn, "Do Parents Get the Schools They Want?" *Equity and Choice* 9 (Fall 1992): 47–49; Charles Glenn, "The Cambridge-Controlled Choice Plan," *Urban Review* 20 (Summer 1988): 75–94; Charles Glenn, "The New Common School," *Phi Delta Kappan* 69 (December 1987): 290–94; Charles Glenn, "Letting Poor Parents Act Responsibly," *Equity and Choice* 3 (Spring 1987): 52–54; Charles Glenn et al., "Parent Information for School Choice: The Case of Massachusetts," *Massachusetts Report* no. 19; Charles Glenn, "Rich Learning for All Our Children," *Phi Delta Kappan* 68 (October 1986): 133–34; Charles Glenn, "New Challenges: A Civil Rights

Agenda for the Public Schools," *Phi Delta Kappan* 67 (May 1986): 653–56; and Reginald Clark, *Family Life and School Achievement: Why Poor Black Children Succeed or Fail* (Chicago: University of Chicago Press, 1983).

In Chicago, there are dozens of private schools that are predominantly or wholly made up of poor African Americans; see Joe Nathen, "The Rhetoric and the Reality of Expanding Educational Choices," *Phi Delta Kappan* (March 1985): 477. In Oakland, three-fifths of all children in Catholic schools are African Americans; see Stuart Seers, "The Catholic Schools' Black Students," *This World* (23 December 1990): 8; a 1981 study found that Catholic schools and public schools had proportionately equal numbers of poor minority students, with poor African Americans comprising almost one-quarter of all Catholic school students; see Andrew Greeley's 1981 poll, cited in Kirkpatrick, *Choice in Schooling*, 125.

56. For an excellent overview, see J. Henig and S. Sugarman, "The Nature and Extent of School Choice," in *School Choice and Social Controversy: Politics, Policy and Law*, edited by S. D. Sugarman and F. R. Kemerer, 13–35 (Washington, D.C.: Brookings Institution Press, 1999), 13–35. There is also the excellent ABCS (A Brighter Choice Scholarships) program for poor students in the failing school of Giffen Memorial Elementary School in Albany, New York. See Rees, "Public School Benefits of Private School Vouchers," 16–19.

57. Adam Meyerson, "A Model of Cultural Leadership: The Achievements of Privately Funded Vouchers," *Policy Review* no. 93 (January/February 1999): 20–24.

58. Meyerson, "A Model of Cultural Leadership," 20–24. Meyerson goes on to describe the specific programs of J. Patrick Rooney in Indianapolis where the Golden Rule Program has spent $5.7 million on vouchers since 1991; James Leininger in San Antonio began a private voucher program that mushroomed into a national program, which, when he was joined by the Walton Family Foundation, emerged into the CEO America Program and has invested more than $61 million in today' poor children; Michael Joyce, working through the Bradley Foundation, established the PAVE (Partners Advancing Values in Education) Program that has helped more then 15,000 low-income children in Milwaukee with over $20 million in assistance; and Ted Forstmann and John Walton who established the Children's Scholarship Fund, which has pledged more than $100 million of assistance to voucher programs. Summing up the benefit of all the programs, Ted Forstmann said, "The worst that can happen is we help 35,000 kids."

59. For more on the New York program, see P. Peterson, D. Myers, and W. Howell, "An Evaluation of the New York City School Choice Scholarships Program: The First Year," *Mathematica Policy Research and Program on Education Policy and Governance*, Harvard University (1998).

60. Peterson, "Vouchers and Test Scores," 10–15.

61. Jay Greene, "The Surprising Consensus on School Choice," *Public Interest* no. 144 (Summer 2001): 19–35. For a complete text of the study's results see http://data.fas.harvard.edu/pepg.

62. Peterson, "Vouchers and Test Scores," 10–15.

63. Greene, "The Surprising Consensus on School Choice," 19–35.

64. For the full report, see http://data.fas.harvard.edu/pepg.

65. Peterson, "School Choice: A Report Card," 47–80. See R. Kenneth Godwin et al., "Comparing Public Choice and Private Voucher Programs in San Antonio," in *Learning from School Choice*, edited by Paul Peterson and Bryan Hassel, 275 (Washington, D.C.: Brookings Institution Press, 1998).

66. Peterson, "Vouchers and Test Scores," 10–15.

67. Greene, "The Surprising Consensus on School Choice," 19–35.

68. Greene, "The Surprising Consensus on School Choice," 19–35.

69. Greene, "The Surprising Consensus on School Choice," 19–35.

70. Greene calls such choice "The Educational Freedom Index," which is made up of five variables: charter schools, subsidized private school choice, home school choice, district choice by changing residence, and district choice without residency change. He found that school choice correlated directly with student SAP and NAEP scores. For the full report, see www.manhattan-institute.org.

71. Greene, "The Surprising Consensus on School Choice," 19–35. Patrick McEwan sums up the findings of all of the different studies of student success in the Milwaukee program: "The preponderance of evidence from evaluations of the Milwaukee plan suggest that attending a choice school may have produced small annual gains in mathematics scores among a group of low-income children in the elementary or middle school grades. However, it did not improve readings scores." Patrick McEwan, "The Potential Impact of Large-Scale Voucher Programs," *Review of Educational Research*, no. 2 (Summer 2000): 103–149.

72. See also Peterson, "Vouchers and Test Scores," 10–15.

73. Peterson and Greene, "Race Relations and Central City Schools," 3307.

74. 1999–2000 Joint Legislative Audit Committee, "An Evaluation: Milwaukee Parental Choice Program" (February 2000), quoted in "School Choice Facts," *Center for Education Reform.*

75. Similarly, Patrick McEwan points out that Milwaukee's and Cleveland's parents participating in the choice programs were much more involved in their children's education: "The same studies suggest that choice parents were more involved in their children's education (as proxied, for example, by parental involvement in school activities). A similar pattern was found in the Cleveland voucher program." Patrick McEwan, "The Potential Impact of Large-Scale Voucher Programs," 103–49.

76. Peterson, "Vouchers and Test Scores," 10–15.

77. McEwan, "The Potential Impact of Large-Scale Voucher Programs," 103–49.

78. Greene, "The Surprising Consensus on School Choice," 19–35. For more on the cost of private education, see also C. M. Hoxby, "What Do America's 'Traditional' Forms of School Choice Teach Us about School Choice Reforms?" *Federal Reserve Bank of New York Economic Policy Review* 4, no. 1: 47–59; J. S. Coleman and T. Hoffer, *Public and Private High Schools: The Impact of Communities* (New York: Basic Books, 1987).

79. Peterson, "School Choice: A Report Card," 47–80. See Jacques Steinberg, "Students Chosen for Grants to Attend Private Schools," *New York Times*, May 13, 1997: B-3; Improving Educational Opportunities for Low-Income Children: Hearings before the Senate Committee on Labor and Human Resources, 105th Congress (1997).

80. Peterson, "School Choice: A Report Card," 47–80. See Paul Peterson, "A Critique of the Witte Evaluation of Milwaukee's School Choice Program," Harvard University Center for American Political Studies, Occasional Paper 95-2, 1995, 29–36. See also Paul Peterson, "The Milwaukee School Choice Plan: Ten Comments on the Witte Reply," Harvard University, Center for American Political Studies, Occasional Paper 95-3, 1995.

81. Barbara Lewis, "Improving Educational Opportunities for Low-Income Children," prepared remarks for testimony before the U.S. Senate Committee on Labor and Human Resources (July 29, 1997), quoted in Peterson, "School Choice: A Report Card," 47–80.

82. Peterson, "Vouchers and Test Scores," 10–15.

83. Peterson, "Vouchers and Test Scores," 10–15.

84. Since private school students are more likely to attend and graduate from college, we can project with confidence that poor children will be more likely to go to and graduate from college if they have the opportunity to attend a school of choice. Peterson reports, "The probability of graduating from college rises from eleven to twenty-seven percent if such a student attends a Catholic high school." "School Choice: A Report Card," 47–80.

85. Garrett, "Progress on School Choice in the States," *Heritage Foundation Backgrounder* (May 16, 2001): 8, quote taken from press release, "Catholic Schools Outperform Public Schools on State English and Math Exams: New Study Says," *New York University* (March 22, 2001).

86. Garrett, "Progress on School Choice in the States," 8, quote taken from Paul Peterson et al., "Test Score Effects of School Vouchers in Dayton, Ohio, New York City, and Washington D.C.: Evidence from Randomized Field Trials," *Harvard University* (August 2000).

87. Garrett, "Progress on School Choice in the States," 8, quote from Tamara Henry, "Scores up for Charter Schools," *USA Today*, March 28, 2001. For entire study, see Gary Miron and Christopher Nelson, *Autonomy in Exchange for Accountability: An Initial Study of Pennsylvania Charter Schools* (Western Michigan University, October 2000).

88. Kevin Smith, "Policy, Markets, and Bureaucracy: Reexamining School Choice," *The Journal of Politics* 56 (May 1994): 489.

89. Jonathan Kozol and Vicki Kemper, "Rebuilding the Schoolhouse: Author Jonathan Kozol Talks about Education Reform. Choice and Chelsea's School," *Common Cause Magazine* (Spring 1993): 26.

90. Sandra Feldman, "Let's Tell the Truth," *New York Times*, November 2, 1997: 7, quoted in Peterson, "School Choice: A Report Card," 47–80.

91. Poetter and Knight-Abowitz, "Possibilities and Problems of School Choice," 58–62.

92. See David Thornburg, "School Choice: Will It Save or 'Gut' Schools?" *Electronic Learning* (March 1993): 16; M. Allen, "Saying No to School Choice," *Black Enterprise* (July 1991): 16.

93. Similarly, Dan Goldhaber of the Urban Institute has written, "But it is also true that the public school system is relatively segregated today and has become more so as middle-class families have fled inner cities." Goldhaber, "School Choice: Do We Know Enough?" *Educational Researcher* 29 (2000).

94. Arthur Bestor, *Educational Wastelands: The Retreat from Learning in Our Public Schools* (Urbana: University of Illinois Press, 1988); Jonathan Kozol, *Savage Inequalities* (New York: Crown, 1991). See also M. Collison, "Saying Yes to School Choice," *Black Enterprise* (July 1991): 16.

95. Wilson, *The Truly Disadvantaged*, 57, 58.

96. Wilson, *The Truly Disadvantaged*, 58.

97. Peterson, "School Choice: A Report Card," 47–80.

98. Poetter and Knight-Abowitz, "Possibilities and Problems of School Choice," 58–62.

99. Peterson and Greene, "Race Relations," 33–37.

100. Peterson and Greene, "Race Relations," 33–37. And public school teachers know the state of these schools and, consequently, are sending their own children to private schools. In this same article, Peterson and Greene point out that 40 percent of Cleveland public school teachers send their children to private schools compared with 25 percent of the entire population; similarly, the numbers in Milwaukee are 33 percent compared with 23 percent of the entire population, and in Boston, where 45 percent of public school teachers send their children to private school compared with 29 percent of the entire population.

101. Beatriz Clewell and Myra Joy, *Choice in Montclair, New Jersey* (Princeton, N.J.: Educational Testing Service, 1990), 9.

102. Peterson and Greene, "Race Relations," 33–37.

103. Greene, "The Surprising Consensus on School Choice," 19–35. Significantly, Greene goes on to cite different studies, noting that as a direct result of competition, students who remain in traditional public schools see an increase in their test scores because the schools are forced to compete to keep their students. If the schools do not perform better, parents may well pull their children from those schools. So, school choice even helps those students who remain in the traditional public school.

104. Paul Peterson et al., "Initial Finds from the Evaluation of the New York School Choice Scholarships Program," (1997), quoted in Peterson, "School Choice: A Report Card," 47–80.

105. Peterson and Greene, "Race Relations," 33–37.

106. Peterson and Greene, "Race Relations," 33–37.

107. Hoxby's findings are quoted in Rees, "Public School Benefits of Private School Vouchers," 16–19.

108. John Coons, "Is Choice Still a Choice?" *First Things* (August/September 1994): 9. See also Coons and Sugarman, *Scholarships for Children* (Berkeley: University of California, 1992), 54–57.

109. David Osborne, cited in "Pro-Choice: A Progressive Friend of Bill's Argues for Competition within the Public School System," *Mother Jones* (September/October 1993): 53.

110. Diane Ravitch, "Somebody's Children," *The Brookings Review* (Fall 1994).

111. Speech given on March 7, 1990, to the Office of Educational Research and Improvement of the U.S. Department of Education.

112. Garrett, "Progress on School Choice in the States," 9. See Jay P. Greene, "The Effect of School Choice: An Evaluation of the Charlotte Children's Scholarship Fund," *The Manhattan Institute Civic Report*, no. 12 (August 2000).

113. Garrett, "Progress on School Choice in the States," 2, quote from Williams, "Ex-Milwaukee Evaluator Endorses School Choice," *Milwaukee Sentinel Journal*, January 9, 2000, 1.

114. Garrett, "Progress on School Choice in the States," 10. See Robert Aguirre, "The Power to Choose: Horizon Scholarship Program Second Annual Report," *Children First America* (Fall 2000).

115. Edward Marciniak, "Educational Choice: A Catalyst for School Reform," *City Club of Chicago* (August 1989): 1–31. For an excellent discussion of how school choice will concretely assist the poor, see Coons and Sugarman, *Education by Choice*, 109–30.

116. Peterson and Greene, "Race Relations," 33–37.

117. Booker, "School Choice and Government Reform," 9, 10.

Conclusion

For over two centuries, the U.S. educational system has labored under a government monopoly. School choice decentralizes that monopoly and provides genuine reform in education through pluralistic freedom. A system of school choice empowers the national, state, and local governments to act justly by equally protecting diverse schools and by providing fair access to all parents regardless of financial status or religious preference.

The push for choice has burgeoned into a nationwide movement. In Milwaukee and Cleveland, poor children can opt out of their failing schools and their parents can choose a school that will empower their children. Nationwide, thousands of low-income students are now able to choose a new school through dozens of privately sponsored voucher programs; significant grassroots coalitions are working for choice in most states; charter schools are booming; legislation continues to get introduced; and poll after poll show that Americans favor school choice.[1] Increasingly, America is realizing what most Western European countries already know: school choice works.

This momentum for choice makes sense. School choice grants teachers more latitude to innovate by freeing them from a stifling bureaucracy; it enables parents who prefer private or parochial schools to choose without discrimination; and it promotes the growth of new schools to challenge those already in existence.

These positive developments promote a better education for America's children. A system of school choice safeguards religious liberty, promotes social equity, and offers distributive justice to all of America's children. In so doing, it will help promote justice for all Americans. Including poor

Americans—for above all else, school choice empowers poor parents by offering them fair access to their state's finest schools. No longer condemned to failing schools, America's poor children in Milwaukee and Cleveland may now attend excellent schools in their cities. And with that excellence comes hope. Hope for a better future, hope for a way out, hope of becoming a productive member of society. For these children, hope replaces despair.

The issue surrounding justice is one of empowerment for the poor. School choice will help poor families, if they receive sufficient funds to send their children to good schools, and if they have enough support from parent organizations.[2] A school-choice plan will not guarantee a student's success, but it will empower poor parents by giving their children an opportunity. According to the sponsor of the Milwaukee program, Assemblywoman Polly Williams:

> I am one of those people who is supposed to be very stupid because I am black; I live in the inner city, I am poor, and I raised my children in a single-parent home. Well, those are lies. The only thing different about us is that we are deprived of resources and access. When you empower parents like me, there is a major difference. We become responsible for our own lives. We want to be empowered, and that is what the choice program has done.[3]

Many of us long for the day when the poor will be empowered. Many African American leaders see the issue of educational choice as a new civil rights issue. Howard Fuller, former superintendent of the Milwaukee public schools says:

> Should low-income, mostly African American, parents receive vouchers that will empower them to make educational choices that a majority of Americans both cherish and take for granted? . . . [A]ny answer but "yes" is unacceptable. . . . [There is an] urgent need to expand the educational power of low-income, African American parents.[4]

Diane Ravitch summed up the transformation many of us hope for—that many of us believe can and will happen under a system of school choice—that the poor would be "empowered consumers rather than hapless clients ignored by an unresponsive bureaucracy."[5]

School choice is good for America's parents and for America's children. The time has come to dismantle the public school monopoly and to implement a system of school choice. Out of the resulting educational pluralism, a genuine national unity might emerge, one founded on a vigorous debate among contrasting creeds, rather than a false consensus that cries, "peace, peace" when there is no peace.

That peace is certainly lacking for today's poor children. Advocates of justice can no longer sit by and allow another generation of poor children to go through the system, condemning them to their local schools. Justice requires that parents be empowered with the tools to control their children's learning. Justice mandates that the state provide equal educational opportunities to all children. And justice suggests that all parents should have the opportunity to send their child to a school of their choice, including poor parents. School choice can and is empowering the poor. It should move beyond the successes in Milwaukee and Cleveland and become a nationwide system. Justice requires it and the poor desire it. Will we listen to the dictates of justice and the cries of the poor?

· NOTES

1. In 2001, twelve states introduced some type of school choice legislation. See "Breaking Up a Monopoly," *Christianity Today* (August 5, 2002): 28, 29.

2. If school choice is implemented, the poor will have the opportunity to get out of their failing schools. As Patrick McEwan puts it, "Low-income families that were constrained to attend low-quality public schools may be among the first to exit." "The Potential Impact of Large-Scale Voucher Programs," *Review of Educational Research*, no. 2 (Summer 2000): 103–49.

3. Polly Williams, "School Choice Promotes Educational Excellence in the African American Community," *Voices on Choice: The Education Reform Debate* (San Francisco: Pacific Research Institute for Public Policy, 1992), 4–5; see Polly Williams, "Choice Debate Is about Who Controls Education," *National Minority Politics* (January 1994): 7; and "Polly's Plan: New Wisconsin Plan Will Allow Poor Children to Attend Private Schools," *Economist* 316 (August 1990): 21, 22.

4. Howard Fuller quoted in Brian Gill et al., *Rhetoric versus Reality: What We Know and What We Need to Know about Vouchers and Charter Schools* (New York: Rand Education, 2001), 41.

Select Bibliography

"Adult Literacy." *National Center for Education Statistics*. 2001 at http://nces.ed
.gov/fastfacts/display.asp?id=69.

Allen, Jeanne. "Monthly Letter to Friends of the Center for Education Reform,
No. 14." Center for Education Reform (n.d.).

——. *Nine Lies about School Choice*. Washington, D.C.: Center for Education
Reform, 1993.

——. *The School Reform Handbook: How to Improve Your Schools*. Washington, D.C.: Center for Education Reform, 1995.

Ambler, John. "Who Benefits from Educational Choice? Some Evidence from
Europe." *Journal of Policy Analysis and Management* 13 (1994).

American Council of Trustees and Alumni. "The American Education Diet: Can
U.S. Students Survive on Junk Food?" *Center for Education Reform* (2001) at
www.edreform.com/pubs/junkfood.htm.

Armstrong, Larry. "California May Choose School Choice." *Business Week*
(October 18, 1993).

Arons, Stephen. *Compelling Belief: The Culture of American Schooling*. New
York: McGraw-Hill, 1983.

——. "The Myth of Value-Neutral Schools." *Education Week* (November 7, 1984).

——. "Out of the Fire and into the Frying Pan." *First Things* (January 1991).

"Back-to-School Bulletin #1." *Center for Education Reform*. August 28, 2001 at
www.edreform.com/update/2001/010828.html.

Baer, Richard. *Democracy and the Renewal of Public Education*. Grand Rapids,
Mich.: Eerdmans, 1987.

——. "'Strict Neutrality' and Our Monopoly System." *School Choice: What Is
Constitutional?* Grand Rapids, Mich.: Baker Books, 1993.

Barber, Benjamin. *An Aristocracy of Everyone*. New York: Oxford University, 1992.

——. *Strong Democracy: Participatory Politics for a New Age*. Berkeley: University of California Press, 1984.

Barone, Michael. "School Choice: Its Time Has Come." *US News & World Report* (October 18, 1993).

Bastian, Ann. "Which Choice? Whose Choice?" *Clearing House* 66 (November/December 1992).

Bates, Stephen. *Battleground: One Mother's Crusade, the Religious Right, and the Struggles for Control of Our Classrooms.* New York: Poseidon Press, 1993.

Becker, H. J., and C. W. Sterling. "Equity in School Computer Use: National Data and Neglected Considerations." *Journal of Educational Computing Research* 3 (1998).

Belluck, Pam. "Learning Gap Tied to Time in the System: As School Stay Grows, Scores on Tests Worsen." *New York Times*, January 5, 1997.

Bennett, William. *American Education: Making It Work.* Washington, D.C.: U.S. Government Printing Office, 1988.

———. *The Book of Virtues: A Treasury of Great Moral Stories.* New York: Simon & Schuster, 1993.

———. "Golden State Opportunity." *National Review* (November 1, 1993).

———. *James Madison Elementary School: A Curriculum for American Students* (Washington, D.C.: Department of Education, 1988).

Bierlein, Louann, and Lori Mulholland. "The Promise of Charter Schools." *Educational Leadership* (September 1994).

Biskupic, Joan. "Quips, Hypotheses Punctuate Court Arguments in Two Religion Cases." *Washington Post*, February 25, 1993.

Black Alliance for Educational Options. *The Continuing Struggle against Unequal Educational Opportunity* (August 24, 2000).

Blank, Rolf, and Douglas Archbald. "Magnet Schools and Issues of Education Quality." *Clearing House* 66 (November/December 1992).

Boaz, David. "Learning Opportunities." *National Review* (September 12, 1994).

Bolick, Clint. *Changing Course: Civil Rights at the Crossroads.* New Brunswick, N.J.: Transaction, 1988.

Booker, Cory. "School Choice and Government Reform: Pillars of an Urban Renaissance." *Manhattan Institute Civic Bulletin* 25 (February 2001).

Bositis, David. "1999 National Opinion Poll, Education." *Joint Center for Political and Economic Studies* (1999).

Boyer, P. L. *High School: A Report on Secondary Education in America.* New York: Harper & Row, 1984.

Bracey, Gerald. "The Ninth Bracey Report on the Condition of Public Education." *Phi Delta Kappan* 81 (October 1999).

———. "Public and Private Schools Compared." *Phi Delta Kappan* 81 (April 2000).

Brimelow, Peter, and Leslie Spencer. "The National Extortion Association?" *Forbes* (7 June 1993).

"Bringing Racial Integration to the Suburbs." *School Administrator* (May 1993).

Brouillette, Matthew J. "Unused Capacity in Privately Funded Michigan Schools: Survey of Excess School Capacity to Help Ease Overcrowded Classrooms and Accommodate School Choice." *Mackinac Center for Public Policy* (March 1999).

Brouillette, Matthew, and Jeffrey Williams. "The Impact of School Choice on School Employee Labor Unions: Unionization Rates among Private, Charter, and Traditional Government Schools Suggest Reason for Union Opposition to School Choice." *Mackinac Center for Public Policy, Midland, Michigan* (June 1999).

Brownstein, Alan. "Constitutional Questions about Vouchers." *NYU Annual Survey of American Law* 57 (2000).

Cannon, Katie. *Black Womanist Ethics*. Atlanta: Scholars Press, 1988.

Carnoy, Martin. "School Choice? Or Is It Privatization?" *Educational Researcher* 29, no. 7 (October 2000).

———. "School Vouchers: Examining the Evidence." *Economic Policy Institute* (2001).

Carter, Stephen L. *The Culture of Disbelief: How American Law and Politics Trivialize Religious Devotion*. New York: Basic Books, 1993.

———. "Virtue via Vouchers: The Supreme Court's Recent Decision Can Help Prevent More Corporate Scandals." *Christianity Today* (November 18, 2002).

"Charter Status Pays Off, in Cash." *Los Angeles Times*, April 5, 1994.

"Choice School Accountability: A Consensus of Views in Ohio and Wisconsin." *Public Policy Forum Report*, at http://publicpolicyforum.org/pdfs/choice _accountability.pdf.

Chubb, John E., and Terry M. Moe. *A Lesson in School Reform from Great Britain*. Washington, D.C.: Brookings Institution Press, 1992.

———. *Politics, Markets and America's Schools*. Washington, D.C.: Brookings Institution Press, 1990.

———. "Politics, Markets, and the Organization of Schools." *American Political Science Review* (December 1988).

Clark, Reginald. *Family Life and School Achievement: Why Poor Black Children Succeed or Fail*. Chicago: University of Chicago Press, 1983.

Clouser, Roy. *The Myth of Neutrality*. South Bend, Ind.: Notre Dame Press, 1993.

Cobb, Clifford. *Responsive Schools, Renewed Communities*. San Francisco: ICS Press, 1992.

Coeyman, Marjorie. "Charter Schools Dig In: Ten Years Later, What Have We Learned?" *Christian Science Monitor*, January 7, 2003.

——. "The Story behind Dropout Rates." *Christian Science Monitor*, July 1, 2003.

——. "Teacher Quality Lags in Poorer Schools." *Christian Science Monitor*, January 7, 2003.

Coleman, James S., et al. *High School Achievement: Public, Catholic, and Private Schools Compared*. New York: Basic Books, 1982.

Coleman, James S., and Thomas Hoffer. *Public and Private Schools: The Impact of Communities*. New York: Basic Books, 1987.

Cooley, William. "School Choice or School Reform?" *Pennsylvania Educational Policy Studies Series*, no. 12 (November 4, 1991).

Coons, John. "The Healthy Burden of Choice: An Opportunity to Empower the Poor." *ESA Advocate* (January/February 1991).

——. "Intellectual Liberty and the Schools." *Journal of Law, Ethics, and Public Policy* 1 (1985).

——. "Is Choice Still a Choice?" *First Things* (August/September 1994).

Coons, John, and Stephen Sugarman. *Education by Choice: The Case for Family Control*. Berkeley: University of California Press, 1978.

——. *Scholarships for Children*. Berkeley: University of California, 1992.

Copple, James. "When Choice Is Not a Good Choice: Reform on the Backs of the Poor." *ESA Advocate* (January/February 1991).

Counts, Stephanie, and Beverly Lavergneau. "Choice as a Vehicle for Urban Educational Change in the 1990s." *Clearing House* 66 (November/December 1992).

Delattre, Edwin. *Education and the Public Trust: The Imperative for Common Purposes*. Washington, D.C.: Ethics and Public Policy Center, 1988.

Diamond, Linda. "A Progress Report on California's Charter Schools." *Educational Leadership* (September 1994).

Doerr, Edd, and Albert Menendez. *Church Schools and Public Money: The Politics of Parochiad*. New York: Prometheus Books, 1991.

Doherty, Carroll. "How Initiatives Fared." *Congressional Quarterly Weekly Report* (November 7, 1992).

Dooyeweerd, Herman. *A New Critique of Theoretical Thought*. Trans. David H. Freeman. Ontario: Paideia Press, 1984.

Dwyer, James. *Vouchers within Reason: A Child-Centered Approach to Education Reform*. Ithaca: Cornell University Press, 2002.

Encarnation, Dennis. "Public Finance and Regulation of Nonpublic Education: Retrospect and Prospect." In *Public Dollars for Private Schools: The Case for Tuition Tax Credits*, edited by T. James and H. M. Levin. Philadelphia: Temple University Press, 1985.

Evans, D. L. "The Marketplace Mythology in School Choice." *Education Digest* 56 (March 1991).

Finn Jr., Chester E. "A Primer for Education Reform." *Wall Street Journal*, January 13, 1995.

Fliegel, Seymour, and James Macguire. *Miracle in East Harlem: The Fight for Choice in Public Education*. New York: Times Books, 1993.

Foster, James D. "Say Yes to School Choice." *Christianity Today* (19 August 1991).

Fowler-Finn, Thomas. "Why Have They Chosen Another School System?" *Educational Leadership* (December 1993/January 1994).

Fox, Jonathan. "Sending Public School Students to Private Schools: The Untold Story of Special Education." *Policy Review*, no. 93 (January/February 1999).

Freid, Stephen H. "The Constitutionality of Choice under the Establishment Claus." *Clearing House* (November/December 1992).

Fuller, Howard. "Evidence Supports the Expansion of the Milwaukee Parental Choice Program." *Phi Delta Kappan* 81, no. 5 (January 2000).

Garrett, Jennifer. "Progress on School Choice in the States." *Heritage Foundation Backgrounder* (May 16, 2001).

Germino, Dante. *Political Philosophy and the Open Society*. Baton Rouge: Louisiana State University Press, 1982.

Gill, Brian, et al. *Rhetoric versus Reality: What We Know and What We Need to Know about Vouchers and Charter Schools*. New York: Rand Education, 2001.

Gilles, Stephen. "Why Parents Should Choose." In *Learning from School Choice*, edited by Paul Peterson and Bryan Hassel. Washington, D.C.: Brookings Institution Press, 1998.

Glenn, Charles. *The Ambiguous Embrace: Government and Faith-Based School and Social Agencies*. Princeton, N.J.: Princeton University Press, 2000.

——. *Choice of Schools in Six Nations: France, Netherlands, Belgium, Britain, Canada, West Germany*. Washington, D.C.: Office of Educational Research and Improvement, 1989.

——. "Controlled Choice in Massachusetts Public Schools." *Public Interest* (Spring 1991).

——. *Educational Freedom*. Washington, D.C.: CATO Institute, 1995.

——. "Just Schools for Minority Children." *Phi Delta Kappan* 70 (June 1989).

——. *The Myth of the Common School*. Amherst: University of Massachusetts Press, 1988.

——. "Putting Choice to Work in Public Education." *Equity and Choice* 2 (May 1986).

——. "Putting School Choice in Place." *Phi Delta Kappan* 71 (December 1989).

——. "What's Really at Stake in the School Choice Debate." *Clearing House* 66 (November/December 1992).

——. "Who Should Own the Schools?" *Equity and Choice* 9 (May 1986).

————. "Will Boston Be the Proof of the Choice Pudding?" *Educational Leadership* 48 (December/January 1990/1991).

Glenn, Charles, and Joshua Glenn. "Making Room for Religious Conviction in Democracy's Schools." In *Schooling Christians: "Holy Experiments" in American Education*, edited by Stanley Hauerwas and John H. Westerhoff. Grand Rapids, Mich.: Eerdmans, 1992.

Goldberg, Bruce. "A Liberal Argument for School Choice." *American Enterprise* 7 (September 1996).

Goldhaber, Dan. "School Choice: Do We Know Enough?" *Educational Researcher* 29 (2000).

Golle, John. "Advocates of School Choice Undaunted by Setbacks." *Congressional Quarterly Researcher* (March 25, 1994).

Good, Thomas, and Jennifer Braden. *"The Great School Debate: Choice, Vouchers, and Charters.* Mahwah, N.J.: Lawrence Erlbaum, 2000.

Goodlad, J. I. *A Place Called School: Prospects for the Future.* New York: McGraw-Hill, 1984.

Goodman, Jesse. *Elementary Schooling for Critical Democracy.* New York: University of New York Press, 1992.

Greene, Jay P. "Choice and Community: The Racial, Economic, and Religious Context of Parental Choice in Cleveland." *Buckeye Institute* (November 1999).

————. "The Surprising Consensus on School Choice." *The Public Interest*, no. 144 (Summer 2001).

Gresham, April, Frederick Hess, and Robert Maranto. "Desert Bloom: Arizona's Free Market in Education." *Phi Delta Kappan* 81, no. 10 (June 2000).

Guerra, Michael. "A Tale of One City and Two Families." *Momentum* (Washington, D.C.) 32 (April/May 2001).

Gutmann, Amy. "Children, Paternalism, and Education." *Philosophy and Public Affairs* 9 (Summer 1980).

Hardy, Lawrence. "The President's Plan." *American School Board Journal* (April 2001).

————. "Public School Choice." *American School Board Journal* (February 2000).

Heller, Frank. "Lessons from Maine: Education Vouchers for Students since 1873." *CATO Institute Briefing Papers* (September 10, 2001).

Hess, Frederick. *Revolution at the Margins.* Washington, D.C.: Brookings Institution Press, 2002.

Hill, Paul T., Gail Foster, and Tamar Gendler. *High Schools with Character.* Santa Monica, Calif.: RAND, 1990.

Hilton, James J. "Local Autonomy, Educational Equity, and School Choice: Constitutional Criticism of School Reform." *New England Journal Public Policy* (Summer/Fall 1994).

———. "States' School-Spending Disparities." *Education Week* (June 17, 1992).

Howell, William, and Paul Peterson. *The Education Gap: Vouchers and Urban Schools*. Washington, D.C.: Brookings Institution Press, 2000.

Hoxby, Caroline. "Does Competition among Public Schools Benefit Students and Taxpayers?" *American Economic Review* (December 2000).

———. "What Do America's 'Traditional' Forms of School Choice Teach Us about School Choice Reforms?" published by Federal Reserve Bank of New York, *Economic Policy Review* March 1998, 47–59.

Hunter, James. *Culture Wars: The Struggles to Define America*. New York: Basic Books, 1991.

"Indicator 14 (2001) International Comparisons of 8th-Graders Performance in Mathematics and Science" at http://nces.ed.gov/programs/coe/2001/section2/indicator14.html.

"International Comparisons (Student Achievement)," *National Center for Education Statistics* at http://nces.ed.gov/fastfacts/display.asp?id=1.

Jencks, Christopher. *Education Vouchers: A Report on Financing Elementary Education by Grants to Parents*. Washington, D.C.: Center for the Study of Public Policy, 1970.

Kahlenberg, Richard. *All Together Now: Creating Middle-Class Schools through Public School Choice*. Washington, D.C.: A Century Foundations Book, Brookings Institution Press, 2001.

Kant, Immanuel. *The Educational Theory of Immanuel Kant*. Trans. E. F. Buchner. Philadelphia: J.B. Lippincott, 1904.

Kaplan, Melanie. "Education Innovators Make Their Mark." *Christian Science Monitor* (January 7, 2003).

Kemerer, Frank. "Reconsidering the Constitutionality of Vouchers." *Journal of Law and Education* 30, no. 3 (July 2001).

Kemerer, Frank, Joe Hairston, and Keith Lauerman. "Vouchers and Private School Autonomy." *Journal of Law and Education* 21 (Fall 1992).

Kennedy, Sheila Suess. "Privatizing Education: The Politics of Vouchers." *Phi Delta Kappan* 82 (February 2001).

Kirkpatrick, David. *Choice in Schooling: A Case for Tuition Vouchers*. Chicago: Loyola University Press, 1990.

Kozol, Jonathan. *Amazing Grace: The Lives of Children and the Conscience of a Nation*. New York: Crown, 1995.

Kristol, William, and Jay Lefkowitz. "Our Students, Still at Risk." *New York Times*, May 3, 1993.

Lange, Cheryl, and James E. Ysseldyke. "How School Choice Affects Students with Special Needs." *Educational Leadership* (November 1994).

Larson, Lisa. "The Constitutionality of Education Vouchers under State and Federal Law." *Information Brief for the Minnesota House of Representatives* (July 1998).

Lazarus, Stephen. "The Real Religious Establishment." *Capital Commentary* (October 5, 2001).

———. "What's Unconstitutional about School Choice." *Capital Commentary* (July 29, 2002).

"Learner Outcomes," *National Center for Education Statistics* (2001) at http://nces .ed.gov/programs/coe/2001/section2/indicator14.html.

Lee, J. Roger. *Education in a Free Society*. Edited by Tibor R. Machan. Stanford, Calif.: Hoover Institution Press, 2000.

Leigh, Patricia. "Electronic Connections and Equal Opportunities: An Analysis of Telecommunications Distribution in Public Schools." *Journal of Research on Computing in Education* 32, no. 1 (Fall 1999).

Lewis, Anne. "Choice: Vouchers and Privatization." *Phi Delta Kappan* (September 1992).

———. "Private-School Vouchers." *Education Digest* (January 1993).

Lewis, Nathan. "Are Vouchers Constitutional?" *Policy Review* 93 (January/ February 1999).

Ley, Joyce. "Charter Starters Leadership Training Workbook 2: Regulatory Issues" (July 1999).

Lieberman, Myron. *Privatization and Educational Choice*. New York: St. Martin's Press, 1989.

———. "Teacher Unions: Is the End Near? How to End the Teacher Union Veto over State Education Policy." Claremont Institute, Golden State Center for Policy Studies, December 15, 1994 at www.educationpolicy.org/files/ tchrunio.htm.

Lines, P. *Compulsory Education Laws: Their Impact on Public and Private Education*. Denver: Education Commission of the States, 1984.

Loconte, Joe. "Paying the Piper: Will Vouchers Undermine the Mission of Religious Schools?" *Policy Review* no. 93 (January/February 1999).

Lubman, Sarah. "Breaking Away: Parents and Teachers Battle Public Schools by Starting Their Own." *Wall Street Journal*, May 19, 1994.

Lugg, Elizabeth, and Andrew Lugg. "Vouchers as School Choice: An Analysis of *Jackson v. Benson*—The Milwaukee Parental Choice Program." *Journal of Law and Education* 29, no. 2 (April 2000).

MacIntyre, Alasdair. *Whose Justice? Which Rationality?* South Bend, Ind.: University of Notre Dame Press, 1989.

Marciniak, Edward. "Educational Choice: A Catalyst for School Reform." *City Club of Chicago* (August 1989).

Margonis, Frank, and Laurence Parker. "Choice: The Route to Community Control?" *Theory and Practice* 38, no. 4 (Autumn 1999).

McCarthy, Rockne, James Skillen, and William Harper. *Disestablishment a Second Time: Genuine Pluralism for American Schools*. Grand Rapids, Mich.: Christian University Press, 1982.

McCarthy, Rockne, et al. *Society, State and Schools: A Case for Structural Confessional Pluralism*. Grand Rapids, Mich.: Eerdmans, 1981.

McDonald, Dale. "Reclaim the 'V' Word!" *Momentum* (Washington, D.C.) 31, no. 4 (November/December 2000).

McEwan, Patrick. "The Potential Impact of Large-Scale Voucher Programs." *Review of Educational Research*, no. 2 (Summer 2000).

Mead, Sidney. *The Lively Experiment: The Shaping of Christianity in America*. New York: Harper & Row, 1963.

Metcalf, Kim. *Evaluation of the Cleveland Scholarship and Tutoring Grant Program 1996–1999*. Bloomington: Indiana University Press, 1999.

Meyerson, Adam. "Bay State Boomer: Bill Weld Talks Tough on Taxes, Tough on Crime." *Policy Review* (Spring 1993).

——. "A Model of Cultural Leadership: The Achievements of Privately Funded Vouchers." *Policy Review* no. 93 (January/February 1999).

Mizala, Alejandra, and Pilar Romaguera. "School Performance and Choice: The Chilean Experience." *Journal of Human Resources* 35, no. 2 (Spring 2000).

Moe, Terry. *Schools, Vouchers, and the American Public*. Washington, D.C.: Brookings Institution Press, 2001.

Morken, Hubert, and Jo Renee Formicola. *The Politics of School Choice*. Lanham, Md.: Rowman & Littlefield, 1999.

Murphy, Dan. "When You Weigh the Evidence: Voucher Programs in Milwaukee and Cleveland." *American Educator* (Fall 1998).

Nathen, Joe, and James Ysseldyke. "What Minnesota Has Learned about School Choice." *Phi Delta Kappan* (May 1994).

"A Nation Still at Risk: An Education Manifesto." *Center for Education Reform*. April 30, 1998 at www.edreform.com/pubs/manifest.htm.

National Commission on Excellence in Education. *A Nation at Risk*. Washington, D.C.: U.S. Department of Education, 1983.

Neuhaus, Richard, and Peter Berger. *To Empower the People: The Role of Mediating Structures in Public Policy*. Washington, D.C.: American Enterprise Institute for Public Policy Research, 1977.

Newman, Muriel. "Choice of School Is a Fundamental Freedom" February 13, 2002 at www.scoop.co.nz/mason/stories/PO0202/S00052.htm.

Noll, Mark. *A History of Christianity in the United States and Canada*. Grand Rapids, Mich.: Eerdmans, 1992.

"The Notebook." *The Christian Science Monitor*, March 18, 2003.

"The Notebook." *The Christian Science Monitor*, March 28, 2003.

Olsen, Dary Ann, and Matthew J. Brouillette. "Reclaiming Our Schools: Increasing Parental Control of Education through the Universal Education Credit." *Policy Analysis* no. 388 (December 6, 2000).

Pangle, Lorraine, and Thomas Pangle. *The Learning of Liberty: The Educational Ideas of the American Founders*. Kansas City: University of Kansas Press, 1993.

Pattison, Scott. "More School Choice." *Consumer's Research Magazine* (October 1992).

Peterkin, Robert S., and Janice E. Jackson. "Public School Choice: Implications for African American Students." *The Journal of Negro Education* 63 (1994).

Peterson, Paul. "Money and Competition in American Schools." In *Choice and Control in American Education*, edited by William Clune and John Witte. London: Falmer Press, 1990.

———. "School Choice: A Report Card." *Virginia Journal of Social Policy and the Law* 6 (Fall 1998): 47–80.

———. "Vouchers and Test Scores." *Policy Review* 93 (January/February 1999): 10–15.

Peterson, Paul, and Jay Greene. "Race Relations and Central City Schools: It's Time for an Experiment with Vouchers." *Brookings Review* 16 (Spring 1998).

Peterson, Paul, and Bryan Hassel. *Learning from School Choice*. Washington, D.C.: Brookings Institution Press, 1998.

Poetter, Thomas, and Kathleen Knight-Abowitz. "Possibilities and Problems of School Choice." *Kappa Delta Pi Record* 37, no. 2 (Winter 2001).

"Private School Vouchers." *National Education Association Topic Legislative Action Center.* June 2001 at www.nea.org/lac/papers/vouchers.html.

"Projections of Education Statistics to 2011." *National Center for Education Statistics* at http://nces.ed.gov/pubs2001/proj01/tables/table33.asp.

"Public and Private Schools: How Do They Differ?" *Findings from the Condition of Education 1997* at http://nces.ed.gov/pubs97/97983.

Quade, Quentin. "School Reform: Toward Parental Choice." *Current* (February 1993).

Randall, Ruth E. "What's after School Choice? Private-Practice Teachers and Charter Schools." *Education Digest* (April 1993).

Ravitch, Diane. "Somebody's Children." *The Brookings Review* (Fall 1994).

"Reading." *National Center for Education Statistics* (2001) at http://nces.ed.gov/fastfacts/display.asp?id=35.

Rees, Nina. "Public School Benefits of Private School Vouchers." *Policy Review* 93 (January/February 1999).

Rose, Lowell. "The 32nd Annual Phi Delta Kappa/Gallup Poll of the Public's Attitudes toward the Public Schools." *Phi Delta Kappan* 82 (September 2000).

Rudolph, Frederich, ed. *Essays on Education in the Early Republic*. Cambridge: Harvard University Press, 1965.

Russell, Mary Ellen. "Parent Advocacy Spurs School Choice Decisions." *Momentum* (Washington, D.C.) 32, no. 2 (April/May 2001).

Salomone, Rosemary. *Visions of Schooling: Conscience, Community, and Common Education*. New Haven, Conn.: Yale University Press, 2000.

Sandy, Jonathan. "Evaluating the Public Support for Educational Vouchers: A Case Study." *Economics of Education Review* (1992).

Schneider, Mark, Paul Teske, and Melissa Marschall. *Choosing Schools: Consumer Choice and the Quality of America Schools*. Princeton, N.J.: Princeton University Press, 2000.

"Scholastic Assessment Test (SAT) Scores." *National Center for Education Statistics* (2000) at http://nces.ed.gov/fastfacts/display.asp?id=53.

"School Choice Does Not Drain Money from Public Schools." *Center for Education Reform* at www.edreform.com/school_choice/facts/money.htm (accessed June 9, 2002).

Sianjina, Rayton. "Parental Choice, School Vouchers, and Separation of Church and State: Legal Implications." *Educational Forum* 63, no. 2 (Winter 1999).

Sider, Ron. *Just Generosity: A New Vision for Overcoming Poverty in America*. Grand Rapids, Mich.: Baker Books, 1999.

Sizer, T. R. *Horace's Compromise: The Dilemma of the American High School*. Boston: Houghton Mifflin, 1984.

Sizer, Theodore, and Phillip Whitten. "A Proposal for a Poor Children's Bill of Rights." *Psychology Today* (August 1968).

Skillen, James W. "Biblical Principles Applied to National Education Policy." *Biblical Principles and Public Policy: The Practice*. Colorado Springs: Navigator's Press, 1989.

———. "Changing Assumptions in the Public Governance of Education: What Has Changed and What Ought to Change." In *Democracy and the Renewal of Public Education*, edited by Richard J. Neuhaus. Grand Rapids, Mich.: Eerdmans, 1987.

———. *Democracy and the Renewal of Public Education*, edited by Richard J. Neuhaus. Grand Rapids, Mich.: Eerdmans, 1987.

———. *Justice for Education*. Washington, D.C.: Association for Public Justice, 1981.

———, ed. "School Vouchers and the United States Constitution." In *The School Choice Controversy: What Is Constitutional?* Grand Rapids, Mich.: Baker Books, 1993.

Smith, Kevin. "Policy, Markets, and Bureaucracy: Reexamining School Choice." *Journal of Politics* 56 (May 1994).

A Special Report: School Choice. Princeton, N.J.: Carnegie Foundation for the Advancement of Teaching, 1992.

"State of the First Amendment: Freedom of Religion." *Update on Law-Related Education* 22 (Winter 1998).

Steers, Stuart. "The Catholic Schools' Black Students." *This World* (December 23, 1990).

Steiner, David. *Rethinking Democratic Education: The Politics of Reform*. Baltimore, Md.: Johns Hopkins University Press, 1994.

Sternberg, Libby. "Lessons from Vermont: 132-Year-Old Voucher Program Rebuts Critics." *CATO Institute Briefing Papers* (September 10, 2001).

"Student Achievement (National)." *National Center for Education Statistics* at http:nces.ed.gov/fastfacts/display.asp?id=38 (accessed June 11, 2002).

Sweeney, Mary Ellen. "How to Plan a Charter School." *Educational Leadership* (September 1994).

Teicher, Stacy A. "The Case for Single-Sex Schools." *Christian Science Monitor*, July 1, 2003.

Tracy, Stephen. "Charter Schools: Choices for Parents, Chances for Children." *Clearing House* 66 (November/December 1992).

Toler, Mary Lou. "School Choice Works in Cleveland." *Momentum* 32, no. 3 (September/October 2001).

Tribe, Lawrence. "Constitutional Scrutiny." *New York Times*, June 17, 1991.

Tucker, Allyson, and William Lauber. *School Choice Programs: What's Happening in the States*. Washington, D.C.: Heritage Foundation, 1995.

Tucker, Jeffrey. "Evils of Choice." *National Review* (1 March 1993).

·Tweedie, Jack. "The Dilemma of Clients' Rights in Social Programs: Effects of Parental Rights of School Choice in England, Scotland, and Wales." *Law and Society Review* 23 (1989).

U.S. Department of Education. *The Condition of Education 2001*. Washington, D.C.: Office of Educational Research and Improvement.

Vangen, Clara. "Condemned: America's Public Schools." *Buildings* 95 (January 2001).

Viteritti, Joseph. *Choosing Equality: School Choice, the Constitution, and Civil Society*. Washington, D.C.: Brookings Institution Press, 1999.

———. "School Choice and State Constitutional Law." In *Learning from School Choice*, edited by Paul Peterson and Bryan Hassel. Washington, D.C.: Brookings Institution Press, 1998.

Voegelin, Eric. *Autobiographical Reflections.* Baton Rouge: Louisiana State University Press, 1989.

Wallis, Claudia. "A Class of Their Own: Bucking Bureaucracy, Brashly Independent Public Schools Have Much to Teach about Saving Education." *Time* (October 31, 1994).

Walsh, David. *After Ideology: Recovering the Spiritual Foundations of Freedom.* San Francisco: Harper, 1990.

Weicker, Lowell, and Richard Kahlenberg. "The New Educational Divide." *Christian Science Monitor*, October 9, 2002.

Williams, Polly. "Choice Debate Is about Who Controls Education." *National Minority Politics* (January 1994).

———. "Polly's Plan: New Wisconsin We Will Allow Poor Children to Attend Private Schools." *Economist* 316 (August 1990).

———. "School Choice Promotes Educational Excellence in the African American Community." *Voices on Choice: The Education Reform Debate*. San Francisco: Pacific Research Institute for Public Policy, 1992.

Witte, John. *The Market Approach to Education: An Analysis of America's First Voucher Program.* Princeton, N.J.: Princeton University Press, 2000.

Zirkel, Perry. "What Will Be the Supreme Court's Choice on Choice." *Journal of Law and Education* 30, no. 3 (July 2001).

Index

Alexander, Lamar, 165
Allen, Jeanne, 113
American Educational Research
    Association, 111
American Federation of Teachers
    (AFT), 121, 122, 141, 179
Arons, Stephen, 30, 44
Association of Christian Schools
    International, 115

Bache, William, 37
Baer, Richard, 42
Barber, Benjamin, 46
Becker, H. J., 8
Bennett, William, 12, 46
Berger, Peter, 51
Berliner, David, 111
Bestor, Arthur, 179
Black Alliance for Educational
    Options (BAEO), 165, 168–169
Bolick, Clint, 14, 90
Booker, Cory, 21–22, 165, 172, 173,
    185
Borwege, Kim, ix
Bracey, Gerald, 17
Bracey Report, 16

Brown, Willie, 111
Brownstein, Alan, 68

Cannon, Katie, 173
Carnegie Foundation for the
    Advancement of Teaching Report,
    ix, 105, 172
Carnoy, Martin, 145
Carter, Stephen, 48
Catholic Church, 54
Center for Education Reform, 5, 6, 13,
    17, 21, 22, 70
Center on Education Policy, 116
Center on Policy Attitudes, 154
charter schools, 138–142; Academy of
    the Pacific Rim, 140; Advantage
    Charter Schools, 141; Bronx
    Preparatory Charter, 140; City
    Academy in St. Paul, 138; first
    charter law, 139; Maya Angelou
    Public Charter School, 141;
    Minnesota New Country School,
    140; North Star Academy, 140;
    Seventy-First Classical Middle
    Charter School, 155; Vaughn Next
    Century Learning Center, 110, 139

Chubb, John, 49, 110
Civil Rights Act of 1964, 112
Clouser, Roy, 44
Cobb, Clifford, 31, 33, 58, 118
Coeyman, Marjorie, 140
The Condition of Education 2000,
    166, 170
Cookson, Peter, 5
Coons, John, 4, 47, 50, 55, 183
Cordell, Dorman, 109
costs of schooling: choice schools,
    105–110, 151–154; public schools,
    3–10, 105–110, 151, 153

Descartes, René, 37
Dewey, John, 45
Doerr, Edd, 105
Du, Jiangtao, 145, 176

Education Week, 9, 48, 108
Establishment Clause, 67, 68, 69, 71,
    75, 77, 78, 81–83, 86, 88, 91
European countries and school
    choice, 117, 119; Belgium, 119;
    Denmark, 119; Germany, 119;
    Great Britain, 118; Netherlands,
    118–119

Feldman, Sandra, 179
Flake, Floyd, 166
Formicola, Jo Renee, 89, 90
Foster, James, 109
Fowler-Finn, Thomas, 172
Fuller, Howard, 34, 196

Gallagher, Tom, 108
Garrett, Jennifer, 143
Gill, Brian, 22
Gilles, Stephen, 30, 51, 52

Glenn, Charles, 31, 68, 111, 115, 116,
    117, 119, 121, 184
Goldberg, Bruce, 15, 50
Government Accounting Office
    (GAO), 151, 152
graduation rates, 10–11, 16–17, 178
Greene, Jay, 10, 70, 84, 145, 146, 148,
    149, 150, 152, 166, 169, 175, 176,
    177, 180, 182, 184
Guthrie, William, 56–57

Hadderman, Margaret, 171
Harper, William, 37
Holmes, John, 115
Howell, William, 3–4, 15, 32, 52–53,
    58, 149, 169, 171, 176
Hoxby, Caroline, 146, 182
Hurley, Rodger, 67

Institute for Contemporary Studies, 170
International Covenant on Economic,
    Social and Cultural Rights, 55

Jackson, Jesse, 7
James, Estelle, 111
Jefferson, Thomas, 37, 38, 39, 40, 41,
    42, 43, 46
Jencks, Christopher, 15
Johnson, Phillip, 43
Joint Center for Political and
    Economic Studies, 2, 167

Kahlenberg, Richard, 2, 11, 14, 15
Kemerer, Frank, 78
Kirkpatrick, David, 52, 67
Knight-Abowitz, Kathleen, 172, 180
Kozol, Jonathan, 2, 6, 7, 10, 179

Larson, Lisa, 84, 89
Lazarus, Stephen, 73–74

Leigh, Patricia, 8
Lemann, Nicholas, 172
Levin, Henry, 111
Lewis, Nathan, 75, 76, 78
Lieberman, Myron, 30, 43, 122–123
limited school choice in select states:
    Maine, 86, 153; Michigan, 153;
    Vermont, 86, 153; Washington,
    D.C., 153
Locke, John, 37, 49
Loconte, Joe, 117
Lugg, Elizabeth, 90

Mackinac Center for Public Policy,
    121, 153
magnet schools, 137–138
Mann, Horace, 5, 33–34, 38–39, 40,
    41, 42, 43, 49
Marciniak, Edward, 184
Margonis, Frank, 169
Maritain, Jacques, 51
McCarthy, Rockne, 37, 38, 40, 41
McEwan, Patrick, 176
McGroarty, Daniel, 170
McReynolds, James Clark, 57
Mead, Sidney, 41
Menendez, Albert, 105
Metcalf, Kim, 171, 175
Meyerson, Adam, 174
Mill, John Stuart, 44, 45, 52
Moe, Terry, 49, 59, 168, 182
Morken, Hubert, 89, 90

A Nation at Risk, ix, 55
National Assessment of Educational
    Progress (NAEP), 175
National Assessment of Educational
    Progress Report Card, 12, 18–19,
    20

National Center for Education
    Statistics, 15, 20, 21, 106
National Commission on Teaching
    and America's Future, 8
National Education Association
    (NEA), 105, 120–123, 142, 154
National Labor Relations Act, 123
Neuhaus, Richard John, 43, 51
New York Times, 108, 169
Newman, Muriel, 14
No Child Left Behind Act of 2001, 155

O'Malley, Charles, 114
Osborne, David, 183

Pangle, Lorraine, 45–46
Pangle, Thomas, 45–46
parental satisfaction: choice schools,
    146, 150, 170–171, 177; public
    schools, 1, 2, 170–171
Parents in Charge, 154
Parker, Laurence, 169
Peterson, Paul, 3–4, 12, 15, 32, 52–53,
    58, 84, 145, 149, 153, 166, 169, 171,
    175, 176, 177, 178, 180, 181, 182
Poetter, Thomas, 172, 179, 180
Pope John Paul II, 54
privately sponsored choice programs,
    143, 174, 177, 178; Children First
    America, 143, 185; Children's
    Scholarship Fund, 143; Choice
    Charitable Trust, 143; Partners
    Advancing Values in Education,
    143; Scholarship Fund for Inner-
    City Children, 143
public opinion polls regarding school
    choice, 1, 151, 154, 167–168
Public Policy Forum, 151

Quade, Quentin, 31, 120

racial integration in schools: choice
    schools, 148–149, 179–182; public
    schools, 12–13, 69, 149
Raspberry, William, 4, 22
Ravitch, Diane, 69, 184, 196
Rawls, John, 57
regulation of schools: European
    countries, 117–119; private,
    111–117, 145; public, 112–114
Reich, Robert, 102
Report on the Condition of Education,
    8–9
Rouse, Cecilia, 12, 145
Ruenzel, David, 146
Rush, Benjamin, 40

Salomone, Rosemary, 31, 39
school choice programs: Cleveland
    Scholarship and Tutoring Grant
    Program, 69–74, 113, 146–152,
    155, 173, 175, 176, 195–197;
    Florida's A-Plus Opportunity
    Scholarships, 107–108, 152–153;
    Milwaukee Parental Choice
    Program, 87–90, 107, 109,
    112, 113, 116, 144–147, 151,
    152, 155, 175, 176, 177, 183,
    195–197
Sider, Ron, 7, 8, 11, 13, 14, 58
Sizer, Theodore, 16
Skillen, James, 36, 37, 54
Smith, Kevin, 179
state court cases: *Chittenden Town
    School District v. Vermont
    Department of Education*, 86;
    Davis v. Grover, 87; *Jackson v.
    Benson*, 87, 116
Stedman, Lawrence, 13
Sterling, C. W., 8

Sugarman, Stephen, 47, 55

test scores: choice schools, 137, 140,
    141, 145, 149, 175–179; public
    schools, 12, 16–20, 149, 152, 182
Third International Mathematics and
    Science Study (TIMSS), 17, 19–20
Toler, Mary Lou, 150
Tribe, Lawrence, 85
Tucker, Jeffrey, 117

United Nations Universal Declaration
    of Human Rights, 35, 55
Urban League, 166
U.S. Department of Education, 6, 8, 9
U.S. Supreme Court cases: *Abington
    School District v. Schempp*, 35;
    Agostini v. Felton, 84; *Brown v.
    Topeka Board of Education*, 3, 14,
    72, 74, 92; *Committee for Public
    Education and Religious Liberty v.
    Nyquist*, 77; *Everson v. Board of
    Education*, 76, 79, 89; *Lemon v.
    Kurtzman*, 35, 77, 79, 81, 89;
    Meyer v. Nebraska, 55; *Mitchell v.
    Helms*, 84; *Mueller v. Allen*, 78–81;
    Pierce v. Society of Sisters, 30, 35,
    55, 56; *Rosenberger v. Rector and
    Visitors of the University of
    Virginia*, 83, 85; *West Virginia
    Board of Education v. Barnette*, 45,
    55, 57; *Wisconsin v. Yoder*, 35, 48,
    56; *Witters v. Washington*, 78,
    81–83; *Zelman v. Simmons-Harris*,
    69–74; *Zobrest v. Catalina
    Foothills District*, 78, 82

Viteritti, Joseph, 70, 79, 85, 86, 87,
    89, 165, 169, 178

Weicker, Lowell, 15
West, Martin, 153
Western, Bruce, 10
Whitten, Phillip, 16
Williams, Joe, 109

Williams, Polly, 144, 196
Wilson, William J., 180
Witte, John, 9, 15, 145, 146, 171,
    184
Wolf, Patrick, 153

About the Author

David B. Van Heemst is professor of political science at Olivet Nazarene University in Bourbonnais, Illinois. He was the first political scientist hired by the university and built the political science program. He has taught there for the past eleven years and has won both teaching awards the university offers—the Faculty Award for Teaching Excellence in 1998 and the Second Mile Award in 2003. He is the author of the forthcoming *The Significance of Herman Dooyeweerd and Eric Voegelin* and co-author of *Idols of Our Time*, second edition.

Dr. Van Heemst has three master's degrees (two in counseling and one in political science) and earned a doctorate in political theory from the University of Virginia in 1993. He lives in Kankakee, Illinois, with his wife, April, and daughters, Maggie and Ellie. April, a former grade school teacher, is now a stay-at-home mom with their twin toddlers.